LONERGAN
ON
CONVERSION

The Development
of a Notion

Michael L. Rende

UNIVERSITY
PRESS OF
AMERICA

Lanham • New York • London

Copyright © 1991 by
University Press of America®, Inc.
4720 Boston Way
Lanham, Maryland 20706

3 Henrietta Street
London WC2E 8LU England

Library of Congress Cataloging-in-Publication Data

Rende, Michael L., 1946–
Lonergan on conversion : the development of a notion /
Michael L. Rende.
p.   cm.
Includes bibliographical references.
1. Theology—Methodology—History of doctrines—
20th century.   2. Hermeneutics—History—20th century.
3. Lonergan, Bernard J. F.—Contributions in theological
methodology.   4. Lonergan, Bernard J. F.—
Contributions in hermeneutics.   I. Title.
BR118.R45   1989   248.2'4'092—dc20   89–36279 CIP

ISBN 0–8191–7525–0 (alk. paper)

BR
118
.R45
1991

The paper used in this publication meets the minimum requirements of
American National Standard for Information Sciences—Permanence
of Paper for Printed Library Materials, ANSI Z39.48–1984.

DEDICATION

To Jane

and Our Sons

Kevin and Joseph

ACKNOWLEDGMENTS

I want to acknowledge my indebtedness to Professor Matthew Lamb. He opened up the deeper levels of Lonergan's thought for me and revealed its possibilities. His own standard of scholarship, as evidenced in his seminars and publications, has been a beacon for me; he keeps one's ideals high. As a friend and a teacher, Professor Lamb has been uncommonly generous. As a priest, his solidarity with the mystical and suffering body of Jesus Christ shines brightly.

The first section of chapter four of this present work, "Conversion and the Realms of Meaning" has previously appeared in *METHOD: Journal of Lonergan Studies* (Vol. 1, No. 2) under the title, "The Development and the Unity of Lonergan's Notion of Conversion". It appears here with the courtesy of Editor Mark Morelli.

My special thanks to Mrs. Gail Jennings and to my fellow workers in the Religious Studies Department of Gonzaga University. Through their conversation and concern they have shown their support for this work.

TABLE OF CONTENTS

INTRODUCTION

This work is an interpretive investigation. The topic of investigation is the development of Bernard Lonergan's thought on the notion of conversion. For Lonergan, the notion of conversion is the foundation of a contemporary theological method. He writes: "Foundational reality, as distinct from its expression, is conversion: religious, moral, and intellectual."[1] Again, he writes: "What is normative and foundational for subjects stating theology is to be found, I have suggested, in reflection on conversion, where conversion is taken as an ongoing process, concrete and dynamic, personal, communal, and historical."[2] Lonergan's prolonged intellectual labor can be understood as a search for a contemporary theological method and one of the chief results of that search has been the establishment of the notion of conversion at the very heart of contemporary method. Consequently, I felt that the time and effort needed to penetrate more deeply into Lonergan's understanding of the notion of conversion would be well spent.

The key interpretive problem is establishing the context. Contemporary hermeneutical theory contends that meaning functions in a context and that the meaning of the part is to be understood by relating it to the whole. Conversely, there is no short cut to understanding the whole context. One apprehends the whole by successively understanding each of its constituent parts. This is the problem of the hermeneutical circle. This problem is complicated, however, in the case of the notions of conversion and of method. They are not simply related as the part to the whole. Instead, they are notions of equal generality and the understanding of one is coterminous with the understanding of the other.

In order to overcome this impasse, I decided to employ a developmental approach. Further, I was encouraged in this decision by other factors. First, Fr. Frederick Crowe has pointed out the general need for research into the origins of Lonergan's later and more developed conceptions. For example, he has described Lonergan's *Insight* and *Method in Theology* as "two finished products that arrived on the scene like Melchizedek without known ancestry."[3] Similarly, the term "conversion" seemed to appear in Lonergan's later work without sufficient introduction. In fact, he had long been concerned with the notion; in his dissertation he had examined it in the works of St. Thomas.

Secondly, the notion of conversion transcends determinate contexts. Contexts can be fixed by establishing the terms and relations that compose them, by fixing the partial terms of meaning which constitute the basic principles. But conversion pertains to the movement from an established context into a newer and better one, from the principles one presently understands to higher ones. Again, any interpretive investigation will be influenced by the self-understanding of the interpreter. But conversion pertains to the fact that interpreters are people involved in the dynamics of human development. Besides their self-understanding is their need to change and to develop. There is an upper or transcendent context vis-a-vis interpretive investigations wherein one is either facing the challenge of self-transcendence or evading that challenge. Consequently, investigating Lonergan's notion of conversion calls for an approach which focuses on the dynamism which leads human subjects to ever higher and broader perspectives.

These general considerations led me to distinguish three major contexts or periods in Lonergan's career. The first period is concerned with the realm of Thomist theory. The second period is concerned with the realm of cognitional interiority. The third period is concerned with method. While each context is important because of the specific material it treats, the most important factor is the dynamism which leads from one period to the next. The third period or context—Theology and the Methodical Exigence—envisages the operations of a dynamic structure which includes the ongoing investigation and construction of successive contexts. It is within this period that the notion of conversion reveals its foundational significance.

There is a dynamism to be discerned in Lonergan's career. It is a complex dynamism, a movement of desire and of love. One is reminded of Dom Jean Leclercq's felicitous phrase: the love of learning and the desire for God. Those are the elements whose combination seems to permeate Lonergan's work. He has understood the connections between those two elements in a most profound and dynamic way. There is the conception of the light of human intellect as a participated likeness in the divine and uncreated Light. There is the unity of Lonergan's account of wisdom in cognitional terms and the wisdom which is a gift of the Holy Spirit. There is the grounding of human judgment in the grasp of the virtually unconditioned-which itself is an anticipation of Transcendent Being—the formally unconditioned. In so many ways throughout his career, Lonergan has integrated the desire to know and the desire for God. Consequently, his conception of theological method reflects the unity of these two elements. It is the union of contemporary scholarly operations with the dynamic state of other-worldly love which makes his conception of theological method so powerful. It is the union of these two elements which gives the notion of conversion its foundational import. Accordingly, this is an interpretive investigation of the development of Lonergan's thought on the notion of conversion and its foundational significance for theological method.

NOTES

[1] Bernard J. F. Lonergan, S.J., *Method in Theology* (New York: Herder and Herder, 1972), p. 267. Hereafter referred to as *M.i.T.*

[2] Lonergan, "Theology in Its New Context," in *A Second Collection,* ed. William F. J. Ryan and Bernard J. Tyrrell (Philadelphia: The Westminster Press, 1974), p. 67. Hereafter referred to as *2nd Col.*

[3] Frederick E. Crowe, "Creativity and Method: Index to a Movement—a Review Article," *Science et Esprit,* XXXIV, 2 (1982), p. 112.

CHAPTER ONE

EARLY PERIOD: THOMISM AND THE SYSTEMATIC EXIGENCE

The human soul understands itself by its understanding,
which is its proper act, perfectly demonstrating its power
and its nature.

Sum. Theo., I, q. 88, a.2, ad3m.

The General Context of the Early Period

This first chapter investigates the early period of Lonergan's
career with its two major interpretive studies of the thought of
St. Thomas Aquinas: *Grace and Freedom*[1] and *Verbum.*[2]
Grace and Freedom is a rewritten version of Lonergan's doctoral dissertation. *Verbum* first appeared as a series of articles
in *Theological Studies* from 1946 to 1949. Later these articles
appeared in book form with the title *Verbum: Word and Idea in
Aquinas.* Various writings which Lonergan also published during this period have been assembled in his *Collection.*[3] While
they indicate the diversity of topics which engaged his interest
at this time, only a few points made in these writings have
direct relevance to the basic interpretation being offered here.
Perhaps the most significant article in this connection is his
"Theology and Understanding," the final publication of the
early period.

1

Lonergan himself has characterized this early period in various ways. In the conclusion to *Verbum,* he describes his initial purpose as "the Leonine purpose, *vetera novis augere et perficere,* though with this modality that I believed the basic task still to be a determination of what the *vetera* really were."[4] Consequently, both *Grace and Freedom* and *Verbum* are historical rather than theoretical works. From the vantage point of *Insight,* several years later, Lonergan would reflect that the central personal achievement of these years was his "reaching up to the mind of Aquinas."[5] Accordingly, Lonergan's first two major works are Thomist. This early period can be understood, then, as part of the larger Roman Catholic historical-theological retrieval of Aquinas.

In Lonergan's first two major works, the notion of conversion is, for the most part, implicit and even where it is explicitly discussed, it is a secondary consideration. *Grace and Freedom* does trace Aquinas' developing thought on religious conversion. Nevertheless, the general topic is the development of his views on operative grace, of which conversion is but one instance. *Verbum* discusses the nature of human reflectivity. It is within this discussion, I believe, that we can discern the origin of Lonergan's later idea of intellectual conversion. Whenever the word "conversion" is explicitly used, however, it refers to the intellect's conversion to phantasm, an idea which is only indirectly related to intellectual conversion. Notwithstanding this lack of developed data on the notion of conversion, if we are to understand the origin of the more developed ideas, and the way in which the notion of conversion functions within the various realms of meaning,[6] then the earliest statements and contexts must be explored.

In sketching the basic features of the early context, mention must be made of the orientation given to Catholic theology in the first half of the twentieth century by the First Vatican Council and its apostolic constitution, *Dei Filius* (1870).[7] *Dei Filius* reaffirmed and further explicated the Church's teaching on the relationship between faith and reason. While unaided reason can reach certain truths about God, it cannot discover other truths which have been revealed. Nevertheless, once revealed, thse truths can be further penetrated by careful, pious, and sober inquiry. Since these revealed truths are mysteries, their complete intelligibility cannot be exhausted; but speculative theology can attain a fruitful but limited understanding of their content. This definition of the power and limits of reason, as well as the transcendence of faith, was a constituent factor in the early context of Lonergan's development.

In the unpublished first chapter of "Gratia Operans," while discussing the way in which speculative theology mediates between faith and reason, Lonergan describes the "dialectical position:"

> On the one hand, it maintains that different truths of faith—or doctrines of faith and certain conclusions of human reason—cannot be contradictory. Truth is one and God is truth. Hence, no matter how great the opposition may appear to be, it is always possible to attain the negative coherence of non-contradiction.
>
> On the other hand, it maintains that at no point of time will the human understanding enjoy a full explanation of all doctrines of faith.[8]

In the final chapter of *Verbum,* while discussing the *via doctrinae* of the *Summa Theologiae,* Lonergan applauds the ability of Aquinas' theology to maintain the polarity of the dialectical position. Lonergan writes:

> It knows just what the human mind can attain and attains it. It does not attempt to discover the synthetic principle whence all else follows. It knows that principle is the divine essence and that, in this life, we cannot properly know it.[9]

Lastly, even though Lonergan was able to express the dialectical relationship between faith and reason with such clarity in "Gratia Operans," he nevertheless continued to meditate upon its implications in the final publication of this early period, "Theology and Understanding."

In "Theology and Understanding," Lonergan reviews Fr. J. Beumer's *Theologie als Glaubenverstandnis.*[10] Fr. Beumer had distinguished between an understanding of the truths of faith and a science of the truths of faith. As G. McCool points out, this tension between a subjective orientation focusing upon understanding and the objective orientation of an Aristotelian

science of faith was incorporated implicitly within the text of
Dei Filius itself and influenced the issues and development of
subsequent post-conciliar theology.[11] Against a conclusion theology based on a narrow interpretation of the Aristotelian concept of science, Karl Rahner advocated a return to mystery.
Against conceptualist interpretation of Aquinas, Lonergan
maintained the intellectualism of Aquinas and the Thomist
tendency toward the identity of science and understanding.
Lonergan's efforts to retrieve the Thomist-Aristotelian ideal of
science must be understood in relation to this tension inherited
from *Dei Filius*. Another equally significant factor determining
the early context was the encyclical *Aeterni Patris* (1879). Pope
Leo XIII gave official support and encouragement to the re-
vival of scholastic thought as the best vehicle for realizing the
First Vatican Council's clarification of the issue of faith and
reason, as the best integration and expression of a unified
approach to philosophic and theological education, and as the
best instrument for the Christian reconstruction of society.[12] At
the summit of the scholastic achievement stood the wisdom of
St. Thomas. Neo-Thomism would undergo profound development between the time of Liberatore, Sanseverino, and
Kleutgen and the time of Rahner and Lonergan. Still, the whole
spectrum of neo-Thomists would profit from tutelage to Aquinas' epistemology and metaphysics.

It is easy, however, to oversimplify Lonergan's dependence
on St. Thomas. His thought had already undergone considerable maturation prior to any significant exposure to Aquinas.
Lonergan has attempted to put his Thomism in perspective:

> Finally, there is the question whether my prior alle-
> giance to Thomism did not predetermine the results I
> reached. Now it is true that I spent a great deal of tin e
> in the study of St. Thomas and I know that I owe a
> great deal to him. I just add, however, that my interest
> in Aquinas came late.[13]

He also mentions his early study of Newman's *Grammar of
Assent,* his devotion to the early dialogues of Plato, and then St.
Augustine. Lonergan began to approach a unified viewpoint
when he succeeded in correlating St. Augustine's notion of

veritas, Aquinas' *esse,* and Marechal's view of judgment.[14] Even with these diverse influences in mind, however, it is still possible to single out Thomism as an integrating factor for Lonergan in a way in which Newman, Augustine, and Plato were not.

A distinctive feature of Lonergan's early Thomism was its historical character. The 19th century neo-Thomists were, for the most part, interested in the metaphysical rather than the historical analysis of Aquinas.[15] But Lonergan's appraisal of the shortcomings of conceptualism, to which exclusively metaphysical analysis tended with its a-historical perspective, led him to conceive his "basic task still to be the determination of what the *vetera* really were."[16]

Grace and Freedom is an historical work in its resources, method, and goal. *In its resources:* Lonergan utilized the excellent research of an earlier generation of historians to determine the significance of the theological and philosophical developments prior to Aquinas. He wrote: "with great thoroughness Dr. Landgraf has investigated several aspects of the general movement of speculation on grace prior to Aquinas, and Dom Lottin, O.S.B. has furnished what from our point of view is a complementary study of contemporary theories of liberty."[17] *In its method:* Lonergan was concerned to avoid two extremes. The first extreme was the conceptualist approach which, through inadvertence to the historical gap separating the modern interpreter and the medieval context, might tend to read the categories and conceptions of the present into the past. The second extreme to be avoided was a positivist approach to historical research which, through inadvertence to the constitutive role of the interpreter's perspective, might tend to deny the relevance of any type of *a priori* factor. Consequently, Lonergan tried to elaborate an *a priori* scheme, a theoretical framework, which while capable of highlighting the salient features of the data, would also be general enough to respect their integrity. He pointed out that his own proposed theory of speculative development "may be mistaken, but at least it is something tangible which can be refuted."[18] *In its goal: Grace and Freedom* described the precise nature of the development in Aquinas theology of grace. Its immediate consequence was that such a description made available a higher viewpoint between the impasse created by the controversy between the Molinists and Banezians. Lonergan achieved this higher viewpoint precisely by appealing to the historical context and development of Aquinas' thought.

Verbum was a more ambitious undertaking from the historical-hermeneutical point of view. Lonergan lamented that even so prominent a Thomist interpreter as Cardinal Billot had overlooked a central feature of Aquinas' account of intellectual processions, and hence of his Trinitarian theology.[19] That central feature was the reflective nature of human rationality. It was a feature which generally slipped through the net of exclusively metaphysical analysis. But it was a feature to which historical hermeneutical investigations could advert. Aquinas' account of intellectual procession integrated Augustinian data on the interior "speech of spirit within spirit"[20] within an Aristotelian metaphysical framework. By careful historical analysis, Lonergan was able to underscore this Augustinian element in Aquinas' thought and the enrichment it underwent in St. Thomas' hands. It was the specifically historical-hermeneutical approach which permitted this achievement. On a later occasion, Lonergan made the general remark: "It is the development of modern hermeneutics and history that has forced Catholic theology out of manualist tradition."[21] It was his historical-hermeneutical studies which forced the recognition of the intellectualism of Aquinas.[22]

In the remainder of this chapter, I shall reconstruct some of the more significant features of the early context within which Lonergan's first conceptions of conversion were formed. My general approach will be to first focus on *Grace and Freedom* and then on *Verbum*. Before the notion of conversion is discussed in each of these books, the most fundamental concerns of each work are clarified. The statements and ideas about conversion are then set within the context of these more fundamental concerns. In the final section of this chapter, the development from *Grace and Freedom* to *Verbum* is analyzed and proposed as the most basic context within which Lonergan's notion of conversion is to be understood in this early period.

Grace and Freedom

In this first phase of the early period, *Grace and Freedom,* I am concerned with three topics. First, Lonergan approaches his material from a particular standpoint. In the first chapter of his dissertation, he presents a theory of speculative development. This theory provides the basic structure for his approach to St. Thomas' developing thought on grace. Secondly, the most significant aspect of St. Thomas' developing thought was the category of actual grace.[23] Before St. Thomas could advance to his mature views on the division of graces, however, he had to clearly conceive the way in which God operates in His creation in general and in the human will in particular. Thirdly, Lonergan's discussion of St. Thomas' views on conversion occurs in the final chapter of *Grace and Freedom.* It incorporates both St. Thomas' views on divine operation, as well as Lonergan's theory of speculative development. Consequently, it is within the context of Lonergan's interpretation of St. Thomas' speculative theological performance that we can apprehend his earliest ideas about conversion.

The Theory of Speculative Development

There are four elements in Lonergan's proposed account of theological speculative development. They are: theorems, terms, dialectical positions, and technique. The most important of these elements in an account of St. Thomas' theology of grace is the theorem. Before discussing this element, however, I shall say something about each of the others.

Terms result from the speculative effort to advance in clarity. Words which are vague and imprecise eventually take on exact technical definitions. New words may be invented. *Dialectical positions* result from the fact that speculative theology is a science which deals with mystery: "the truths of faith have the apex of their intelligibility hidden in the transcendence of God."[24] Negatively, this means that theology will never fully comprehend its data. Positively, this means that theology can at least advance to the point where apparently opposed truths reach the negative coherence of non-contradiction. *Technique* is based on the fact that speculative theology relies on philosophy. It relies on philosophy for the clarificaton of strictly natural problems, for the analogies necessary to conceive the supernatural dimension, and also for its basic method. Consequently, developments in philosophy can often have immediate effects upon speculative theology.

The *theorem* is the single most important element in Lonergan's analysis of *gratia operans*. The advance of theology as a speculative science is often the result of integrating two or more theorems into a higher unity. In outline form, Lonergan describes the development of a theological explanation by a compound theorem in seven phases. His description can be paraphrased as follows:

> First, an initial theorem is discovered which seems to explain some problem in the tradition.
> Second, the initial theorem is generalized and has its implications worked out.
> Third, the initial theorem is perceived as capable of solving the whole of the problem on its own.
> Fourth, the limitations of the initial theorem are revealed and a second more general theorem is discovered.
> Fifth, the general theorem is expanded and has its implications worked out.
> Sixth, the general theorem is perceived as capable of solving the whole of the problem on its own.
> Seventh, the limitations of the general theorem are revealed, the necessity of the initial and more specific theorem is rediscovered, and the solution is reached when the general and specific theorems are integrated into a compound theorem.[25]

This scheme is abstract. In the concrete, explanations may involve a series of successively more general theorems. Further elements such as terms, technique, and dialectical positions have to be included. Regardless of concrete complexity, however, the general principle remains the same.

In order to illustrate this scheme more clearly, Lonergan applies its general outlines to the movement of speculation from St. Augustine to St. Thomas on the necessity of grace.

The specific theorem takes account of the condition of fallen humanity. The general theorem is the theorem of the supernatural. Lonergan sketches the various phases in the emergence and integration of these two theorems.[26]

The first phase is constituted by the emergence of the specific theorem. In St. Augustine's *De Corruptione et Gratia,* one can find numerous points which bear on the distinction between our own need for grace and its necessity for our first parents. While these points are not specifically formulated into a scientific theorem, they are, nevertheless, an attempt to explain. Lonergan remarks that "throughout Augustine's many writings on grace, there is not only positive theology but also such a penetration of thought and understanding that one must affirm the development of speculative theology to already have begun."[27] Still, St. Augustine is not attempting to elaborate a speculative system. Instead he deals with notions which are the common possession of all.

The second phase is illustrated by Peter Lombard's formulation of the four states of human liberty: paradise, humanity's fallen condition, humanity's redeemed condition, and heaven. In this phase the implications of the basic distinction are being worked out.

The third phase results from the limitations of the specific theorem with respect to the speculative problems inherent in our need for grace. Without the theorem of the supernatural, it is virtually impossible to separate grace and liberty. Grace tends to be conceived psychologically as the liberation of liberty.

The fourth phase witnesses the emergence of the second and more general theorem. In this case, it is Philip the Chancellor of the University of Paris formulating the theorem of the supernatural. Lonergan describes the significance of that development in this manner:

> What Philip the Chancellor systematically posited was not the supernatural character of grace, for that was already known and acknowledged, but the validity of a line of reference termed nature. In the long term and in the concrete the real alternatives remain charity and cupidity, the elect and the *massa damnata.* But the whole problem lies in the abstract, in human thinking:

> the fallacy in early thought had been an unconscious
> confusion of the metaphysical abstraction, nature, with
> concrete data which do not quite correspond; Philip's
> achievement was the creation of a mental perspective,
> the introduction of a set of coordinates, that eliminated
> the basic fallacy and its attendant host of anomalies.[28]

Now one could distinguish between, on the one hand, the order
of grace, faith, charity, and merit; and on the other hand, the
order of reason, nature, and the natural love of God. As Lonergan notes, the supernatural character of grace was well accepted, but the problem remained—why was not everything
grace? Philip responded by positing an abstract line of reference termed nature. Now one could speculate on liberty without bringing in problems of divine providence and speculate on
grace without threatening human liberty.[29] All of this did not
happen at once. Nevertheless, it was the breakthrough which
allowed for the development of the theology of grace which we
find in Aquinas.

In the fifth phase, the theorem of the supernatural is expanded in the attempt to provide the single source of the
solution to the problem. Thus we find St. Albert, St. Bonaventure, and St. Thomas' early works focusing upon sanctifying
grace as the principle of supernatural life.

In the sixth phase, the inadequacies of the general theorem
begin to reveal themselves. In St. Thomas' work this is manifested in his discovery of the significance of moral impotence
and the limitations of habitual grace.

In the seventh phase, the general theorem of the supernatural
and the specific theorem on humanity's fallen state are integrated into an explanation by a compound theorem. The presence of both theorems, as well as their integration into a
synthesis, can be discerned in the following passage concerning the necessity of grace.

> Hence in the state of the integrity of nature, man
> needs a gratuitous strength superadded to natural
> strength for one reason, viz., in order to do and will
> supernatural good; but in the state of corrupted nature
> he needs it for two reasons, viz., in order to be healed
> and, furthermore, in order to carry out works of super-
> natural virtue, which are meritorious.[30]

Generally speaking, humanity's final goal is not proportionate to its nature. Hence, whether in the state of integral nature or in the state of corrupted nature, the human person needs to be elevated in order to attain his or her transcendent finality. More specifically, humanity has in fact fallen. Consequently, we need grace in order to be healed, viz., in order to be restored even to our natural dignity. The full answer is, neither of these two theorems taken singly, but their integration into a synthesis.

The basic point to be noted is the central significance which Lonergan accords to explanation by theorem. Speculative theology is advancing from common sense notions to explanation by a scientific ordering of the data.[31] The development of thought on the issue of grace and freedom is but a microcosm of the larger development of theological method itself.

Religious Conversion

Lonergan specifically discusses St. Thomas' views on religious conversion in the context of the final chapter of *Grace and Freedom* on actual grace. He writes: "St. Thomas found the idea of the habit ready made, but he had to think out for himself the analogy of nature that corresponds to actual grace."[32] Thus, St. Thomas could appeal to a developed theory of habits to provide the underpinnings for his speculation on habitual grace, but he had to develop his own theoretical underpinnings for the notion of actual grace. Further, and this is the important point, St. Thomas' developing thought on actual grace paralleled his developing thought on conversion.[33] In chapters four and five of *Grace and Freedom,* Lonergan clarified the speculative background for St. Thomas' thought on actual grace by investigating two key topics: St. Thomas' theory of universal instrumentality and his developed theory of will. Consequently, before I discuss Lonergan's treatment of religious conversion in *Grace and Freedom,* I shall review these two key topics.

The theorem of universal instrumentality is: God applies all agents to their activity. Again, God operates through the operations of His creatures. As the artist applies the brush to the canvas, so God applies the creature to its creaturely activities.

Again, as the pianist plays the piano, so the Creator operates through the operations of the creature. More precisely, the piano produces the musical sounds and the pianist causes the piano to operate. Thus, the pianist causes the causation of the piano; similarly, God causes the causation of all created things. In the *Summa contra gentiles* St. Thomas writes: "Hence it is clear that in all things that operate God is the cause of their operating."[34]

In St. Thomas' view of the universe, God operates with a plan. As the plan exists in God's mind, it is termed providence; as it exists and unfolds in the created universe, it is termed fate. Both providence and fate are certain. What God wills has come to pass, is coming to pass, and will come to pass. For St. Thomas, Lonergan points out, "providence was certain in each case because it was the cause of all cases."[35] In other words, God's plan pertains to the universe as a whole and it is relevant to each of the parts in the manner and measure that they are related to the whole. Fate is not some entity imposed upon creatures and the created order from the outside. Instead, it exists in the category of relations and is the intrinsic order of secondary causes. Fate is the seriation of contingent causes and effects which, in their mutual conditionality, combine to constitute the actual order and unfolding of creation. Accordingly, St. Thomas' view of providence includes both the idea of an order of contingent causes and effects, as well as the certitude of the divine plan.

The second topic is St. Thomas' developed theory of will. According to the theorem of universal instrumentality, God operates in the operations of his creatures. According to St. Thomas' developed theory of will, God operates in the voluntary operations of the human will.[36] The key issue is the combination of divine and human activity in the human act of choice.

In his later writings, St. Thomas distinguished between the determination and the exercise of the act of will. He writes:

> Now a power of the soul is found to be in potentiality to different things in two ways: first, with regard to acting and not acting; secondly, with regard to this or that action. . . . It needs therefore a mover in two respects:

viz., as to the exercise or use of the act, and as to the determination of the act.[37]

The determination of the act of will is provided by the intellect. The intellect moves the will by presenting the objects which it apprehends. The exercise of the act of will is provided by the power of the will to move itself. Thus, one cannot choose an object which one does not first know about; however, simply knowing about an object does not necessitate choosing it. The exercise of the act of will is ultimately grounded in the self-movement of the will.

The self-movement of the will is not absolute. The human will can move itself to choose this or that particular object because its self-movement originates in and proceeds from a prior movement by God. St. Thomas writes:

> God moves man's will, as the Universal Mover, to the universal object of the will, which is the good. And without this universal motion man cannot will anything. But man determines himself by his reason to will this or that, which is a true or apparent good.[38]

Thus, God causes people to will their highest good and final end, and on the basis of this prior movement, the will moves itself to choose the means.

The theorem of universal instrumentality and the developed theory of the will provide the speculative background for St. Thomas' developed thought on conversion. According to the theorem of universal instrumentality, people are always instruments in God's plan. God applies them to their activity and operates through their operations. According to the developed theory of will, volitional activity occurs in two phases. In the first phase, the will does not move itself, but rather is moved by God's direct operation. In the second phase, the will, initially moved by God to will the end, moves itself to will the means. Still, people are called to an end which transcends their nature; they are called to supernatural life, to a vision of God. Such an end requires God's grace. Consequently, by habitual and by actual graces, God operates within the human will to turn it or convert it to Himself.

In order to understand St. Thomas' conception of conversion, we must distinguish three types of movement towards God. First, there is a general, all-pervasive movement of the totality of creation back to the Creator. Secondly, within this general movement, each creature moves according to its own nature and mode of operation. Thirdly, God moves some people to seek Him in a special way. Conversion must be understood within this third category. St. Thomas writes:

> Since God is absolutely the First Mover, it is by His motion that everything seeks Him under the common notion of the good, whereby everything seeks to be likened to God in its own way. . . . But He directs just men to Himself as a special end, which they seek and to which they wish to cling.[39]

Lonergan explains that "grace moves the will to God, who is determinate indeed but also the *bonum universale* beyond all limitation or classification; further, grace moves the will to God not by adding "potency" in the sense of limitation and con-traction, but by being a further actuation, and so giving expan-sion and enlargement.[40] Consequently, conversion is a movement which presupposes the general movement of each creature according to its nature. Conversion goes beyond these, however, by adding a movement towards God vivified by charity.

In the *Pars Tertia* of the *Summa Theologiae,* St. Thomas discusses conversion in terms of the justification of the sinner. He distinguishes six acts within the process of conversion. He writes:

> The first source of such acts is God's operation con-verting the heart. As we read, "Convert us, O Lord, to thee and we shall be converted." The second act is a movement of faith. The third is a movement of servile fear, by which the person withdraws from sin by fear of punishment. The fourth is a movement of hope, by which he makes a firm purpose of amendment, in the hope of obtaining pardon. The fifth is a movement of charity whereby sin itself is displeasing, and not in view of punishment. The sixth act is a movement of

filial fear whereby a person freely offers amendment to God out of reverence for Him.[41]

The first act in the process of conversion is an operative grace. The will has not responded to an intellectually apprehended object. Instead, God has moved it directly, turning the will towards Himself.[42]

It is not certain which of the movements are due to actual grace or habitual grace. Lonergan comments that the first act, God's operation converting the heart, may be an actual grace since it occurs prior to justification.[43] The fifth act, I believe, is the infusion of habitual grace and it grounds the movement towards God vivified by charity. This is the response of the free will of the justified person towards God. Perhaps the first act is related to the fifth act as the act of charity to the habit of charity.[44] That is, God first acts on our will, inspiring a pious thought or a holy aspiration. Subsequently, what began as a momentary desire, fixes itself into a permanent disposition or orientation. Thus the act of charity so implants itself in the person that it becomes the habit of charity. Accordingly, both by operative and cooperative graces, God converts the person to Himself.

St. Thomas distinguishes between two kinds of sequence.[45] In the sequence of time, sinners must first turn from their sins before they can freely respond towards God. In the sequence of the order of meaning, however, the movement towards God vivified by charity is prior to the movement away from sin. In other words, we are not moved by God's love because we have turned from sin, but rather we can turn from sin because we are converted by God's love. Thus, temporal sequence is not strictly applicable to the movements of the will. In summary, conversion is chiefly a movement towards God vivified by charity and secondarily a movement away from sin motivated by fear and reverence.

Prior to the discussion in the *Pars Tertia,* St. Thomas had distinguished three types of conversion. First, a preparatory conversion initiates us into the spiritual life. Secondly, a meritorious conversion enables us to persevere on the road to perfection. Thirdly, perfect conversion is the possession of the souls of the blessed in the presence of God in heaven. St.

Thomas writes: "Every movement of the will towards God can be termed a conversion to God."[46] I would say that the first conversion is primarily due to an actual grace, the second to habitual grace, and the third requires a consummate grace.

In summary, St. Thomas' developed view of conversion is a synthesis of his conception of the way in which the Creator operates in His creation, of the way in which He operates within the human will, and of the way in which He draws just people to Himself. Lonergan had studied the development of St. Thomas' thought on operative grace in *Grace and Freedom;* he concluded that study with a summary statement:

> The general law is that man is always an instrument; that his volitional activity deploys in two phases; that in the first phase he is governed . . . while in the second he governs . . . and finally that, inasmuch as motions to the *bonum meritorium* and its supernatural goal are graces, the general law of instrumentality then becomes the special gift of *gratia operans et cooperans.* Now this adaptation of the speculative materials of instrumental and voluntary theory into a doctrine of grace not only implies that conversion is but a single instance of *gratia operans* but also involves that good performance is but one instance of *gratia cooperans.*[47]

Consequently, in this earliest work, we see the initial conception of the notion of religious conversion within the context of a speculative theology which proceeds, as Lonergan points out, through the scientific ordering of theorems.

Verbum

In this second phase of the early period, *Verbum,* I am dealing with four related topics. While it is my primary intention to discuss the topic of intellectual conversion, direct discussion of that topic will have to await the development of the various contexts of meaning. First, it is my contention that intellectual conversion began as the notion of reflective self-knowledge. The relevant initial context of meaning for this notion is Lonergan's discussion of the psychological fact of understanding. Thus, the first section investigates the psychological context.

Secondly, Thomist statements on *verbum,* while employing introspective data, are primarily theological in intent. In other words, the psychological context itself is merely the subjective pole of a higher context, the objective pole of which is Thomist trinitarian theory. A second section, therefore, discusses the theological dimension of intellectual conversion. Thirdly, the aforementioned higher context of meaning for the emerging concept of intellectual conversion is to be found in Lonergan's ideal of science. He labels that ideal as intellectualist.[48] His intellectualist views serve as the basis for his entire approach and organization in these *Verbum* articles. Finally, once these various contexts have been investigated and interrelated, the proper dimensions of the emerging concept of intellectual conversion can be traced.

The Psychological Fact

THE DIVISION OF INNER WORDS

Inner words are of two types: the definition and the judgment. Both types of inner word proceed from acts of understanding which Lonergan terms direct understanding and reflective understanding respectively. Aquinas had his own, more metaphysical reason for this twofold division of inner words. Reality is properly divided into essence and existence. Related to this point, St. Thomas was following Aristotle when he wrote: "We must realize that, as the Philosopher says, the intellect has two operations: one called the understanding of indivisibles, by which it knows what a thing is; and another by which it joins and divides, that is to say, by forming affirmative and negative statements."[49] As might be gathered from these points, the inner word of definition proceeds from the act of direct understanding which responds to the question, What is it? The question, Is it so? precedes the act of reflective understanding which, in turn, is the source of the inner word of judgment. Consequently, Lonergan begins his study of Aquinas' treatment of *verbum* with a first chapter entitled "Verbum: Definition and Understanding," and follows with a second chapter entitled "Verbum: Reflection and Judgment."

While there are two intellectual operations and two corresponding inner words, both types of processions manifest a common quality. Aquinas characterized the general nature of intellectual procession as intelligible emanation.[50] Lonergan discusses three factors which distinguish the procession of an intelligible emanation from a natural procession. First, natural procession is passive. While it can be understood, it is not what is meant by the term understanding. It is intelligible but not intelligent. Secondly, natural process manifests the intelligibility of some specific law. It may reveal, for example, the law of gravity. But natural process never reveals the intelligibility of law itself. Thirdly, natural process proceeds intelligibly because of some law imposed from without.

Conversely, because it is active, general, and native, the procession of the inner word of human understanding is an intelligible emanation. First, the procession of the inner word is not merely intelligible, it is also actively intelligent. It is what is meant by the term "understanding". Secondly, the procession of the inner word does not proceed according to some specific law, but rather is itself the general principle from which the various laws of science proceed. Thirdly, the procession of the inner word proceeds, not with an imposed intelligibility, but with the native intelligibility of intellect in act.

The contrast between natural and intellectual procession is paramount to these *Verbum* articles. In order to underscore the significance which this distinction has for trinitarian theory, Lonergan writes:

> Now it is only to restate the basic contention of this and subsequent articles to observe that the human mind is an image, and not a mere vestige, of the Blessed Trinity because its processions are intelligible in a manner that is essentially different from, that transcends, the passive, specific, imposed intelligibility of other natural process.[51]

Aquinas expressed a related point. He wrote that since God is the Supreme Being, and above all created perfection, our attempts to conceive Him should be not in terms of what is lowest in creation—namely bodies, but in terms of what is highest—namely intellectual substances. Similarly, the procession of divine persons is not to be conceived on an analogy with natural procession. "Rather it is to be understood by way of an intelligible emanation, for example of the intelligible word which proceeds from the speaker, yet remains in him."[52]

Lonergan designates this threefold characterization of the procession of the inner word (active, general, and native) by using the term rational. "The human mind offers an analogy to the trinitarian processions because it is rational in its conceptualizations, in its judgments, in its acts of will."[53] Furthermore, the rational character of the inner word implies that it is reflective; in other words, self-expressive and self-possessive. What else is implied by such a designation cannot be conveyed in any simple manner. Yet, in the rational and reflective nature of human intelligence lies the whole point.

THE LEVEL OF DIRECT UNDERSTANDING

The procession of the inner word on the level of direct understanding terminates in an essential definition. Such procession occurs neither spontaneously nor automatically. The human intelligence must labor to grasp and express essences. Lonergan elaborates this feature by recalling the questioning of Socrates. Socrates was fond of asking such questions as What is justice? or courage? or piety? Aristotle saw that a significant portion of the difficulty in answering Socrates' questions lies in the prior difficulty of determining exactly what one is seeking when asking a question such as What is it? Aristotle concluded that one is seeking a cause, and most often and most significantly, the formal cause. When one asks What is a house? or a man? or anything? One is attempting to grasp the formal cause.

Lonergan interprets Aristotle's concept of form in two sections of this first chapter. His point is that what Aristotle means by formal cause can best be settled by reference to the act of insight into sensible or imaginable data. The heart of Lonergan's interpretation is contained in the following quotation:

> What is a man? What is a house? The clue lies in the fact of insight into sensible data. For an insight, and act of understanding, is a matter of knowing a cause. Presumably, in ultimate and simple cases, the insight is knowledge of a cause that stands between the sensible data and the concept whose definition is sought. . . . What is a man? What is a house? The meaning is, Why

is this sort of body a man? Why are stones and brick arranged in a certain way, a house? What is it that causes the matter sensibly perceived to be a thing? To Scholastics the answers are self-evident. That which makes this type of body to be a man, is a human soul. That which makes these stones and bricks to be a house, is an artificial form. That which makes matter in general, to be a thing, is the *causa essendi,* the formal cause.[54]

How does one know the formal cause? It is by an act of insight. Certainly, one must perceive the sensible data, but grasping the form requires more than simple staring. One grasps the form by the further act of direct understanding. One grasps the form by grasping what is significant about the data, yet can never itself be a mere datum. One grasps the form by an act of insight into the sensible or imaginable data.

While the formal cause can be understood in terms of insight into sensible or imaginable data, insight itself is difficult to isolate for inspection. Aquinas dropped the effort to isolate the act of understanding prior to the procession of the inner word of definition. Lonergan suggests that his reason must have been that the act of understanding "is prior to and cause of conceptualization, [and] because expression is only through conceptualization, any attempt to fix the act of understanding, except by way of introspective description, involves its own partial failure; for any such attempt is an expression, and expression is no longer understanding and already concept."[55] How can one say what one means prior to expression in language?

Nevertheless, the preconceptual act of understanding, insight into phantasm, can be indicated in some fashion. It can be somewhat described and examples can be offered wherein presence can be discerned. Evidence of intellect turning to, or converting to, phantasms can be found in the process of learning. As Aquinas notes: "anyone can experience this of himself, that when he tries to understand something, he forms certain phantasms, to serve him by way of examples, in which as it were he examines what he is desirous of understanding."[56] Further, a picture is worth a thousand words, and every teacher has had the experience of searching for the apt example in order to avoid the necessity of lengthy explanations. Again, we need phantasms, not simply when we are learning something for the first time, but also when we are actualizing knowledge which we habitually possess. Finally, even in such an abstract subject as theology, the intellect relies on phantasms. Although we remove from God everything which can be imagined, we could not "know that God causes bodies, or transcends all bodies, or is not a body, if we do not form an image of bodies."[57] Aquinas agreed with Aristotle that without phantasms the soul can understand nothing.

There are more metaphysical reasons, however, for the Thomist insistence of the role of phantasms. Since the human person is a soul united to a corruptible body, and his or her own powers partake of that composite condition; the proper object of human intellect must be composite as well, that is to say, the quiddity of a material thing.[58] Knowledge of the quiddity of a material thing occurs when intellect converts to the phantams "as objects in which it sees whatever it sees, either through a perfect representation or through negation."[59] Consequently, for Aquinas, the necessity of phantasms is grounded in the prior necessity of the human person, as incarnate spirit, having an object proportioned to his or her power of knowing.

THE LEVEL OF REFLECTIVE UNDERSTANDING

The procession of the inner word on the level of reflective understanding terminates in the judgment. Judgment is the answer, in the affirmative or negative, to the question, Is it so? Like the inner word of definition, judgment also proceeds from an act of understanding. In this case, however, the act of understanding is termed reflective because of its self-possessed and critical nature. Comparatively, we characterize the act of direct understanding from which the definition proceeds as a type of ecstatic wonder. Reflective understanding is that wonder having become critical of its own ground. Lonergan distinguishes two components within the mechanism of judgment: the synthesis and positing the synthesis.

The synthetic component of judgment is rooted in the prior level of direct understanding. On that level, the act of insight into phantasm is expressed in a simple definition or quiddity. Several discrete insights can be expressed in several distinct definitions. There are, however, more elaborate operations than the production of simple definitions. For example, the several insights may coalesce into a higher and more comprehensive insight expressed in a more complex definition. Hence the definition of a circle comprises the simpler concepts of a line, a point, and a curve. This synthesis of simple quiddities into the unity of a higher intelligibility is the material upon which reflective understanding reflects. Again, the synthesis which is a product of direct understanding, becomes the hypothesis which is a question for reflective understanding.

For St. Thomas, the synthetic power of intelligence is a central factor in his hierarchical conception of the universe. Higher angels grasp more objects, more profoundly, with fewer intelligible species. The divine act of understanding, which is identical with the divine being, embraces the universe in its entirety. In one act of understanding, God knows everything about everything. It is to this summit of perfection that the human intellect aspires.

Although our aspiration is high, we must struggle in order to understand even basic definitions. We must reason. First we understand one thing. Then we understand another. Knowledge of principles, for example, leads to knowledge of conclusions. Finally, in one synthetic sweep, we can understand one thing in another. We can grasp the conclusion as it pre-exists in and flows from the principles.

Reason is often distinguished from understanding as if the two were unrelated. In such cases, reason is usually identified with its formalized presentation in certain logic textbooks. But reason and understanding are more intimately related. First, our reasoning begins in understanding; for unless we understood something we would never begin to reason at all. Secondly, reason terminates in understanding. Thus, the consideration of elements, which at first seemed merely disparate, terminates in one intellectual act which is the apprehension of diversity and interdependence. In Aquinas' view, reason is understanding in process. Again, reason is related to the act of understanding as motion is to rest. Nevertheless, if we reason only in order to understand, we are best characterized as rational animals. The point behind this characterization is that "the human intellect is only potential in the genus of intelligible beings."[60] In order to reduce the potentiality to act, reason is required.

The synthesis of direct understanding, which becomes the hypothesis of reflective understanding, requires a further operation before it provides knowledge of reality. As hypothesis, it may be true, but it is not yet known to be true for there has been no judgment. Judgment is the positing of synthesis, not simply because it is true; but primarily because it is known to be true. Consequently, to the mental synthesis must be added the further act of positing or assenting.

The act of assent is the inner word expressing the act of reflective understanding. Lonergan contrasts the act of assent with the act of the will. "Consent is the motion of the will with respect to the thing, but assent is a motion of the intellect with respect to conception."[61] More precisely, assent is a motion of the intellect with respect to the correspondence between mental and real synthesis. By what criterion, asks Lonergan, does judgment posit the synthesis, or assent?

The criterion by which judgment posits the synthesis, gives its assent, utters its inner word, is the intellect itself. The act of applying this criterion to the mental synthesis is the act of *resolutio in principia*. This act involves intellect in using the light of its own principles as standard. Lonergan explains: "There are truths that are naturally known; they form the touch-stone of other truth; and judging is a matter of reducing other issues to naturally known first principles."[62] In another context, Lonergan refers to these "naturally known first principles" as the intellect's own light. It must be noted that these preliminary remarks on the criterion of judgment are sketchy and are filled out by later remarks on the nature of intellectual light. At this point, however, Lonergan is merely trying to indicate a starting point by dealing with what he terms the mechanism of judgment.[63]

In order to begin to fill out these elementary points, we should note that although Aquinas focused chiefly on reduction to the first principles of the intellect, or intellectual light, Lonergan draws attention to other factors as well: sensitive, imaginative, and psychological. He summarizes the process of reduction to principles in the following way:

> Hence the reflective activity whence judgment results is a return from the synthesis effected by developing insight into their sources in sense and in intellectual light.[64]

He continues:

> The reflective activity of reason returning from the synthesis of intelligibilities to its origin in sense and in naturally known principles terminates in a reflective act of understanding, in a single synthetic apprehension of all the motives for judgment, whether intellectual or sensitive, in a grasp of their sufficiency as motives and so of the necessity of passing judgment or asserting.[65]

Resolutio in principia, then, is a return to sources. Further, it is a grasp of the sufficiency of those sources to ground the inner word of judgment. That is the key point. The rationality of intelligible procession lies in its self-expressive and self-possessive character. What reflective understanding grasps in the sources is not simply fuller understanding, but the sufficiency of present understanding for the utterance of the judgment. Human rationality, and the reflective character of judgment, provide a clue to the procession of the divine persons because of the ability of reflective understanding to express and possess itself and the sufficiency of its own ground.

We are now in a position to summarize Lonergan's analysis of the Thomist conception of the procession of the inner words of human intellect. In the following quotation Lonergan offers a review of both levels of intellectual operation and consequently the substance of the first two chapters of *Verbum:*

> The general outline of Thomist analysis of human intellect is now, perhaps, discernible. There are two levels of activity, the direct and the reflective. On the direct level there occur two types of events: there are insights into phantasm which express themselves in definitions; there is the coalescence or development of

insights which provide the hypothetical syntheses of simple quiddities. On the reflective level these hypothetical syntheses are known as hypothetical; they become questions which are answered by the *resolutio in principia*. Thus return to sources terminates in a reflective act of understanding, which is a grasp of the necessary connection between the sources and the hypothetical synthesis; from this grasp there proceeds its self-expression which is the *compositio vel divisio*,[66] the judgment, the assent.[67]

This is the summary analysis of the two levels of human intellectual activity with the corresponding twofold processions of the inner words. We can proceed now to the related issue of self-knowledge.

SELF-KNOWLEDGE

In Lonergan's view, Aristotle and Aquinas were correct in their account of knowledge in terms of identity. "Hence the Philosopher says that the sensible in act is the sense in act, and the intelligible in act is the intellect in act."[68] Aristotle maintained this position against the Platonist view that knowledge is inherently knowledge of other. On the Platonist view, it is difficult to account for divine self-knowledge. On the Thomist account, based on the Aristotelian knowledge by identity, it is a problem that God knows things other than Himself. Lonergan concludes that the central problem with an account of knowledge in terms of the identity of intelligibility and intelligence in act, is knowledge of other. How does one move from knowledge as subjective perfection to knowledge as a grasp of some aspect of reality?

St. Thomas' full account of knowledge goes beyond the Aristotelian account. To knowledge by immateriality, St. Thomas added knowledge by the intentionality. While the sensible in act is sense in act, and while the intelligible in act is intellect in act; the act of being of the known is not identical with the act of being of the knower. Rather, the act of being of the known is the object of human intentionality. It is what is intended by the reflective questions Is it so? and Is such and such actually the case? It was in rational reflection that Aquinas placed the burden of this transition from knowledge as perfection to knowledge of other.

Only rational reflection terminates in knowledge of the truth. Sense knowledge may be either true or false. For example, we often check to be sure that we have heard or seen something correctly. Of itself, however, sensation does not include knowledge of its own truth or falsity. Similarly, the act of direct understanding may be either true or false. We often review our evidence to be sure we have not misunderstood. Yet, the act of direct understanding terminates not in truth or falsity, but in hypothesis. Only on the level of reflective understanding does intellectual knowledge, reduced to its sources in sense, imagination, and intellectual light, not merely take possession of its content but of its own validity as well. In reviewing the role of intellectual light in reflective understanding, intellect returns to itself. It was in relation to the return of intellect to itself, in the self-expressive and self-possessive act of reflection, that Aquinas tried to understand the procession of the divine word.[69]

The judgment proceeds from a reflective act of understanding which always includes some self-knowledge. But not every judgment includes a knowledge which penetrates to the very essence of the person. Aquinas maintained, however, that knowledge of our acts of understanding could lead to such knowledge. "The human soul understands itself through its own act of understanding which is proper to it, showing perfectly its power and nature."[70] Aristotle had provided St. Thomas with a scientific approach to the soul in terms of its objects, acts, potencies, and essence.[71] But Aristotle also spoke of a more direct route to self-knowledge. We are present to ourselves, he maintained, in each of our acts. For example, we not only speak, move, hear, and understand; we are also immediately aware of ourselves in each of these acts. Aquinas agreed but emphasized that it was the last of these acts, the act of understanding, which properly revealed our natures to us.

Following Aquinas, Lonergan distinguishes two elements within the act of understanding. There is the element of determination and the element of light. First, the element of determination is present because human understanding is never simply pure act. It is understanding of this or that particular thing. Secondly, the element of light is present as the actualizing element in every act of understanding, rendering actual the intelligibility of this or that particular thing. No matter how divergent may be the content of the particular intellectual acts, this element of light is an ever present common factor. Lonergan compares it to the light of the sun. As the sunlight is not properly the object of human vision, but rather that which makes particular object visible to our eyes; so too, intellectual light is not properly the object of human intellect, but rather the medium through which objects become intelligible to our minds.

Lonergan correlates the element of determination and the element of light with the two levels of intellectual operation of the earliest analysis:

> On the division enounced above, these two types of expression have their grounds respectively in the two elements of determination and light found in the act of understanding. Inasmuch as the act of understanding grasps its own conditions as the understanding of this sort of thing, it abstracts from the irrelevant and expresses itself in a definition of essence. But inasmuch as the act of understanding grasps its own transcendence-in-immanence, its quality of intellectual light as a participation of the divine and uncreated Light, it expresses itself in judgment, in a positing of truth, in the affirmation or negation of reality.[72]

In this passage Lonergan relates intellectual light to the ground of judgment. In other places, he identifies it generally with the capacity for reflection and specifically with the agent intellect.

In summary, I have been sharpening the focus on the central factor in self-knowledge. Aquinas affirmed that we can understand ourselves by grasping the nature of our acts of understanding. From this general consideration, I focused further on the level of reflective understanding. In the act of reflective understanding, intellect returns to itself. I drew attention to Lonergan's characterization of this reflective act of understanding in terms of intellectual light. In this last context, self-knowledge involves the apprehension of intellectual light. Lonergan synthesizes the various aspects of this complicated matter in the following manner: "In the measure one grasps the character and implication of the act by which intellectual light reflects by intellectual light upon intellectual light to understand itself and pronounce its universal validity, in that measure one grasps one of the two outstanding analogies of the procession of an infinite Word from an infinite understanding."[73] In the reflectivity of intellectual light lies the key both to self-knowledge and to knowledge of the Trinity. The foregoing analysis provides at least the elements necessary to grasp the psychological fact which serves as the basis of the analogy for the trinitarian processions.

The Psychological Fact and Theology

When Aquinas spoke of God as *ipsum intelligere,* he meant that God is absolute understanding. That is one of Lonergan's central contentions in the *Verbum* articles.[74] Further, God is not to be conceived on an analogy with ideas or concepts. He is rather to be thought of as analogous to the human act of understanding. In contrast, the Platonic separate ideas are what is known through confrontation with concepts. Aristotle advanced beyond this position considerably when he conceived separate substances by extrapolating, not from the human concept, but from the act of insight into phantasm. The separate substance is the act of understanding without the determination of sensitive conditions. This is much closer to the Thomist view of God as *ipsum intelligere.*

In the Thomist view, in addition to the extrapolation from insight into phantasm, there is an Augustinian dimension. St. Augustine grounded his account of judgment in the Eternal. But for Aquinas, we know by what we are. Our judgments are valid not because of anything we may spiritually "see," but rather because we are by nature participated likenesses in God. Aquinas insisted that our immanent intellectual light is a participated likeness in the Uncreated Light.[75] While God is the act of understanding everything about everything, our flashes of insight are participation in that absolute act of understanding.

These points can be summarized in the following manner. God as Uncreated Light is ontologically prior and we are participated likenesses of Him. On the other hand, our immanent intellectual light is the element which most properly manifests the nature and power of our souls. Intellectual light is prior for us. Our wisdom consists in a dialectical interplay between the poles of grasping our own nature, as intellectual light, and grasping, in a limited act of understanding, God as Uncreated Light. Increased self-knowledge provides an expanded basis upon which to extrapolate to knowledge of God. Knowledge of God, as *ipsum intelligere,* provides the clue to deeper self-knowledge.

From these considerations of the divine essence, we turn to Trinitarian speculation. Aquinas had relied on introspective knowledge of his own mind when he tried to conceive the divine essence; he would also rely on introspective knowledge when he undertook the task of conceiving the Trinitarian processions. Looking at the order of questions in the *Pars Prima,* one sees that Aquinas turned his attention to God as triune only after some twenty-five questions on the divine unity.[76] Once turned to Trinitarian theory, his first question was whether there is procession in God. He answered in the affirmative. There is procession in God and it is an intelligible procession; but what is meant by that designation is best shown by the process of elimination. First, divine procession is not a *processio operationis,*[77] that is, not a process of the emergence of a perfection from and in what is perfected. Examples of *processio operationis* are: generally speaking, the emergence of an act from a potency; more specifically, the emergence of the act of understanding from the intellect. Secondly, the divine procession is a kind of *processio operati,* that is, the emergence of one thing from another. There are, however, two serious qualifications.

In human understanding, the emergence of the judgment, for example, from the act of reflective understanding is a *processio operati.* It is the emergence of one act from another act. There are two elements in this procession which should be distinguished. The first element is efficient causality. Its presence is accounted for on the grounds that the second act is the effect of the first act. The second element is procession as intelligible. Its presence is accounted for on the grounds that the judgment proceeds from the act of reflective understanding, not merely as from a sufficient ground, but more significantly, as from a ground that is grasped and known to be sufficient. This is the element of reflectivity. In the divine act of understanding, the procession of the Word from its Principle is a *processio operati,* but without the element of efficient causality. It is analogous to the procession of the inner word of human thought primarily because of its reflectivity.[78] However, whereas human intellect is a conditioned reflectivity, God is pure reflectivity.

There is a second qualification to be stipulated. The human act of understanding and utterance of the inner word involves two acts. The divine Word and its Principle are not two distinct acts. Aquinas offers the following explanation for this difference: "Whatever proceeds within by an intelligible procession is not necessarily distinct; indeed, the more perfectly it proceeds, the more closely it is one with the source whence it proceeds."[79] In God, there is an identity of principle and term. While in most acts of human understanding, the principle and the term differ, there is an exceptional case. At the height of human reflection there is an approximation to identity of principle and term. When intellectual light reflects upon intellectual light, there is duplication. It is a duplication, however, with a dynamism toward identity. I quoted Lonergan previously on this point: "For in the measure one grasps the character and implication of the act by which intellectual light reflects by intellectual light upon intellectual light to understand itself and pronounce its universal validity. . . ."[80] Nevertheless, given our material limitations, and the fact that our intellects are chiefly potential; we are never identical with any one of our acts of understanding. This is why our reflectivity is conditional.

The relevance of the psychological analogy is limited in Thomist Trinitarian theory. It takes us beyond what can be affirmed of God solely on the basis of natural reason. But since it is based on analogy, it is limited by the very attempt to measure the Creator in terms of the creature. But it does achieve partial success. It brings us further in our limited understanding of the mysteries of faith. Lonergan remarks that "the psychological analogy is just the side door through which we enter for an imperfect look"[81] at the divine essence. That view, however, is paled by the Beatific Vision which is the possession of the blessed in heaven. That brings us to our next point which is the Thomist view of theology as science.

Understanding and Science

Lonergan's approach to the interpretation of the concept of *verbum* is intended to promote the development of understanding. The articles are organized around three hermeneutical circles: the psychological, the metaphysical, and the theological.[82] One theme is developed repeatedly through each of the contexts: the centrality of the act of understanding for Thomist rational psychology. Instead of proceeding to his conclusion by the direct route of logical deduction, Lonergan is content to "explore separately the several hermeneutical circles that in cumulative fashion are relevant to an interpretation.[83] He intends his method to be consonant with his purpose. Since his purpose is to underscore the centrality of the act of understanding, his method emphasizes the development of understanding rather than the deduction of certitudes.

The reason for Lonergan's approach lies in the intellectualist concept of science.[84] For the intellectualist, the ideal of science is understanding. There are three important aspects to this view which need to be distinguished.

First, for Aquinas, science is one of the three habits of the speculative intellect. The other two are understanding[85] and wisdom. Each of these three habits possesses its own proper operation as well as a dependence on each of the others. Aquinas writes:

> The principles of demonstration can be considered by themselves, without the conclusion being considered at all. They can also be considered together with the conclusions, in so far as the principals are extended to lead to conclusions. Accordingly, to consider principles in this second way belongs to science, which considers the conclusions also; while to consider principles in themselves belongs to understanding . . . science depends on understanding as on a virtue of higher degree. So too, both of these depend on wisdom as obtaining the highest place; for it contains beneath

itself both understanding and science, as judging both
of the conclusions of science and of the principles on
which they are based.[86]

Lonergan correlates these speculative habits with his earlier
analysis of intellectual acts. Whereas Aquinas distinguished
between the habits of understanding, science, and wisdom,
Lonergan distinguishes the corresponding acts. Therefore, in a
parallel manner we have: the act of direct understanding, the
development of direct understanding, and the act of reflective
understanding. Specific implications of this correlation should
be noted. First, as the habit of understanding is related to the
act of direct understanding, so the habit of science is related to
the development of understanding. Secondly, as I pointed out
above,[87] Aquinas regarded reason as developed understanding.
Consequently, as it is unnecessary to restrict reason to the
formal exercise found in certain logic textbooks, so too it is
unnecessary to restrict science to the demonstration of certitudes. In short, the Thomist conceptions of both reason and
science are implicit in the notion of developing understanding.

Secondly, the general conception of science is, of course,
relevant to the more specific conception of theology as science.
Lonergan remarks: "Nor was understanding as the ideal of
scientific theology unknown to Aquinas whose principles,
methods, and doctrine the Church bids us follow."[88] But if
other sciences proceed from principles which are known, theology proceeds from and to a principle which is shrouded in
mystery, that is, God Himself. Consequently, theology aspires
to and must be content with a limited but fruitful understanding. For example, the psychological analogy for the Trinitarian
processions is only meant to provide a possibly relevant understanding. It does not deny the possibility of alternative explanations. Further, even on its own terms, the psychological
analogy is meant to help develop understanding only to a
certain point. Then, it is "transcended and we are confronted
with mystery."[89] Thus, while Thomist theology does not claim
that we can know God's essence, it does aim at limited analo-
gical understanding of the mysteries of faith.

Finally, Lonergan's own approach to historical investigation
in these *Verbum* articles is consonant with the Thomist scien-

tific ideal. There are two errors which he is most concerned to avoid. First, there is the positivist concept of historical inquiry which simply excludes the goal of reflective understanding. Secondly, there is the conceptualist approach to Aquinas' which overlooks the historical distance between Aquinas' habitual understanding and the preunderstanding of the twentieth century investigator. But it is Lonergan's goal to establish the intellectualism of Aquinas.[90] His method must be consonant with that goal. Consequently, he describes his basic approach as "the task of developing one's understanding so as to understand Aquinas' comprehension of understanding and its intelligibly proceeding inner word."[91] Lonergan accepts as his own, then, the Thomist conception of science as the development of understanding.

The scientific aim of developing understanding is so basic that the conclusion of these *Verbum* articles seems almost anticlimatic. Lonergan states that conclusion in the following proposition: "Aquinas adverted to the act of understanding and made it central in his rational psychology."[92] If the appropriate insights and development of understanding have occurred, the conclusion is significant indeed. Nevertheless, the central point is not the assertion of the conclusion. Rather, the central point is the occurrence of the relevant acts of understanding. Only if one has understood is the conclusion meaningful.

Intellectual Conversion

Within *Grace and Freedom* we find the beginning of Lonergan's thought on religious conversion and within these *Verbum* articles we find the conception of intellectual conversion beginning to emerge. Its presence is most easily detected in discussions of the psychological fact, more specifically in the conception of reflective self-knowledge. Its presence is also to be discerned, however, in discussions of the procession of the divine word from infinite understanding. Lastly, although not as obviously, I believe we can find intellectual conversion implied in Lonergan's treatment of the Thomist conception of science. Let me expand on each of these points.

First, there is intellectual conversion as reflective self-knowledge. In the more developed treatment to be found in *Method in Theology*,[93] Lonergan makes two points relevant to the present discussion. First, intellectual conversion is a "radical clarification."[94] Secondly, intellectual conversion involves the realization that knowing is essentially a process of self-transcendence.[95] Although not expressed in this more contemporary language, Lonergan had made the same points earlier. When intellectual light reflects upon intellectual light, what becomes manifested and grasped is intellect's openness to the fullness of being, its native infinity. Although such language is not routine, Lonergan does specifically correlate the level of reflective understanding, our intellectual light, and the intellect's capacity for self-transcendence. He writes:

> But inasmuch as the act of understanding grasps its own transcendence-in-immanence, its quality of intellectual light as a participation of the divine and uncreated light, it expresses itself in judgment, in a positing of truth, in the affirmation or negation of reality.[96]

Merely to be aware of the quality of intellectual light does not, however, constitute intellectual conversion. Awareness is a beginning. To mere awareness, one must add the understanding of its implications and the reflective grasp of its nature and existence. Intellectual conversion can be a "radical clarification" because of the reflective nature of intellectual light. Intellectual light can express and possess itself almost to the point of identity of principle and term. Thus, in intellectual conversion, self-transcendence grasps its own nature.

Secondly, intellectual conversion has implications for Thomist trinitarian theory as well. If the beginning of the conception of intellectual conversion is to be located in the idea of reflective self-knowledge, then as Lonergan remarks, and as I have previously quoted:

> In the measure one grasps the character and implication of the act by which intellectual light reflects by intellectual light upon intellectual light to understand itself and pronounce its universal validity, in that measure one grasps one of the two outstanding analogies to the procession of an infinite Word from an infinite Understanding.[97]

If intellectual conversion is to be understood as the act whereby intellectual light reflectively returns to itself in self-possession and self-expression, then it finds its infinite analogue in the procession and interrelation of the Father and the Son. It is to be recalled, however, that in human reflectivity, principle and term are never identical. Since we are mostly potential in the genus of intellectual substances, our intellects are never fully actualized by any particular act of understanding, no matter how reflective. Nevertheless, the more closely the act of understanding approximates total reflectivity, the more closely it approximates the procession of the divine Word. As a postscript to this point, it should be noted that we shall never achieve such total reflectivity until "God Himself slips into and mysteriously actuates a finite intellect."[98] Then, we shall know both God and ourselves; for we shall be like Him. There is, then, a distinctly *theological* dimension to intellectual conversion.

Thirdly, intellectual conversion has implications for the intellectualist concept of science. The Thomist habit of science is correlated with the development of understanding and is rooted in the habit and act of direct understanding. The Thomist habit of understanding, Lonergan points out, is in turn grounded in the habit of wisdom. In this sequence of dependency, wisdom is foundational. It validates not only the conclusions of science but even the first principles of understanding. While science proceeds from understanding according to the principles of demonstration, it is the task of understanding to grasp indemonstrable principles. Moreover, Aquinas contends:

> The truth and knowledge of indemonstrable principles depend on the meaning of the terms; for as soon as we know what is a whole, and what is a part, we know at once that every whole is greater than its part. Now to know the meaning of being and non-being, which are the terms of which indemonstrable principles are constituted, is the function of wisdom.[99]

Thus, science depends on understanding for its basic principles, but wisdom, by grasping component terms, validates even understanding's apprehension of the principles. Chief among the component terms of basic principles, of course, is "the meaning of being and non-being." This raises the key question: On what basis does wisdom claim to know being?

Since both the habit of science and the habit of understanding depend ultimately upon wisdom in order to validate the knowledge of being, wisdom is necessarily thrown back upon itself. What aspect of itself must wisdom reflect upon in order to grasp and express its access to knowledge of being? Lonergan points out that it is the prerogative of wisdom to contemplate the highest cause in the universe. But this is not the aspect of wisdom upon which he focuses reflection. He points out again that there is an epistemological aspect to wisdom which is most relevant here. It is in reflection upon the native infinity of the intellect that wisdom's knowledge of being is to be grounded. When Lonergan adverts to the intellect's native infinity and characterizes it as *potens omnia facere et fiere*,[100] he is not simply asserting an aspect of Thomist theory. He is drawing attention to a point which can be immediately verified in any number of ways. The native infinity of the intellect manifests itself in the restless spirit of inquiry; in the continual search for causes; in the dissatisfaction with partial answers; in the Aristotelian philosophical wonder; in the realization that personally, communally, and historically the source of questioning will never dry up; and even in the wonder and doubt whether this list has any point or validity.

There is a kind of infinity to the questioning of the human intellect. The source of such questioning is constituted by a potential infinity and it is that source which is grasped and expressed in intellectual conversion. That source may be further characterized as a potential openness to the fullness of being. Note that intellectual conversion does not reflectively grasp the fullness of being. What intellectual conversion apprehends is questioning as the immanent source whose only proportionate object can be being itself. In reflection upon the native infinity of the intellect, intellect conversion moves toward the realization of both the nature of intellectual light and its proportionality to the fullness of being.

It follows that intellectual conversion is relevant to the intellectualist concept of science. As science is dependent upon understanding's grasp of component terms, so too the grasp of component terms is dependent, in part, on intellect's knowledge of itself as naturally infinite. Consequently, a science, which intends to be reflectively aware of itself and its own conditions, will have to, at some point, take account of the nature of intellect and, hence, reach some approximation to intellectual conversion.

In summary, these were the major contexts in which the concept of intellectual conversion began to emerge. The most obviously fertile soil for the germination of such a conception was in Lonergan's discussion of the psychological fact. Related immediately to that discussion were the points concerning Thomist trinitarian theory. Informing both of these contexts was an intellectualist ideal of science and the precondition of such an ideal of science was an intellect reflectively aware of its native infinity—that is, an intellect which has been converted.

Lonergan's Development in the Early Period

In the span of years between *Grace and Freedom* and *Verbum*. Lonergan's thought underwent considerable development. How can the nature of this development be best expressed? My approach to both phases has been to distinguish the material from the formal elements. In *Grace and Freedom,* Lonergan organized his material according to a theory of speculative development. In *Verbum,* he approached the Thomist inner word in terms of three hermeneutical circles. The more significant movement is not the material one from the Thomist theology of grace to the Thomist theology of the Trinity. The more significant development occured on the formal level. What has changed about Lonergan's formal approach to Thomist material?

As early as "Gratia Operans," Lonergan was meditating on theological method. In the first chapter, he apologizes for the difficulty of his method, explaining that it demands of the reader a capacity to discern in "several hundred pages which discuss a great variety of points a single argument with a major premise in the theory of development and a minor in a number of facts."[101] The conclusion of his study, then, is the result of integrating a theory of the way theological speculation develops with statements on the nature of *gracia operans*. I was best able to understand Lonergan's earliest writings on conversion by placing them within this context. Summarily stated, conversion is the result of God's grace acting directly on the will. Aquinas' successive statements on it can be understood in terms of the development of his theorems on the universal instrumentality, on the nature of the human will, and on the relationship between the natural and supernatural orders.

Besides distinguishing the theorems which Aquinas used in any given explanation, Lonergan also reflected on the general nature of speculative theology. I have mentioned his understanding of speculative theology as constituted by theorems, terms, dialectical positions, and technique. He distinguishes a further feature, however, when he notes:

> The content of speculative theology is the content of a pure form. It is not something by itself but the intelligible arrangement of something else. It is not systematic theology but the system in systematic theology.[102]

I do not think it far fetched to suggest that this interpretation of speculative theology was rooted in Lonergan's earlier devotion to Plato.

Around 1928 or 1929, when confronted with the possibility that his superiors might at some time want him to teach philosophy or theology, Lonergan admitted that he was a nominalist. However, he added:

> As Fr. Bolland had predicted, my nominalism vanished when I read J. A. Stewarts' *Plato's Doctrine of Ideas* . . . It contained much that later I was to work out for myself in a somewhat different context, but at that time it was a great release. My nominalism had been an opposition, not to intelligence or understanding, but to the central role ascribed to universal concepts. From Stewart I learned that Plato was a methodologist, that his ideas were what the scientist seeks to discover, that the scientific or philosophic process toward discovery was one of question and answer.[103]

Two main points in Stewart's book are possibly relevant to Lonergan's development beyond nominalism and his approach to theological method in *Grace and Freedom*. First, Stewart rejected the interpretation of the Platonic idea as a static thing. Rather, the Platonic idea is the "context grasped," the "scientific point of view taken," and "more properly regarded as having a dynamic than having a static existence."[104] For Stewart, then, the Platonic idea is the dynamic scientific viewpoint from which some matter is regarded. Secondly, the primary means for discovering the idea is not the simple reception of an intuition. Rather, ideas are discovered only by

> . . . reflection, hard thinking, stirred by dialectic. . . . Mental activity is the one thing needful, which no degree of receptivity can make up for lack of. And it is by mental activity, by hard thinking, by connected not desultory thinking that the notion or idea is grasped.[105]

The idea, therefore, is the result of the dialectical labor of rational discourse.

In the conclusion of *Grace and Freedom,* Lonergan writes that the synthesis of general and specific theorems cannot be stated in a few words. It is like the soul's relationship to the body, "everywhere at once, totally in each part and yet distinct from every part."[106] The synthesis itself is difficult to apprehend and maintain.

If we can understand nominalism roughly as the apprehension of only arbitrary connections between experience and concept, then the clarification of the deeper dimensions of intelligence would be "a great release." From Stewart, Lonergan learned that what lies between the material world and the immaterial is the living process of question and answer. Correspondingly, Aquinas' synthesis of theorems was the goal toward which his reasoned discourses aimed. I credit Stewart with opening up the deeper dimensions of the level of direct understanding for Lonergan.

To summarize: if we distinguished the material from the formal elements in *Grace and Freedom,* we can focus on the theory of speculative development which is operative. That theory accounts for the way scientific theorems emerge from common notions and from each other. A key feature of this interpretation of Aquinas' performance lies in Lonergan's emphasis, not upon any particular theorem, but rather upon the arrangement of theorems in terms of a central synthesis.

In *Verbum*, the formal approach has evolved considerably. Materially, the study focuses on Thomist statements on understanding and its intelligibly proceeding inner word. Formally, Lonergan investigates the several contexts in which the Thomist statements occur. He is not primarily concerned with relating Thomist statements to one another in terms of general and specific theorems. Rather, he is concerned with relating Thomist statements to the dimensions of the act of understanding. As he had done in *Grace and Freedom*, he contrasts his approach with both positivism and conceptualism:

> A method tinged with positivism would not undertake, a method affected by conceptualist illusion could not conceive, the task of developing one's own understanding so as to understand Aquinas' comprehension of understanding and its intelligibly proceeding inner word.[107]

Materially, Lonergan seeks to apprehend "Aquinas' comprehension of understanding." Formally, such apprehension will be accomplished through "the task of developing one's own understanding."

In *Grace and Freedom*, the synthetic power of understanding was a central explanatory factor. In *Verbum*, it is understanding itself which is being investigated. *Verbum* does not seek to explain the act of understanding in terms of something else. Rather, it seeks to gradually develop understanding. Through such a development, understanding can proceed to a reflective grasp of its own nature. Hence, *Verbum* is a reflection, in both the technical and common sense meanings, upon the act of understanding. Its formal approach is designed to promote such reflection. The material and formal elements both converge on the act of understanding.

The origin of Lonergan's notion of intellectual conversion can be found in the reflective character of intelligible procession, in the act whereby understanding grasps of its own nature. What is implicit in the procedure of *Verbum* will be explicated in later works. Accordingly, Lonergan's evaluation of Aquinas can be applied to his own development as well: "For performance must precede reflection on performance, and method is the fruit of that reflection. Aquinas had to be content to perform."[108] So too, in Lonergan's performance of developing understanding, lies the materials for his later idea of intellectual conversion.

Besides Lonergan's later development, there is to be considered his earlier influences. Lonergan has noted the influence of Cardinal Newman upon his conception of the act of reflective understanding. He writes: ". . . the *intelligere* from which the judgment proceeds is a reflective and critical act of understanding not unlike the act of Newman's illative sense;"[109] and even more positively, "his illative sense became my act of reflective understanding."[110] As Stewart opened up the level of direct understanding, I believe Newman was responsible for leading Lonergan into the deeper dimensions of the level of reflective understanding.

The level of reflective understanding is central to the procedure of *Verbum*. The argument of *Verbum* is inductive. Lonergan wants to proceed from what Aquinas had to say about *verbum* to what he meant. He writes:

> The present article concludes the first three sections of the investigation. All that has been said so far and all that remains to be said can be reduced to a single proposition that, when Aquinas used the term, *intelligibile,* his primary meaning was not whatever can be conceived, such as matter, nothing, and sin, but whatever can be known by understanding. The proof of such a contention can only be inductive, i.e., it increases cumulatively as the correspondence between the contention with its implications and, on the other hand, the statements of Aquinas are found to exist exactly extensively, and illuminatively.[111]

It is the act of reflective understanding which reviews the evidence for judgment and which grasps its sufficiency for the assent. This is the same function which Newman assigned to his illative sense. Lonergan described the illative sense as "proceeding along ways unknown to the syllogism from a cumulation of probabilities—too manifold to be marshalled, too fleeting to be formulated—to a conclusion that is nonetheless certain."[112] Newman thought about his illative sense in the context of the concrete world of common sense.[113] Lonergan's meditations on the act of reflective understanding occurred within the technical context of Thomist trinitarian theory. Both the illative sense and the act of reflective understanding, however, represent the way the mind proceeds from a cumulation of probabilities to a valid affirmation of reality.

In the decade from the completion of his doctoral dissertation (1940) to the publication of the last *Verbum* article (1949), Lonergan's thought underwent significant development. I have located the most important aspect of that development on the formal level. In *Grace and Freedom* he organized his material in terms of a theory. In *Verbum* he organized his material in terms of the development of understanding. In the former, he focused on the way theorems develop from common notions and from each other. In the latter, he focused upon the way inner words develop from acts of understanding. In *Grace and Freedom* he emphasized the structure of the objects of thought. In *Verbum* he emphasized, not objects, but intellectual acts. On the formal level, the movement was from the generation of theorems to the generating intellect, from theory to interiority.

Consequently, when we turn to our central concern—the development of the notion of conversion—we must be aware of the deeper development occurring in Lonergan's thought. In *Grace and Freedom,* conversion is one of the material elements discussed. In *Verbum,* although conversion, in the relevant sense, is not explicitly discussed, its presence can be discerned in the way Lonergan approaches his material. The concept of intellectual conversion will become still more explicit in the major work of Lonergan's next period—*Insight*.

NOTES

[1] There are three versions of this material on the development of St. Thomas' theology of grace. First, Lonergan's doctoral dissertation is entitled "Gratia Operans: A Study of the Speculative Development in the Writings of St. Thomas Aquin" (a thesis undertaken under the direction of the Rev. Charles Boyer, S. J., and submitted at the Pontifical Gregorian University, Rome, towards partial satisfaction of the conditions for the Doctorate in Sacred Theology, 1940). Secondly, this thesis was rewritten and submitted to *Theological Studies* for publication. It appeared as "St. Thomas' thought on Gratia Operans" in a series of four articles: *Theological Studies* 2 (1941) pp. 289–324; 3

(1942) pp. 69–88, 375–402, 533–78. Thirdly, this material has been published as a book under the title *Grace and Freedom: Operative Grace in the Thought of St. Thomas Aquinas,* ed. J. Patout Burns (London: Darton, Longmans and Todd; New York: Herder and Herder, 1971). Much of the analysis in this chapter relies on the unpublished introduction of the dissertation. When referring to this material I shall use the dissertation title, "Gratia Operans." Otherwise references will pertain to the book *Grace and Freedom.*

2 There are two versions of the material on St. Thomas' notion of the inner word. Originally, this material appeared in *Theological Studies* 7 (1946) pp. 349–92; 8 (1947) pp. 35–79, 404–44; 10 (1949) pp. 2–40; 359–93. This series of articles was entitled "the Concept of Verbum in the Writing of St. Thomas Aquinas." Subsequently, the articles appeared in book form: *Verbum: Word and Idea in Aquinas,* ed. David Burrell (Notre Dame: 1967; London: 1968). References will pertain to the 1967 edition, hereafter referred to as *Verbum.*

3 *Collection: Papers by Bernard Lonergan, S.J.,* ed. F.E. Crowe (New York: Herder and Herder, 1967). I conceive this first period of Lonergan's career to include the first eight of the sixteen papers assembled in *Collection.* They are: "The Form of Inference," (1943); "Finality, Love, Marriage," (1943); "On God and Secondary Causes," (1946); "The Assumption and Theology," (1948); "The Natural Desire to See God," (1949); "A Note on Geometrical Possibility," (1949–50); "The Role of a Catholic University in the Modern World," (1951); and "Theology and Understanding," (1954). Hereafter referred to as *Col.*

4 *Verbum,* p. 215.

5 *Insight: A Study in Human Understanding.* (London: Longmans, Green and Co.; New York: Philosophical Library, 1957) p. 748. Hereafter referred to as *Insight.*

6 On the realms of meaning, see *Method in Theology* (New York: Herder and Herder, 1972) pp. 81–89. The phrase "realms of meaning" is more properly located in the later period of Lonergan's development and I have tried to avoid the anachronism of using later terminology in earlier periods. I have made an exception with the "realms of meaning" because I am, not simply concerned with its location in its own proper period, but am also concerned with its relevance to Lonergan's overall development. It is my hypothesis that the development of Lonergan's ideas on conversion is best understood as part of his ongoing penetration into the realms of meaning. For example, in this early period, conversion must be understood against the background of his deeper movement from the systematic to the critical exigence of meaning, from the realm of theory to the realm of interiority. Lonergan formulates his ideas on the exigencies and the realms of meaning in *Method in Theology.*

7 For the impact of *Dei Filius* on subsequent theological development, see Gerald A. McCool, *Catholic Theology in the Nineteenth Century: The Quest for a Unitary Method.* (New York: The Seabury Press, 1977), pp. 216–26.

[8] Gratia Operans," p. 15.

[9] *Verbum, p. 213.*

[10] Johannes Beumer, *Theologie als Glaubensverstandnis* (Wurzburg: Echter-Verlag, 1953).

[11] *Catholic Theology in the 19th Century,* pp. 224–26.

[12] Ibid., pp. 226–36.

[13] Lonergan, *A Second Collection,* ed. William F. J. Ryan and Bernard J. Tyrrell. (Philadelphia: The Westminster Press, 1974). Hereafter referred to as *2nd Col.* This citation is from the third paper, "Theories of Inquiry: Responses to a Symposium," p. 38.

[14] "*Insight* Revisited," in *2nd Col.,* p. 265

[15] In his *Catholic Theology in the 19th Century,* Fr. McCool comments: "*Aeterne Patris* also expressed the serene conviction of the nineteenth century neo-Thomists that scholastic philosophy was a single metaphysical system, common to all the scholastic doctors, and that scholastic philosophy could gather up, preserve, and represent the essence of the patristic thought which it has superseded. . . ."

"Kleutgen had taken the same metaphysical approach to the history of theology in his *Die Theologie der Vorzeit.* According to Kleutgen's norm of philosophical evaluation and according to the norm proposed by *Aeterni Patris,* the metaphysics of Francis Suarez could be considered one of the pure 'streams flowing from [Thomas'] spring,' and the reality of the act of existence, which Suarez denied and Cajetan affirmed, was reduced to the status of an accidental point on which modern scholastics could agree or disagree without compromising the purity of their Thomistic philosophy and theology." pp. 233–34.

[16] *Verbum,* p. 215.

[17] *Grace and Freedom,* p. 1.

[18] "Gratia Operans," p. 36.

[19] *Verbum,* p. xiv.

[20] Ibid., p. x.

[21] Lonergan, *Philosophy of God and Theology* (Philadelphia: The Westminster Press, 1973) p. 32.

[22] As Lonergan points out in the conclusion to *Verbum,* his efforts to establish the intellectualism of Aquinas had been preceded by Pierre Rousselot's excellent *L'Intellectualisme de Saint Thomas* which "had contended that in the writings of Aquinas it was not the rarely treated concept but the perpetually recurring intellect that was central and basic." *Verbum,* p. 217. Also anticipatory of Lonergan's contention and approach was J. Pegaire's classic *Intellectus et Ratio selon S. Thomas.*

[23] Lonergan points out that the term *gratia actualis* does not occur in St. Thomas' work; instead he writes of the *auxilium divinum.* "Gratia Operans," p. 14 and *Grace and Freedom,* p. 3, n. 5.

[24] *Grace and Freedom,* p. 8.

[25] "Gratia Operans," pp. 33–34.

[26] Ibid., pp. 36–45.

27 *Grace and Freedom*, p. 5.

28 Ibid., p. 16.

29 In *Method and Theology*, written thirty years later, Lonergan summarized the significance of Philip's achievement: "Again, the middle ages inherited from Augustine his affirmation of both divine grace and human liberty. For a long time it was difficult to say that there existed any finite thing that was not God's free gift. Though it was obvious that grace named not everything but something special, still lists of graces properly so called not only differed from one another but also betrayed not a little arbitrariness. At the same time it was very difficult for a theologian to say what he meant by liberty. Philosophers could define it as immunity from necessity. But theologians could not conceive liberty as free from the necessity of grace, or good without grace, or even evil with it. But what tortured the twelfth century found its solution in the thirteenth. About the year 1230 Philip the Chancellor completed a discovery that in the next forty years released a whole series of developments. The discovery was a distinction between two entitatively disproportionate orders: grace was above nature; faith was above reason; charity was above human good will; merit before God was above the good opinion of one's neighbors. This distinction and organization made it possible (1) to discuss the nature of grace without discussing liberty, (2) to discuss the nature of liberty without discussing grace, and (3) to work out the relations between grace and liberty." *M.i.T.*, pp. 309–10.

30 *Summa Theologiae*, 1–2, q. 109, a. 2.

31 In his book *The Achievement of Bernard Lonergan*, (New York: Herder and Herder, 1970), David Tracy emphasizes this point by observing that "Lonergan's recovery of the particular theorems of Aquinas on grace led to his further articulation of the very heart of the medieval enterprise as a search for a scientific theology" (p.33). Further, he explains that medieval theologians were attempting to construct "a *Begrifflichkeit* (i.e., a related and structured set of cognate theorems, terms, operations and relations)" (p. 36). Lonergan notes that the content of speculative theology is very peculiar. It is not some datum but rather, the process of ordering something else. "Thus the content of speculative theology is the content of a pure form. It is not something by itself but the intelligible arrangement of something else. It is not systematic theology but the system in systematic theology." "Gratia Operans," p. 12. Thus, the basic movement of thought on grace is but a minor theme in the larger development toward the systematic ordering of all dogmatic data. See *Grace and Freedom*, p. 136.

32 *Grace and Freedom*, p. 63.

33 In the *Commentary on the Sentences*, St. Thomas did not yet understand the need for the category of actual grace. Conversion was conceived in terms of an external divine intervention, perhaps an admonition or an illness. He even conceives St. Paul's conversion as due to an external rather than an internal light. In *De Veritate*, St.

Thomas conceives an actual grace that is cooperative. He expands his view of the conversion preparatory to justification to include divine motions internal to the mind. By the time of the *Summa Theologiae,* St. Thomas understands actual grace as both operative and cooperative. His earlier explanation of conversion in terms of external causes is dismissed as Pelagian. Only God's operation within the will is accepted as a sufficient ground for conversion. Consequently, we see that St. Thomas tended to conceive the graces causing conversion as operating ever more internally on the will.

34 *Summa contra gentiles,* Book 3, Chapter 67.

35 *Grace and Freedom,* p. 76.

36 Lonergan writes: "The will has its strip of autonomy, yet beyond this there is the ground from which free acts spring; and that ground God holds and moves as a fencer moves his whole rapier by grasping only the hilt." Ibid., pp. 142–143.

37 *Summa Theologiae,* 1–2, q. 9, a. 1.

38 Ibid., a. 6, ad 3m.

39 Ibid., a. 6.

40 *Grace and Freedom,* p. 123, n. 29

41 *Summ Theologiae,* 3, q. 85, a. 5.

43 St. Thomas uses conversion to illustrate an operative grace that is not habitual. "First, there is an interior act of the will, and with regard to this act the will is as something moved, and God is the mover; and especially so when, the will, which hitherto willed evil, begins to will good." *Summa Theologiae,* 1–2, q. 111, a. 2.

43 *Grace and Freedom,* p. 124, n. 33.

44 In the *Summa Theologiae,* the long development of St. Thomas' thought on the division of actual and habitual grace comes to fruition. He writes: "Grace may be taken in two ways. First as a divine help, whereby God moves us to will and to act; secondly, as an habitual gift divinely bestowed on us. Now in both these ways grace is fittingly divided into operating and cooperating." *Summa Theologiae,* 1–2, q. 111, a. 2.

45 *Summa Theologiae,* 3, q. 85, a. 6.

46 Ibid., 1, q. 62, a. 2, ad3m.

47 *Grace and Freedom,* p. 137.

48 For a discussion of the term "intellectualist" see *Verbum,* pp. 142, 151–52, 155–56, 184–89 and 210–13. Briefly stated, the intellectualist ideal of science is understanding. Lonergan contrasts intellectualism with conceptualism: "Conceptualists conceive human intellect only in terms of what it does; but their neglect of what intellect is, prior to what it does has a variety of causes. Most commonly they do not advert to the act of understanding but the intellectualist knows and analyzes not only what intelligence in act does but also what it is." *Verbum,* pp. 186–87.

49 Aquinas, *Commentary on the "De Trinitatae" of Boethius,* q. 5, a. 3.

50 "Procession, therefore, is not to be understood from what it is in

bodies, either according to local movement, or by way of a cause proceeding forth to an exterior effect: as, for instance, like hot proceeding from the agent to the thing made hot. Rather it is to be understood by way of an intelligible word which proceeds from the speaker, yet remains in him." *Summa Theologiae* 1, q. 27, a. 1.

[51] *Verbum*, p. 34.

[52] *Summa Theologiae* 1, q. 27, a. 1.

[53] *Verbum*, p. 45.

[54] Ibid., pp. 14–15.

[55] Ibid., p. 25.

[56] *Summa Theologiae* 1, q. 84, a. 7.

[57] *In Boet, de Trin.* q. 6, a. 2, ad. 5.

[57] *Summa Theologiae* 1, q. 84, a. 7.

[58] *In Boet. de Trin.* q. 6, a. 2, ad. 5.

[59] *Summa Theologiae* 1, q. 87, a. 1.

[60] *Verbum*, p. 61.

[62] Ibid., p. 62.

[63] Lonergan comments: "We have now to penetrate more deeply into our subject. The finer points of Thomist trinitarian theory cannot be grasped from the analogy of the mere mechanism of human intellect. . . . Accordingly, an attempt is to be made to integrate with the foregoing what Aquinas has to say of the habit and virtue of wisdom." *Verbum*, p. 66.

[64] Ibid., pp. 64–65.

[65] Ibid., p. 65.

[66] The phrase *compositio vel divisio* refers to the fact that an affirmative or negative judgment joins or divides, respectively, the two components of subject and predicate.

[67] *Verbum*, pp. 65–66.

[68] *Summa Theologiae* 1, q. 14, a. 2.

[69] The procession of the Holy Spirit from the Word and Its Principle is conceived on an analogy with the intelligible procession of love from the inner word of human intellect. For the discussion of the procession of love, see *Verbum*, pp. 201–05.

[70] *Summa Theologiae* 1, q. 88, a. 2, ad 3.

[71] The contrast between the Aristotelian knowledge of soul in terms of its objects, acts, potencies, and essence and an Augustinian introspective self-knowledge is an interpretive key to Lonergan's approach to the Thomist *verbum*. Aquinas was attempting to fuse the two approaches: to sublate the Augustinian material into the fundamentally metaphysical scheme and to fill out the Aristotelian framework with introspective data. Lonergan remarks that Aquinas was attempting "to fuse together what to us may seem so disparate; a phenomenology of the subject with a psychology of the soul." *Verbum*, p. vii. Also see the entire introduction to the 1967 *Verbum* for Lonergan's analysis of the issue fifteen years after the appearance of the original articles.

[72] *Verbum*, p. 83.

[73] Ibid., p. 87.

[74] Lonergan writes: "When Aquinas spoke of God as *ipsum intelligere,* did he mean that God was a pure act of understanding? To that conclusion we have been working through four articles." *Verbum,* p. 190.

[75] *Summa Theologiae* 1, q. 84, a. 5.

[76] Lonergan remarks: "The significance of this procedure is that it places Thomist trinitarian theory in a class by itself." *Verbum,* p. 206. "Aquinas did not conclude that the principle by which the Father generates is the divine intellect or the divine understanding . . . in God substance, being, understanding, thought, willing are absolutely one and the same reality. Accordingly, Aquinas not merely in his *Commentary on the Sentences,* but also in his *Summa* makes the divine essence the principle of divine generation." *Verbum,* p. 209. The psychological analogy only complements the divine essence as a principle of explanation.

[77] For Lonergan's interpretation of the distinction between a *processio operati* and a *processio operationis,* see *Verbum,* pp. 98–102.

[78] For the relevance of human reflectivity for an understanding of trinitarian processions, see *Verbum,* pp. 34, 45; and above, nn. 50, 51 and 73.

[79] *Summa Theologiae* 1, q. 27, a. 1, ad. 2.

[80] *Verbum,* p. 87.

[81] Ibid., p. 209.

[82] In another context, Lonergan made a general remark about the *Verbum* articles: "So about 1943 I began collecting materials for an account of Aquinas' view on understanding and the inner word. The result was a series of articles that appeared in *Theological Studies* from 1946 to 1949. They took into account the psychological, metaphysical and trinitarian aspects of Thomist thought on the subject." "*Insight* Revisited," in *2nd Col.,* p. 267.

[83] *Verbum,* pl. xiii.

[84] See above note 48.

[85] Lonergan uses the term "intellect" to designate the speculative habit of understanding. *Verbum,* p. 67. For consistency with the edition of the *Summa Theologiae* which I am using here, I use the term "understanding." Aquinas, *Summa Theologiae,* edited and annotated, with an introduction by Anton C. Pegis.

[86] *Summa Theologiae* 1–2, a. 57, a. 2, ad. 2.

[87] For the relationship between understanding and reason, see above, p. 35.

[88] *Verbum,* p. 212.

[89] Ibid., p. 208.

[90] Lonergan writes: "It seems to me that intellectualism, if once it gains a foothold, never will be dislodged from the interpretation of Thomist trinitarian theory. If that is correct, I have reached my objective." *Verbum,* p. 219. Supportive of this point, Lonergan sums up his intention in the *Verbum* articles: "Their basic point was that Aquinas

attributed the key role in cognitional theory not to inner words, concepts, but to acts of understanding." "*Insight* Revisited," in *2nd Col.*, p. 267

91 *Verbum*, p. 217.

92 Ibid.

93 *M.i.T.*, pp. 238–40.

94 Ibid., p. 238.

95 Ibid., p. 239.

96 *Verbum*, p. 83.

97 Ibid., p. 87.

98 Ibid., p. 212.

99 *Summa Theologiae* 1–2, q. 66, a. 5, ad. 4.

100 *Verbum*, pp. 32, 45, 85–86.

101 "Gratia Operans," p. 3.

102 Ibid., p. 12.

103 *Insight* Revisited," in *2nd Col.*, p. 264.

104 J.A. Stewart, *Plato's Doctrine of Ideas* (Oxford: Clarendon Press, 1909) pp. 7, 26–27.

105 Ibid., p. 25.

106 *Grace and Freedom*, p. 143.

107 *Verbum*, p. 217

108 Ibid., p. xiii.

109 Ibid., p. 47.

110 "*Insight* Revisited," in *2nd Col.*, p. 263.

111 *Verbum*, pp. 180–181.

112 "The Forms of Inference," in *Collection*, pp. 1–2.

113 Lonergan writes that it was Newman, together with St. Augustine, Descartes, and Pascal, who revealed the possibility of a non-metaphysical, common sense approach to self-knowledge. It seems that of this group, Newman was first in Lonergan's affection. *M.i.T.*, p. 261.

CHAPTER TWO

THE MIDDLE PERIOD: THE PROBLEM OF INTEGRATION AND THE CRITICAL EXIGENCE

> The crucial issue is an experimental issue, and the experiment will be performed not publicly but privately. It will consist in one's own rational self-consciousness clearly and distinctly taking possession of itself as rational self-consciousness. Up to that decisive achievement, all leads. From it, all follows.
>
> Bernard Lonergan,
> "Introduction" to *Insight,* p. xviii.

The General Context of the Middle Period

Insight: A Study of Human Understanding is the single work which dominates the middle period of Lonergan's career.[1] Lonergan began *Insight* in 1949; he worked on it until 1953. It was not, however, published until April of 1957. *Collection* is an assemblage of various articles also published during this period.[2] For example, the article "Theology and Understanding" provides a transition from the Thomist concerns of the early period to the modern methodological issues of the middle period. The article "Cognitional Structure" concludes this middle period with a summary statement of *Insight*'s cognitional theory. Chronologically, then, I would locate the middle period between the years 1949 and 1964.

In the middle period Lonergan both continued to explore some earlier issues and also opened up some new territory. For example, as in the early period, he continued to understand his work as part of the Leonine program "vetera novis augere et perficere." In the early period, however, Lonergan conceived his main task to be the determination of what the *vetera* really were; now he conceives his main task to be the discovery of new possibilities.[3] Again, whereas in the early period Lonergan was attempting the hermeneutical task of reaching up to the mind of Aquinas; now he is attempting the creative task of erecting new structures upon that prior achievement. Again, as in the early period, the act of understanding is the pivotal issue. In *Verbum* however, Lonergan had written of a development of one's understanding so as to understand Aquinas' comprehension of understanding; in *Insight* he writes of the self-appropriation of one's own rational self-consciousness. The conceptual categories are different, but *Verbum*'s development of understanding and *Insight*'s self-appropriation are notionally identical. Thus, Lonergan can substitute the latter for the former in the following statement: "It is only through a personal appropriation of one's own rational self-consciousness that one can hope to reach the mind of Aquinas and, once that mind is reached, then it is difficult not to import his compelling genius to the problems of this later day."[4] There is a significant continuity between the early and middle periods; the difference lies in the concern to address the "problems of this later day."

Lonergan's approach to a variety of modern problems reveals a unity. To articulate that unity is difficult. It is the unity of a basic problematic from which a multiplicity of particular problems in specialized fields emanate.[5] Still, I must offer some approximate description of the basic problematic, even though it involves a number of generalizations which leave the particularities of concrete situations unclear.

Generally speaking, the problematic arises from the differentiation of the field of the empirical sciences from the field of common sense. We have already encountered one aspect of this problematic in "Gratia Operans." Aquinas sought to transpose earlier literary treatments of grace and freedom into a technical system of theorems.[6] More generally, Aquinas was credited with the integration of Aristotelian philosophy and science into a theological synthesis. Since Aquinas wrote, however, there have been profound developments both in common sense and science.

One can maintain with Lonergan that ultimately the two realms do not conflict. Still, applying that principle and reconciling the multiplicity of apparent contradictions is a staggering task. For example, *Insight* contrasts the apparently contradictory statements: from the point of view of science, the planets move in approximately elliptical orbits with the sun at their focus. From the point of view of common sense, the earth is at rest and the sun rises and sets.[7] How can we reconcile the testimony of our senses and the scientific account of our solar system? This is a single example of the tension between common sense and scientific viewpoints. The dichotomy can be extended to include Aristotle's distinction between what is prior for us and what is prior in itself, to include Galileo's distinction between secondary and primary qualities, to include Newton's distinction between apparent motion and true motion, and to include Kant's distinction between phenomenon and noumenon.[8] Reconciling the conflicts between the fields of common sense and science is a philosophic problem because it is global in significance.

There is a further related aspect to the basic problematic. As I have just described it, the tension between the fields of common sense and science seems remote and theoretical. However, the problem with which *Insight* is specifically concerned is not solely theoretical. Lonergan writes: "the development of empirical, human sciences has created a fundamentally new problem. . . . Now it is this problem that in large measure has dictated the structure of the present work."[9] The problem created by the emergence of the empirical human sciences manifests the basic problematic in its most acute form.

If the conflict between science and common sense initially seems remote and theoretical, the emergence of empirical human sciences makes it immediate and practical. The human sciences, because they intend to be empirical, study people in the concrete. Instead of borrowing their basic terms and relations from philosophy or theology, they imitate the natural sciences. They work out their basic terms and relations from the resources of their own investigations. The human sciences are entitled to autonomy. However, imitation of the natural sciences presents a two-fold danger. First, the natural sciences investigate electrons, atoms, molecules, and so on. There are many aspects of the human person, of course, which cannot be reduced to these basic terms. Secondly, the natural sciences have in fact tended to be positivist, pragmatist, and influenced by mechanist determinism.[10] While the physical universe has managed to survive this type of scientific methodology, the human spirit may be less resilient. These two dangers conspire to create the immediate and practical problem of the empirical human sciences.

If the human scientist overlooks peoples' intelligences, their wills, and their souls; still these spiritual elements exist and operate in the political realm. The advertising firm or ministry of culture can use the knowledge gained in human scientific investigations to increase their control over people, to implement their social engineering, to speed up the drift toward totalitarianism. The immediate and practical problem is that the human sciences study people in the concrete. If their vision of the human person is distorted, then their conclusions will prove all the more useful to biased minds and cynical purposes.

The distinction, tension, and reconciliation of the fields of common sense and science is a philosophic problem. Philosophy evades its responsibility if it does not provide the integrating principles.[11] Lonergan points out that insofar as philosophy deserts the field of science and attempts to take its stand as a specialization of common sense, it is evading its responsibility. While there is certainly a need for philosophic analysis of human existence in the concrete, philosophy cannot ignore the problem of integration.

Lonergan believes that the problem of integration cannot be met without a full and detailed account of how we know.[12] It will not do to retreat to a small island of certainty which includes the few epistemological and metaphysical principles upon which we can all agree. We need a full and detailed account of how natural scientists proceed when they set out to know, of how mathematicians proceed, of how people of common sense proceed, of how philosophers proceed, and so on. Lonergan writes:

> We have a problem. It is not a problem of the existence of knowledge, but a problem of some detailed account of knowledge. That is where the problem lies. It is not a problem of existence but of fruitful existence. It was this idea that was in the back of my mind in writing *Insight*.[13]

Since the content of scientific theories is revisable, and since the conclusions of scientific investigations can be corrected, complemented, and sometimes overturned, it is to scientific method we must turn. Scientific method is a permanent structure. It must be studied critically, however, Lonergan recalls Einstein's advice: "pay very little attention to what scientists say and a great deal to what they do."[14] We must determine what scientific method reveals about human intelligence and what it reveals about human baises. It is a full and detailed account of the invariant and recurrent procedures of the human mind that can provide the integrating principle for science and common sense.

There is also a theological dimension to the problematic of the middle period. Although *Insight* is a philosophic work, in the "Epilogue" Lonergan draws out some of its theological implications.[15] Traditionally, theology has been considered queen of the sciences. However, without a philosophy which aims at a comprehensive integration of the departments of knowledge, theology lacks the necessary means to exercise her sovereignty. Moreover, even an adequate philosophy would not be enough to integrate the current scientific situation. The human sciences investigate people in the concrete and there are elements in peoples' concrete situations which cannot be mediated philosophically. For example, people suffer from sin; they stand in need of God's grace to enlighten their minds and to strengthen their wills; the efficacy of God's grace depends on its acceptance or rejection. These factors have positive consequences, but they are not open to direct empirical investigation. Lonergan writes: "the fact is that the human sciences are empirical, that they are engaged in understanding all the data on man as he is, and that the only correct general form of that understanding is theological."[16] Consequently, only theology can fill out an empirical, but partial, picture of the human person.

Theology can most effectively address the problem of integration by contributing to the clarification of scientific methodology.[17] Theology knows the general principle that all things seek God. Aquinas affirmed the epistemological aspect of this general principle: people naturally desire to see God.[18] Lonergan will exploit the methodological implications of this general principle by revealing the ground of scientific method in the detached, disinterested, unrestricted desire to know. The pure desire to know is both a general principle and a concrete reality. It provides, not only the basis for a unification of the sciences, but also the reality which generates and criticizes all particular scientific and common sense procedures.

In conclusion, this middle period of Lonergan's career is concerned with a problematic which can be generally characterized as one of integration.[19] There is a theoretical side to the problematic: what is the principle which is capable of unifying the field of the sciences and of integrating that field with the field of common sense? There is a practical side to the problematic and it is the more profound: how can scientists and people of common sense be brought to understand and affirm this principle and how can they apply it to all of the diverse fields in which it is relevant?

The General Structure of Insight

In the "Preface," Lonergan explains that *Insight* proceeds on three levels. First, it is a study of the act of human understanding: it pursues insight into insight. The insights of mathematicians permit us to study it with precision; the insights of scientists permit us to study the dynamic flow of consciousness in which insights most readily occur; the insights of people of common sense permit us to study the way in which alien concerns intrude into the dynamic flow of consciousness. Each of these fields contributes the materials for an understanding of understanding.

Secondly, *Insight* unfolds the philosophic implications of understanding. To paraphrase Lonergan's words, insight into insight yields:

> a clear and distinct idea of clear and distinct ideas; an apprehension of the meaning of meaning; the range of *a priori,* synthetic components in our knowledge; a philosophic unification of mathematics, the sciences, and common sense; a metaphysical account of what is to be known through the various departments of human inquiry.[20]

If statements within the various departments of knowledge are not to be repeated as a parrot unintelligently utters its pronouncements, then such statements must proceed from acts of understanding. Consequently, *Insight* constructs a method of metaphysics based upon the centrality of human understanding.

Thirdly, *Insight* wages a campaign against the flight from understanding: it seeks insight into oversight. As insight into insight reveals profound philosophic implications, equally insight into oversight reveals the origin of the multiplicity of philosophies and the source of aberrant views on knowing, being, and objectivity.

In the "Introduction," Lonergan provides a more detailed account of his task and goal in *Insight*. His chief question is not whether knowledge exists, but what is its nature? He asks: how can one account for both an elementary type of knowing in which the world of objects is already-out-there-now real, as well as a fully human type of knowing in which the world of things is a synthesis of both subjects and objects? His approach to this problem is, not to focus upon the content of the known, which is variable, but to focus upon the activity of knowing. Thus he seeks an understanding of the act of understanding— an insight into insight. Still, the most important aspect of *Insight* is its personal character. Lonergan emphasizes that he is offering, not a theory, but an invitation. One is invited to perform a personal and decisive act. He writes:

> It will consist in one's rational self-consciousness clearly and distinctly taking possession of itself as rational self-consciousness. Up to that decisive

> achievement, all leads. From it all follows. No one
> elese, no matter what his knowledge or his eloquence,
> no matter what his logical rigour or persuasiveness,
> can do it for you.[21]

One is invited to take possession of a most personal part of
oneself—one's rational self-consciousness.

With so personal a goal as self-appropriation, the reader
could properly ask, why does *Insight* begin with excursions
into mathematics and science? Initially, *Insight* concentrates
on these fields because of the clarity and precision they possess. The clarity and precision of mathematical and scientific
objects can be transferred to clear and precise determinations
of cognitional acts. In turn, clearly and precisely determined
cognitional acts can be used to determine levels of consciousness. Hence, knowledge of objects leads to knowledge of
cognitional acts and knowledge of cognitional acts leads to the
self-appropriation of the knower.

There is a second reason for the initial concentration on
natural science. The shift in contemporary science from "the
old mechanism to relativity and from the old determinism to
statistical laws"[22] is a most precise piece of evidence. It provides the images and clues for insight into the two types of
knowing and the inherent tension of their relationship.

There is a third reason for beginning with illustrations from
natural science. The particular illustrations provide access to
understanding the general nature of scientific method. This
point will be further explained in the following paragraphs on
Insight's moving viewpoint. For the present, the key point is
that although *Insight* is fundamentally an invitation to a personal act, the preconditions and implications of the act reside,
in part, in an analysis of mathematics and natural science.

The excursions into mathematics and natural science serve a
higher purpose. They provide access into a higher viewpoint.
However, moving into a higher viewpoint, according to Lonergan's strategy, is a matter of human development. It is a matter
of the steady accumulation of insights into particular problems
within limited contexts. Thus, *Insight* proceeds slowly and
painstakingly from a minimal context through the process of
questioning to the emergence of a higher viewpoint, and so on

to ever expanding contexts. Lonergan remarks: "a book designed to aid development must be written from a moving viewpoint."[23]

The moving viewpoint of *Insight* reveals a strategy which unfolds on successive levels. Initially, one needs to apprehend some of the elementary features of the fields of mathematics, natural science, and common sense. Again, the elementary features provide for an understanding of the recurrently operative cognitional procedures of these fields. The goal of this strategy, however, is the reflective grasp and rational affirmation of the basic structure of each and every instance of knowing. At this point, one has reached "an upper context that logically is independent of the scaffolding of mathematics, science, and common sense."[24] One has slowly and painstakingly been developing an elementary apprehension of various fields of inquiry, a comprehensive grasp of the nature of understanding, and the reflective grounds for affirming one's empirical, intelligent, and rational consciousness.

Lonergan summarizes the positive context of *Insight* in the slogan-like formulation which appears at the end of both the "Introduction" and the "Epilogue".

> Thoroughly understand what it is to understand, and not only will you understand the broad lines of all there is to be understood but also you will possess a fixed base, an invariant pattern, opening upon all further developments of understanding.[25]

As the act of self-appropriation requires a prior development of the subject, so too the act of self-appropriation provides a new basis for future development. It is a new beginning. One can now pursue new understanding from the position of having already grasped the basic form of all human understanding. The understanding of understanding becomes, in some sense, the knowledge of knowing. Hence, self-appropriation provides a criterion of the real.

From the self-appropriated structure of human understanding and doing, one can develop a method of ethics. From the understanding and affirmation of inner dynamism of our desire to know, its transcendent orientation, and its infinite potentiality, one encounters the question of transcendent knowledge.

From the notion of an all knowing, all powerful, completely good, loving, and wise God, one encounters the problem of evil.

Insight is divided into two parts: "Insight as Activity" and "Insight as Knowledge." First, the subject is invited to appropriate the invariant structure of his or her cognitional activity. The key question in this first part is, what do I do when I know? Secondly, the subject is shown how that appropriated structure provides an integrating principle for the totality of what is known and what can be known. The key question in this second part is, how does our appropriated structure fix the general features of the known and the to be known? Finally, the specific factor which accounts for the transition from cognitional activity to cognitional content, from part one to part two, is the personal act of self-appropriation.

The act of self-appropriation is central to the structure of *Insight,* and it is central to my interpretation of the book. Lonergan writes: "*Insight* may be described as a set of exercises in which, it is hoped, one attains self-appropriation."[26] However, there is an important difference between the procedures of *Insight* and my procedure in this interpretation. *Insight* is intended to aid development and is written from a moving viewpoint. It begins from a minimal context and proceeds slowly toward a basic and invariant context. My interpretation of *Insight* proceeds in the opposite direction. It is my thesis that the pure desire to know is the hermeneutical key to *Insight*. When Lonergan writes about self-appropriation, he means the appropriation of the pure desire to know. Self-appropriation is a matter of distinguishing the various levels and operations of cognitional structure; it is a matter of grasping the way in which that structure is underpinned, penetrated, and constituted by the pure desire to know. Again, self-appropriation is a matter of realizing that one's pure desire to know possesses, not merely private and interior significance; but is in fact the intention of being. While Lonergan moves slowly and proleptically towards that realization through a painstaking analysis of empirical science and of common sense my interpretation moves from above downward. I am writing from the thesis of the foundational significance of the pure desire to know towards fuller empirical nuance. The task of the interpreter is different from the task of the interpreted author.

The pure desire to know is the interpretive key to *Insight*'s procedure. It is the pure desire to know which orients us toward being. Most important, for our purpose of interpreting this middle period of Lonergan's development, it is the pure desire to know which is appropriated in intellectual conversion. Intellectual conversion will move the person beyond the false dichotomy, on the one hand, of a merely "objective" account of knowing that overlooks insight and the necessity of the development of understanding in the subject; and, on the other hand, of a merely "subjective" account of knowing that overlooks the intentionality which permeates cognitional operations. In brief, it is intellectual conversion that meets the critical exigence. Still, without Lonergan's analysis of the realms of mathematics, of empirical science, and of common sense, the notion of the pure desire to know risks becoming emptied of all content. Without his explanations of the natural and inevitable connections between the pure desire to know and the various levels of consciousness, the notion of being risks becoming the notion of nothing at all. Lonergan provides, then, the framework to give us a full, critical, and reflective grasp of the pure desire to know through his detailed account of cognitional operation as it occurs in the various fields of human knowledge. There is no way in which I could recount his analysis here.

My procedure in the following sections of this chapter will be as follows. First, I will offer a brief summary of the account of cognitional structure informing the first part of the book— "Insight as Activity". Secondly, I will analyze in detail chapters eleven through thirteen—"Self-Affirmation of the Knower", "The Notion of Being", and "The Notion of Objectivity". These chapters are the most important ones for understanding the overall argument or logic of the book. Finally, there remains the implications of these analyses for metaphysics.

The notion of conversion is the notion of a profound act of transformation in the subject. In one sense, the pure desire to know exists and operates whether the subject adverts to it or not. It is an *existential* and a permanent part of the structure of consciousness. The notion of conversion, then, refers to more than the mere existence of the pure desire to know. It refers to the change that occurs in the subject when the pure desire to know has been identified, named, and made one's own. That appropriation is an *existentiell* and pertains to the subject in his or her own personal and free discovery of the cognitional self. What is meant by that kind of self-appropriation can only be communicated in and through the cognitional activity of the person.

A Summary Account of Cognitional Structure

The first part of *Insight*, "Insight as Activity" discusses the acts by which and through which we come to understanding and knowledge. It focuses on acts of direct and of reflective insight. Lonergan's account of cognitional structure is fundamentally consistent with his account in *Verbum*. He distinguishes among experiential, intelligent, and rational levels of conscious operation. He offers the following schema of the three levels of cognitional process:

1. Data Perceptual Images	Free Images	Utterances
2. Questions for Intelligence	Insights	Formulations
3. Questions for Reflection	Reflection	Judgment[27]

Whereas, *Verbum* had clarified this structure in terms of the framework of Thomist metaphysical psychology; in *Insight* Lonergan turns more directly to the immediate data of consciousness—to acts of understanding. He relies on the procedures of empirical method and of common sense to provide the details and the clarification necessary for a full account of human cognitional operation. The first part of *Insight*, then, presents a nuanced discussion of the cognitional operations of experiencing, understanding, and judgment within the fields of empirical method and of common sense.

In the field of common sense living and in the field of empirical method, cognitional operation is based on experience. Of course, experience in each of these fields is different. Generally, common sense operates within the dramatic pattern of experience and science operates within the intellectual pattern of experience. Thus, for the common sense or the scientific subject, experience generally emerges into consciousness as already patterned. In the field of common sense, the key factor which determines the way in which experience is organized for the subject is a prior interest or concern. The chief concern of the common sense subject is the concern of daily living. It is this prior concern which will enable him or her, for example, to pick out a friend's face within a crowd of strangers. In the field of the empirical sciences, the key factor which determines the way in which experience is organized is also a prior concern. This time, however, the chief concern which determines the context of scientific experience is the pure desire to know. Both scientists and people of common sense want to know; but for the scientist the detached and disinterested desire to know is the dominant concern.

We next turn to the intelligent level and to consider common sense and science as different ways of understanding. Empirical science finds its experiential object in the sensible data and common sense finds its experiential object in the perceptions of daily living. In both fields, however, intelligence is discontented with mere experience. It seeks insight; it seeks to understand. Moreover, there is an important difference between the types of intelligibility sought in these two fields. Empirical scientific investigation seeks a type of formal intelligibility which correlates elements with one another.[28] Common sense intelligence seeks a type of unformulated intelligibility which is correlative to a subject who wants to know, not purely for the sake of knowing, but for the sake of living.[29] Hence, science tends to be theoretical and common sense tends to be practical.

Common sense intelligence does not seek to precisely formulate what it knows. It tends to be an habitual but unformulated core of insights which needs to be complemented by further insights as one turns to the particular and to the individual circumstances. Most generally, common sense relates individual situations to a subject whose primary concern is, not knowledge, but living. Empirical science can be understood as a developing and formulated system of hypotheses and laws which tend toward the invariance of an abstract totality. Within this abstract system, terms which originally emerge from the data of sense are more and more implicitly defined with respect to one another. Thus, common sense is materially dependent on the percept emerging within the dramatic pattern of experience and formally dependent on an incomplete and unformulated core of insights dominated by the concerns of daily life. Science is materially dependent on the sensible data emerging within the intellectual pattern of experience and formally dependent on the tendency toward an abstract and universal system dominated by the detached and disinterested desire to know. Lonergan writes: "Rational choice is not between science and common sense; it is a choice of both, of science to master the universal and of common sense to deal with the particular."[30]

Finally, we turn to the rational level of cognitional operation, the level of reflection and judgment. Lonergan offers a general analysis of the form of the reflective insight. This is the type of insight which grounds the rationally proceeding judgment; this is the type of insight which enables the cognitional subject to reach beyond understanding as mere subjective perfection to understanding as the basis of objective knowledge.

In general, judgment is rationally grounded when it proceeds from the reflective grasp of a virtually unconditioned.[31] A formally unconditioned has no conditions; God is formally unconditioned. A virtually unconditioned has conditions, but they are fulfilled. Thus, in grasping the virtually unconditioned, the reflective insight:

1. grasps a conditioned which is
   a. the content of an act of understanding, or thinking, or formulating,
   b. as scrutinized by the questioning of critical reflection,
   c. and thereby revealed as in need of evidence, support or argument;
2. grasps the link between the conditioned and its conditions which
   a. can be established differently in different contexts,
   b. for example, by an act of understanding, or conceiving, or defining;
3. grasps the fulfillment of conditions which

    a. can occur differently in different contexts,

    b. for example, as the content of sensation, or imagination, or thought.

In one sweep, then, reflective understanding grasps the validity of its intelligent and rational procedure, the existence of its data, "and by rational compulsion there follows the judgment."[32] The general form of reflective insight, as the grasp of the virtually unconditioned, determines the basic elements of any judgment. The establishment of the link and the fulfillment of conditions will vary with different contexts. Since the contexts of science and common sense differ, scientific and common sense judgments can be expected to differ.

The key factor which will contribute to the solidity and the objectivity of our judgments will be the consideration of further, pertinent questions. If all of the further, pertinent questions have been addressed; then one's reflective insight, and hence one's judgment, is correct. Of course, the number and the kind of further, pertinent questions will differ for common sense and for science. Still, Lonergan's analysis of the grounds of judgment remains in principle the same for the field of common sense and for the field of science. The following outline schematizes the invariant structure of cognitional operations and the variable contents from science and common sense.

FIGURE 1

Common Sense and Cognitional Structure

Experience: the dramatic subject and the percept.

Understanding: an unformulated core of habitual insights complemented by additional insights into concrete situations.

Judgment: the absence of further pertinent questions arising in a mind which is alert and intellectually master of a concrete situation.

Science and Cognitional Structure

Experience: the intellectual subject and the data of sense.

Understanding: an abstract system of terms and relations defined implicitly and complemented by statistical investigations.

Judgment: the absence of further pertinent questions arising in a mind which is approaching mastery of a particular field of empirical inquiry.

Three Pivotal Chapters

The next three chapters of *Insight* move us to a higher viewpoint. Is this cognitional structure of experiencing, understanding, and judging really the way I know? What do I know when I perform these operations? Why is performing these operations properly called knowing? These are the three questions asked in chapter eleven, "Self-Affirmation of the Knower", chapter twelve, "The Notion of Being", and chapter thirteen, "The Notion of Objectivity". The following section analyzes this pivotal part of *Insight*.

SELF-AFFIRMATION OF THE KNOWER

Generally, the eleventh chapter of *Insight* discusses whether correct judgments occur. More specifically, it discusses this question, not in terms of necessity, but in terms of fact. Do correct judgments in fact occur?[33] The two prior chapters of *Insight* ("The Notion of Judgment," ch IX; and "Reflective Understanding", ch X) have prepared the reader to answer this pivotal question. They have examined the notion of judgment, the general form of reflective insight, and the way in which we make concrete judgments of fact. Thus, we are familiar with the form which a concrete judgment of fact will take. Since the first part of *Insight* has been a study of the activity of human understanding, the content of the judgment which we should be best prepared to make is whether we too understand, whether we understand correctly, whether we are in fact knowers.

Lonergan discusses the self-affirmation of the knower in three sections. The tripartition is based on the nature of a virtually unconditioned.[34] The first section examines the proposition, I am a knower, as a conditioned. The second section discusses the proposition, I am a knower, as a virtually unconditioned. The third section discusses the proposition, I am a knower, as a virtually unconditioned which conditions other instances of the conditioned.

First, the proposition, I am a knower, is a conditioned. It may be true; it may not be true; it stands in need of argument, support, and evidence. This first section clarifies the conditions of the possible affirmation that I am a knower. There are two types of conditions: those grounded in the general form of reflective understanding, viz., a virtually unconditioned, and those linked with the specific content to be affirmed, viz., cognitional process. First, any reflective grasp of a virtually unconditioned will involve.

1. a conditioned
2. a link between the conditioned and its conditions
3. the fulfillment of conditions.[35]

Secondly, the specific content to be affirmed is the concrete and intelligible unity of cognitional process. Hence, the conditioned is the proposition, I am a knower. The link between the conditioned and its conditions is a statement of meaning. "I am a knower, if I am a concrete and intelligible unity-identity-whole characterized by acts of sensing, perceiving, imagining, inquiring, understanding, formulating, reflecting, grasping the unconditioned, and judging."[36] The fulfillment of conditions is given in consciousness. This last element, the notion of consciousness and the fulfillment of conditions, is the most intractable element.

Initially, Lonergan illustrates what he means by consciousness by contrasting a cognitional act with an unconscious act. Thinking, for example, is a cognitional act; there is not only a succession of contents, or thoughts, but also a concomitant awareness of activity. The growth of a beard, for example, is an unconscious biological act; there is an occurrence, but there is no concomitant awareness. Further, cognitional acts can be of several types. They can be empirical: sensing, imagining, or perceiving. They can be intelligent: wondering, inquiring, or conceiving. They can be rational: reflecting, weighing evidence, or judging. Each type of cognitional act is accompanied by a different type of consciousness: empirical, intelligent, or rational. Still, if the type of consciousness can vary, consciousness as given is the underlying unity and "identity immanent in the diversity and the multiplicity of the (cognitional) process."[37] Consciousness, then, is a quality of awareness manifested and differentiated in cognitional acts.

Consciousness may be either rational, intelligent, or empirical. The conditions as formulated occur in rational and intelligent consciousness; but they also occur, although as un-formulated, in empirical consciousness. Lonergan writes:

> By an experiential fulfillment, then . . . one does mean that the conditions, which are formulated, also are to be found in a more rudimentary state within cognitional process . . . so there is a reverse shift by which one moves from the perceived and understood to the merely perceived.[38]

Verification is constituted by this reverse shift. It can take diverse forms. Empirical science shifts from the formulated to the more rudimentary data of sense. Cognitional analysis shifts from the formulated to the more rudimentary data of consciousness.

The second section of the eleventh chapter of *Insight* discusses the proposition, I am a knower, as a virtually unconditioned. It invites the reader to advance from the prior clarifications to affirmation, from cognitional theory to practice, from his or her understanding to correct judgment. The crucial question is: Am I a knower? Initially, the answer is maybe yes and maybe no. It is a question of fact and so the experiential aspect plays an important role. However, the intelligent aspect plays an important role as well. Am I a knower? It depends on what one means by "knower." The prior ten chapters have been busy clarifying precisely that issue. "I am a knower, if I am a concrete and intelligible unity-identity-whole, characterized by acts of sensing, perceiving, imagining, inquiring, understanding, formulating, reflecting, grasping the unconditioned, and judging."[39] The foregoing definition is a formulation. Prior to it there was the process of formulating. If one has read the previous ten chapters of *Insight* attentively and participated in the generation, clarification, and interrelation of the various cognitional terms, then one has been operating on the intelligent level. Further, to entertain the question, Am I a knower?, and to consider a possible "Yes" and a possible "No" as answers, that is an example of operating on the rational level. Ultimately, one must ask and answer these types of questions for oneself.[40] Only the specific and concrete consciousness of the reader can provide the field of fulfilling conditions.

The third section of this chapter of *Insight* discusses the proposition, I am a knower, as a virtually unconditioned which conditions other instances of the conditioned. That is, the fact that I am a knower manifests certain factual implications. They are both direct and indirect. Most directly, certain conditions must be reflectively understood before I can transform the conditioned proposition into an unconditioned. Before I can grasp that it is a virtually unconditioned that I am a knower, I must, for example, understand the nature of intelligent and rational procedure. But once I make the affirmation that I am a knower, then the conditions which contributed to that affirmation share in its newly acquired factual status. Lonergan writes: "The contingent, if you suppose it as a fact, becomes conditionally necessary, and this piece of elementary logic places the merely factual self-affirmation in a context of necessity."[41] Accordingly, if it is a fact that I am a knower; then empirical, intelligent, and rational consciousness, cognitional process, and all that it implies are factual too. These implications directly follow from the self-affirmation of the knower.

Skeptics may doubt whether they are knowers. But empirical, intelligent, and rational consciousness are factual. The "natural spontaneities and natural inevitabilities"[42] of experiencing, wondering, and criticizing will condition their very doubting. As Aristotle suggested, get skeptics to talk and their natural, although unacknowledged, intelligence and rationality will be revealed.

Cognitional facts and self-understanding can be consistent or inconsistent.[43] The statements, I am a knower, and, I know that fact, are consistent. The statements, I am not a knower, and, I know that fact, are contradictory. Self-negation is incoherent. The incoherence is ultimately between spontaneous cognitional practice and mistaken self-understanding. If skeptics rise above elementary animal knowing, their very attempts to explain their position, to offer reasons, to excuse their hesitations, will involve them in the spontaneities and inevitabilities of fully human knowing. If one cannot know, then one cannot know explanations, reasons, or excuses.

The first type of implication, then, is factual and follows directly from the fact that I am a knower. It includes the conditions which most directly contributed evidence for the judgment. Prior to the judgment, prior to self-affirmation, they were the hypothetical formulations of direct understanding. But once the knower affirms himself or herself as virtually unconditioned, the conditions of that judgment take on a factual status.

The second type of implication is a more indirect result of self-affirmation. The self-affirmed knower is a fact and as such participates in the conditioning of other facts. Lonergan explains that the virtually unconditioned stands within an interlocking field of conditioning and conditioned. The virtually unconditioned "has conditions; it itself is among the conditions of other instances of the conditioned."[44]

Revisions occur in the fields of natural and human sciences. Revision itself, however, is no necessity; it is factual; it is conditioned. Revision may presuppose the discovery of new data, the formulation of a better theory, or a closer approximation to the virtually unconditioned. It certainly presupposes a revisor who experiences, understands, and judges. In other words, the act of revision is conditioned and a major condition of its possibility is the existence of the cognitional self as it has just been affirmed. Consequently, although the cognitional process of the knower is among the concrete conditions of revision, the cognitional process as affirmed is not itself within the field of the potentially revisable. Since any revision would presuppose some new knowledge, and "since every other known becomes known through the [cognitional] process, no known could impugn the process without simultaneously impugning its own status as known."[45]

We began by reviewing the conditions for the possibility of a judgment of fact. Am I, in fact, a knower? It was a factual judgment based upon a general analysis of cognitional process and a specific account of the form of reflective insight. The conditions for this particular judgment of fact were limited in number, determinate in nature, and capable of being experientially fulfilled. "Further, though self-affirmation is no more than a judgment of mere fact, still it is a privileged judgment."[46] It was not privileged in the sense that it required special pleading, for it conformed to the general form of reflective insight. But it was privileged in the position it occupied in the interlocking field of conditioning and conditioned—the field of facts. Since every other fact we know is known through this cognitional process, cognitional process itself is always among the concrete conditions of any other virtually unconditioned. Lonergan writes: "The making of judgments is a determinate process, and one does not have to make all judgments to grasp the nature of that process."[47] We have, then, in the self-affirmation of the knower, the establishment of an extremely significant fact.

THE NOTION OF BEING

Lonergan begins this twelfth chapter of *Insight* with a definition. "Being, then, is the objective of the pure desire to know."[48] He expands on each of the partial terms of this explanatory definition: what he means by "the desire to know," by its purity, and by "being" as its objective.

First, by the desire to know is meant, not any single element within cognitional process, but the dynamic orientation of the process as a whole.[49] The desire to know, as a dynamic orientation, promotes experience into the material for intelligent inquiry, then transforms the products of our thinking into the material for critical reflection, and finally weaves our rationally grounded judgments into the fabric of our habitual knowledge. Moreover, it is the desire to know which moves us beyond our habitual knowledge to further questioning and thence to new knowledge.

Secondly, the desire to know is pure. Its purity appears differently in different fields. It is the cool shrewdness of the person of common sense; it is the disinterestedness of the scientist; it is the detachment of the philosopher. Its purity consists in giving free reign to intelligence and rationality.

Thirdly, the pure desire has an objective. It is satisfied when the objective is reached. But the pure desire seeks, not satisfaction, but content. Being is the anything and everything that is the objective of intelligent and rational desiring.[50] Initially, being is the totality of the unknown. But one does reach partial answers: the darkness slowly diminishes, and light increases. Being, as the objective of the pure desire to know, includes the little bit that we already know and the vast expanse we could ask about. The range of the pure desire to know, and hence the range of being is unrestricted.[51]

In order to emphasize this last point, Lonergan considers the impossibility of measuring being by any finite standards. Could there not exist something apart from being, apart from the range of the pure desire to know? For example, we can imagine a circle encompassing all that is meant by being. Something could possibly exist outside that circle, if only empty space. Still, being is defined not in terms of an imaginative picture of what could possibly lie within or without a circle, but in terms of the pure desire to know. Hence, anything about which we could wonder, anything which we could desire to know, is included within being.

There is an important technical point involved in the definition of being. Lonergan writes:

> Our definition of being, then, is of the second order. Other definitions determine what is meant. But this definition is more remote for it assigns, not what is meant by being but how that meaning is to be determined.[52]

This point is a technical implication of the more elementary point that, for Lonergan, being is not a conceptual content. It cannot be comprehended by any human act of understanding. Still, although being is not directly determinate, neither is it merely indeterminate. It is defined in terms of a relationship to the pure desire to know; but the pure desire to know can be understood in terms of its unfolding in cognitional process.

The definition of being as the objective of the pure desire to know relates the terms "being" and "pure desire to know" to one another in an explanatory fashion. The theory is: if you wish to understand what being is, then investigate the pure desire to know. Although the pure desire to know is not the whole of being, it is a strategically chosen and extremely significant part. But besides explanation there is description. How do they relate to our spontaneity?

Lonergan distinguishes between theoretical accounts of being and the spontaneously operative notion of being. Theoretical accounts of being are multiple, often conflicting, and differ with various philosophic contexts. The spontaneously operative notion of being is one and the same for scientists and for people of common sense; it is indifferent to one's philosophic predilections.

Lonergan locates the notion of being in our experience by identifying it with the functioning or the pure desire to know. The pure desire to know, as the notion of being, is experienced as the initiator of cognitional process. It arises in consciousness as intelligent questioning. It sustains cognitional process through intelligent questioning to critical reflection. Further, it extends beyond all immanent cognitional operation to the affirmation and knowledge of the universe of being.

As an illustration, Lonergan discusses how the notion of being is at once prior to reflective understanding and yet extends beyond it. Extending beyond what we presently know, the notion of being grounds our affirmation that there is much that exists of which we have no knowledge, understanding, or even experience. Operating prior to judgment, the notion of being raises the reflective question Is it so? In other words, prior to knowing being, there is a capacity to determine what an example of "knowing-being" would be like. That capacity is the notion of being.

Similarly, the notion of being is at once prior to conception and yet extends beyond it. We can, of course, think of almost anything we like. Still, for the most part, our thinking is purposive. We think things out in order to clarify our concepts preparatory to judgment. In other words, thinking is thinking of being insofar as it is a moment in a process which begins in experience and heads for knowledge of being.

The notion of being is most clearly manifested by the dynamic aspect of cognitional process. In the intellectual pattern of experience, data is selected and organized for the purpose of thinking; thinking is for the purpose of judging; judging is for the purpose of knowing being. Each of the elements of cognitional process Lonergan has analyzed in the first part of *Insight* reveals a different aspect of the pure desire to know. But it is the "dynamic orientation"[53] of cognitional process; and it is the "immanent dynamism (that) both underlies actual attainment and heads beyond it with ever further questions,"[54] and again, it is the "universal intention of being;"[55] it is all of these phrases together which locates in experience the more rudimentary form of what is meant by the notion of being.

How does the notion of being differ from being as being? Being as being is the whole and notion of being is a part of that whole. The notion of being is oriented toward the whole of being as being. For example, a foetal eye is oriented toward seeing. It does not presently see, but given the proper develop-ment of its present structure, it will see. Similarly, the notion of being is oriented toward knowing being. But there is a fuller dimension which this parallel with foetal eye does not capture.

The notion of being is conscious. As hunger motivates one to seek food and is a consciously felt desire, the notion of being motivates one to seek knowledge in an open-eyed, conscious fashion. One consciously desires to know and to know some aspect of being. There is, however, a fuller dimension which eludes this parallel with hunger.

The notion of being is more than an orientation toward being, more than a felt desire to know being; it is intelligent and rational. The notion of being is an intelligently and rationally conscious orientation towards being as being. It initiates and sustains one's cognitive journey, not in the manner of a salmon returning up a river to spawn, but intelligently and rationally.

The notion of being is also the core of all acts of meaning. Lonergan distinguishes between formal acts of meaning and full acts of meaning. The former include acts of thinking, con-ceiving, and formulating. The latter include acts of judging. Lonergan further distinguishes between formal terms of mean-ing and full terms of meaning. The former include the concept, thought, or definition. The latter include judgments. The key point is that the final and all-inclusive term of meaning is being. Being is the totality towards which all formal and full acts of meaning are heading.

As being is the all-inclusive term of meaning, so the notion of being is the core of all acts of meaning. Again, the notion of being is the universal intention of being. It can be described as the all-pervasive, underpinning, and constituting dynamism of all our formal and full acts of meaning.

To illustrate the notion of being as the core of meaning, let us consider the individual judgment. Any given judgment is both determined and determining. As determined, the individual judgment participates in the meaning of the prior context of insights and judgments. Thus, certain relevant insights and judgments fix its meaning. Further, each individual judgment is but a partial increment to our knowledge of being. As determin-ing, the individual judgment "is but an element in the determination of the universal intention of being."[56] Thus, the meaning of a given judgment is determined by the prior context of judgments, while the intention of the judgment is to realize a single moment in the universal anticipation and intention of being. In other words, the distinction between the meaning of a given judgment and its intention is equivalent to the distinction between the determinate meaning and the determining act of judgment as a partial increment to the universal intention of being.

Accordingly, in a true judgment there is a harmony between the determinate elements of meaning and the actualization of the universal intention of being. In a false judgment, "there is conflict between intention and meaning."[57] One intends to affirm an aspect of being, but one affirms what is not. There is a conflict between the intention of being and the meaning of the judgment.

The notion of being has traditionally been troublesome to formulate. Lonergan singles out several puzzling aspects of the notion of being and reduces them to a common source. The source of the difficulty in the notion of being is the manner in which it diverges from other concepts and the rules which govern their formulation.

First, the formulations of other concepts proceed from acts of insight. But the notion of being seems to proceed from no discoverable insight. The only insight it could directly proceed from would be an act of understanding everything about everything. But since we possess no such insight, our notion of being could not proceed from it.

Secondly, from whence emerges our notion of being? It cannot emerge from experience alone, otherwise we would know being before we began to think. What point or purpose, then, could thinking have? It cannot emerge from understanding alone, otherwise we would know being before we reflectively asked, Is it so? What point or purpose, then, could judgment have if understanding was automatically correct? It cannot emerge from the single judgment alone, for in the single judgment we affirm or negate this or that being, but by being we mean everything, the totality.[58] Still, if the notion of being cannot originate in any of these cognitional levels taken singly, it can and does originate in understanding the dynamic manner in which the combination of cognitional processes proceed, coalesce, and terminate in a single knowing, and especially in the way judgment follows judgment in an intelligent and rational succession toward an intelligent and rational goal. Hence, Lonergan understands being as "what is to be known by the totality of true judgments."[59]

Thirdly, if the level of intelligence is not sufficient to produce the notion of being, neither is that notion to be had without our insights, thinking, formulations, or conceptions. Although judgment transcends all conceptual content, judgment is always an act with respect to conceptual content. Although our judgments of fact are affirmations or negations of beings, our judgments of fact are never pure affirmations or negations. Our judgments are always answers to determinate questions; it is our insights, concepts, and previous judgments which determine our reflective questions. Referring to Aquinas, Lonergan notes:

> It is in and through essences that being has existence. Hence being apart from essence is being apart from the possibility of existence; it is being that cannot exist; . . . the notion of being apart from essence in the notion of nothing.[60]

In *Insight,* Lonergan chooses to speak of the cognitional levels of intelligence and reflection rather than of essences and acts of existence, but the point is the same. The notion of being, even though it transcends any and all conception, is not to be grasped without conception.

Thus, Lonergan strategically places the chapter on the self-affirmation of the knower prior to this chapter on the notion of being. The earlier chapter provides the ground for the latter. It provides the ground for the notion of being, not because it contains a concept of knowing, or a theory of knowing, or a definition of knowing, but because it contains a concrete judgment of fact—the self-affirmation of the knower. To be sure, self-affirmation presupposes the grasp and formulation of many conceptual contents. The notion of being, however, is only indirectly connected to those particular conceptual contents; it is directly connected to self-affirmation as a judgment of fact.

Fourthly, if cognitional process reaches a full increment only in the judgment, the notion of being reaches its full determination only in the total context of correct judgments. Lonergan writes of the notion of being:

> It becomes determined only as correct judgments are made, and it reaches its full determination only when the totality of correct judgments are made. However, the making of judgments is a determinate process and one does not have to make all judgments to grasp the nature of that process. It is this fact that makes cognitional theory a base for operations for the determination of the general structure of the concrete universe.[61]

Hence, since the full meaning of the notion of being is identical with the totality of true judgments, we must be modest about actual intellectual achievement. Yet, in the process of making a single judgment, we have revealed the invariant form of all subsequent judgments. While there may be an enormous range of being remaining to be known, for us, it is not to be known in any other way than our already experienced, understood and affirmed cognitional process. Accordingly, while modesty is appropriate, so too is confidence in our intellectual and rational progress.

THE NOTION OF OBJECTIVITY

This thirteenth chapter of *Insight* discusses what principally is meant by the notion of objectivity and by the three partial aspects of the principle notion. The unity grounding the principal notion and the partial notions of absolute, normative, and experiential objectivity is the pure desire to know. The notion of objectivity is basically understood as the manner in which the pure desire to know proceeds towards towards its unrestricted objective.

The complexity of the notion of objectivity arises from the complexity of cognitional process. To use a simile, a wheel not only revolves around its center, but when attached to a cart, also moves down the road towards its objective. Similarly, cognitional process not only proceeds in a cycle of experiencing, understanding, and judging, only to revert to experiencing and proceed to another judgment, but it also moves down the road towards being. Our acts of knowing are related cumulatively; we cover ground. We accumulate experiences, we add to our cluster of insights, we progressively deepen our habitually possessed knowledge.

The pure desire to know unifies the notion of objectivity and the procedures of cognitional process differentiate it. The pure desire to know initiates cognitional process by inquiring into the given; thus, there is an experiential notion of objectivity.[62] The pure desire to know unfolds according to its own intrinsic demand for intelligent and rational procedure; thus there is a normative notion of objectivity. The pure desire to know has a terminal objective in knowing by grasping a virtually unconditioned; thus there is an absolute notion of objectivity. The pure desire to know has a final objective in being as a whole; thus there is a principal notion of objectivity.

This is an overview of the chapter but there remain important specific points to be appreciated. The principal notion of objectivity is located in a patterned context of judgments. It presupposes that correct judgments occur and that they can coalesce into a determinate pattern. Further, it is from the determinate pattern of judgments that the terms "object" and "subject" are implicitly defined. Lonergan writes: "In brief, there is objectivity if there are distinct beings, some of which both know themselves and know others as others."[63] Accordingly, the principal notion of objectivity presupposes that one has already made a number of correct judgments: the affirmation of the existence of several objects, the self-affirmation of the knower, the affirmation of the implicit relations which hold between objects and subjects.

Lonergan points out that the principal notion of objectivity is closely related to the notion of being. While neither notion can be formulated without the occurrence of particular judgment, viz., the self-affirmation of the knower, still the single judgment as single is not enough to establish the respective notions. Instead, both notions arise from a plurality of judgments. In the case of the notion of being, the particular content of each judgment is less important than the dynamism which the aggregate of judgments reveals. In the case of the principal notion of objectivity, the content of the judgments is more important and the aggregate of judgments must reveal a determinate pattern which implicitly defines the terms "object" and "subject."

Lonergan's strategy has placed the problem of the self-transcendence of the knower in a unique context. First, he has established that correct judgments occur (Ch. XI). Secondly, he has established that each correct judgment is only a minimal increment to a dynamic orientation toward the unrestricted objective named being (Ch. XII). Thirdly, within that pure and dynamic orientation towards being occurs the several correct judgments which distinguish and relate such beings as subjects and objects (Ch. XIII). In contrast, consider the problem of the self-transcendence of the knower in another context. First, there is a subject who knows himself or herself through intuitive self-presence. Secondly, there are objects which from different viewpoints appear differently to the subject. Thirdly, there is now the question of how the knower, who is intuitively present to his or her own being, can know the being of objects.

Lonergan approaches the question of cognitional self-transcendence with two aspects in mind:

> Our answer involves two elements. On the one hand, we contend that, while the knower may experience himself or think about himself without judging, still he cannot know himself until he makes the correct affirmation, I am. Further, we contend that other judgments are equally possible and reasonable, so that through experience, inquiry, and reflection there arises knowledge of other objects both as beings and as beings other than the knower. Hence, we place transcendence not in going beyond a known knower but in heading for being within which there are positive differences and, among such differences, the difference between object and subject.[64]

The two aspects which Lonergan emphasizes are complementary. First, the being of the subject is not known by intuition. It is not known merely in experience nor in the compound of experience and understanding. It is not known until the act of judgment occurs. Secondly, the being of the object is possibly known when the data on it are understood, and actually known when the data on it are understood correctly. Hence, it is really and truly the being of the object that is known by experience, understanding, and judging.[65] Cognitional self-transcendence is a matter of partially knowing an aspect of being in experience. It is a matter of more fully grasping the possible dimensions of a being in understanding. Finally, it is a matter of actually knowing the being of a particular being in judgment. It is a secondary consideration whether that being is an object or a subject.

There remains the three partial notions of objectivity. First, the absolute notion of objectivity is located in the notion of judgment as proceeding from the reflective grasp of a virtually unconditioned. The principal notion of objectivity pertained to a plurality of judgments in a patterned context; the absolute notion pertains to the single judgment as single. Lonergan writes:

> The formally unconditioned, which has no conditions at all, stands outside the interlocked field of conditioning and conditioned; it is intrinsically absolute. The virtually unconditioned stands within that field; it has conditions; it itself is among the conditions of other instances of the conditioned; still its conditions are fulfilled; it is a *de facto* absolute.[66]

It is the absolute aspect of judgments which accounts for their ability to be understood apart from the subject that utters them and apart from the time and place of utterance. The absolute notion of objectivity gives judgments their public status.

Secondly, the normative notion of objectivity is located in the manner in which the pure desire to know unfolds itself in intelligent inquiry and critical reflection. The absolute notion of objectivity pertains to the terminal object of cognitional process—the judgment. The normative notion of objectivity pertains to the cognitional process as intelligent and rational procedure, prescinding from its terminal or final object. Accordingly, this aspect of objectivity focuses upon the purity of the pure desire to know. It is purity as an unrestricted process opposing all obscurantism, as a detached process resisting the interference of wishes and fears, and as a disinterested process refusing to serve as the instrument of some lesser desire. Further, the validity of all logic and methods is ultimately grounded in this normative notion of objectivity. That is, a logical or methodical procedure is valid if it proceeds from and remains faithful to the prior demand of the pure desire to know for intelligent and rational procedure.

Thirdly, the experiential notion of objectivity is located in the relation of the pure desire to know to the materials of inquiry. The experiential notion of objectivity pertains to the given. What are the given? For the natural scientists, they are the data of sense. For the psychologist, the methodologist, and the cultural historian, they include the data of consciousness. Although the given is the starting point for inquiry, the given as given is constituted prior to questioning, insight, or formulation. Thus, Lonergan characterizes the given as unquestionable, residual, and diffuse. One may object that this does not approach an adequate description of the flow of empirical consciousness. But, it is Lonergan's intention merely to fix the meaning of the given in terms of the pure desire to know. In that sense, the given is the material starting point for intelligent inquiry and critical reflection.

In summary, all three aspects of objectivity, and the principal notion as well, are to be understood in terms of the manner in which the pure desire to know proceeds toward knowledge of being. Experiential objectivity pertains to the starting point. Normative objectivity pertains to the manner in which intelligence and rationality proceed. Absolute objectivity pertains to the nature of judgment as the terminal object of cognitional process. The principal notion of objectivity pertains to the manner in which the pure desire to know proceeds to its final object-being.

The Method of Metaphysics

Lonergan observes that any discussion of metaphysics is threatened by the fallacy of begging the question.[67] The object of metaphysics is the unified totality towards which the various departments of knowledge are collectively heading. In Lonergan's words, "the only question to be settled in metaphysics is the general nature of the goal of knowledge, for all questions of detail have to be met by the sciences and by common sense."[68]

The goal of metaphysics, then, is a kind of totality.[69] On the other hand, a method is only as good as its ability to guide a process to its desired goal. Accordingly, a method, in some way, anticipates the as yet unachieved goal; a method already contains within itself some view of the goal towards which it is tending. Hence, in selecting a method, would not a metaphysician use as a principle of selection some view of totality, some view of the ideal towards which the method is tending? Would not a metaphysician's choice imply that the only question metaphysics seeks to settle is already in some sense settled? In order to avoid the fallacy of begging the question, Lonergan points out that metaphysics is unique: "In metaphysics, however, methods and results are of equal generality and tend to be coincident."[70] The metaphysician does not first choose some method and then proceed to its goal. Rather, the advance of metaphysics has been simultaneous with the search for a fundamental method.

Lonergan chooses human consciousness as the fundamental factor in determining the proper method for metaphysics. Human consciousness is the starting point, the guiding agent, and the terminal goal of metaphysical method. Lonergan writes:

> Just as metaphysics can exist only in a mind and can be produced only by the mind in which it is to be, so also metaphysics can begin only in minds that exist and it can proceed only from their actual texture and complexion. Bluntly, the starting-point of metaphysics is people as they are.[71]

Metaphysical method starts from the human mind that exists. That is clear; but what is not clear is—what is the human mind? Human consciousness, as *Insight* convincingly shows, is a complex reality. The initial problem of metaphysical method is not the establishment of self-evident principles, but the clarification of human consciousness to itself. No principle is self-evident to a consciousness bewildered by its own complexity.[72]

Lonergan characterizes the complexity of mind as "the polymorphism of human consciousness." Human experience flows in any of several basic patterns.[73] For example, there are the biological, the practical, the dramatic, the artistic, the intellectual, and the mystical patterns of experience. Different patterns possess their own proper conscious procedures. The pure desire to know properly dominates the intellectual pattern of experience. It is peripheral in the biological pattern of experience; it plays an intermediate role in the dramatic pattern of experience. In every pattern of experience, however, the pure desire to know exists in tension with other concerns. We are not pure intellects; we are concrete unities-in-tension.

Lonergan's account of the polymorphism of consciousness is, of course, the product of reflection. One can conceive and affirm the existence and significance of a pure desire to know only after prolonged labor. Further, it is only in and through that intellectual labor that one becomes secure and familiar with what is meant by "the intellectual pattern of experience." For the existential subject, prior to that intellectual labor, the tension between the pure desire to know and other concerns is simply bewildering. It is experienced, but it is neither understood nor affirmed. For the existential subject, prior to differentiation, the various paterns of experience easily flow together, interfere with one another, or break down. The starting point of metaphysics is human consciousness; but it is human consciousness as existing in bewildering tension.

For Lonergan, metaphysical method begins with a preliminary phase in which the subject is invited to self-knowledge.[74] Although *Insight* begins by investigating the procedures of mathematics, science, and common sense, the point of that investigation is to make available to the initially bewildered subject the insights which ground the diverse procedures of diverse fields of investigation. Through understanding those insights, the bewildered subject can advance to an understanding of his or her own acts of understanding. Through reflecting on the structure and procedure of reflective insight, the subject can advance to a reflective grasp of the invariant and recurrent structure of his or her own correct understanding. The person can affirm himself or herself as a knower. While this does not make the subject into a scientist, or even a person of common sense, it does advance the cognitional subject from the bewildering tension of polymorphic consciousness to the clarified and affirmed tension of self-knowledge.[75]

Self-affirmation is only the beginning of the cognitional subject's self-knowledge. Through reflection upon the act of self-affirmation, the cognitional subject can affirm being as the object of the pure desire to know, and the subject can affirm his or her knowledge of being to be objective insofar as he or she conceives and affirms the experiential, the normative, the absolute, and the principle notions of objectivity. The most important aspect of self-knowledge, however, is the grasp and affirmation of the significance of the pure desire to know. The cognitional subject reaches a high moment of intelligent and rational self-possession when he or she reflectively grasps and affirms the pure desire to know as the universal intention of being. Thus, the subject reflectively grasps and affirms the underlying, penetrating, transforming, and unifying intention of all his or her cognitional operations to be the desire to know being. That reflective grasp is self-knowledge; it is knowledge of a partial, but extremely significant, aspect of being.

From that high moment of reflective self-appropriation, the cognitional subject can return to the diverse fields of intellectual inquiry with a transformed self-understanding. It was through the content of intelligent inquiry and critical reflection that the subject was able to achieve the act of self-appropriation; it will be through the act of self-appropriation that those acts of intelligent inquiry and critical reflection with their corresponding contents can be integrated and unified. Lonergan writes: "The detached and disinterested desire to know and its unfolding in inquiry and reflection not only constitute a notion of being but also impose a normative structure upon man's cognitional acts."[76] The key point here is that the act of self-appropriation constitutes a pivot between the highest point in interior reflection and the formal principle of metaphysical method. The highest point in interior reflection is the reflective identification of the pure desire to know and the intention or notion of being. The formal principle of metaphysical method is that the pure desire to know proceeds toward being through its self-appropriated, invariant, and normative structure. This, I believe, is the same point which Lonergan makes in the Introduction to *Insight*. There he discusses the act whereby rational self-consciousness takes possession of itself as rational self-consciousness. He writes: "Up to that achievement, all leads. From it all follows."[77] From this highest point in reflective self-possession, we turn now to the second explicit phase of metaphysical method.

In the initial phase, the pure desire to know and its unfolding in intelligent inquiry and critical reflection existed and operated. In this second phase of metaphysical method, the pure desire to know not only exists and operates, but also has been conceived and affirmed. Metaphysics was latent and now it becomes explicit. In the explicit phase, cognitional process as a normative structure functions as an integrating principle for the diverse materials of scientific investigation and common sense. In order to better conceive the relationship of this normative structure to its materials, let us recall a point which Lonergan had made in his dissertation:

> Thus, the content of speculative theology is the content of a pure form. It is not something by itself, but the intelligible arrangement of something else. It is not systematic theology but the system in systematic theology.[78]

Similarly, cognitional process as a normative structure is a type of pure form. It is not common sense or science. Rather, it provides the integrating structure for an intelligible arrangement of those fields. Nevertheless, the normative structure of cognitional process is not the type of pure form to be discovered by Platonic reminiscence. It is discovered by thinking about and reflecting upon our cognitional operations as they exist in tension with other human concerns. Consequently, as a normative principle, cognitional structure exists independently of the materials provided by common sense and science; as a principle intimately involved with concrete matters of fact, cognitional structure cannot be conceived or affirmed apart from an understanding of the structures of common sense and science.[79]

In *Insight*, Lonergan does not use the phrase, "the content of a pure form." He characterizes cognitional process as an integral heuristic structure. The word "heuristic" is used to indicate the fact that we can anticipate an unknown content by understanding the general type of cognitional act through which it will become known. Thus, classical scientific procedure is heuristic because through direct insights, it anticipates the emergence of systematic intelligibilities immanent in the data. Statistical scientific procedure is heuristic because through the direct insights of classical science and its own brand of inverse insights, it anticipates the way in which data will non-systematically diverge from abstract formulations.[80] Lonergan's analysis of both scientific and common sense procedures is intended to reveal the general nature of the types of cognitional acts through which knowledge in those various fields occurs. Hence, he defines a heuristic notion as "the notion of an unknown content and it is determined by anticipating the type of act through which the unknown would become known."[81] However, *Insight* seeks to reveal to and in the cognitional subject, not simply the anticipation of particular types of insights, but also the general anticipatory structure of all cognitional activity. The integral heuristic structure is the pattern of intelligible and intelligent relations which exists among empirical, intelligent, and rational levels of consciousness.

Lonergan defines explicit metaphysics as "the conception, affirmation, and implementation of the integral heuristic structure of proportionate being."[82] By the term "proportionate being" Lonergan means what is known and what is to be known through human experiencing, understanding, and judging. It can be contrasted with transcendent being which, although it can be affirmed and to a limited degree understood, is not an immediate object of human experience. Integral heuristic structure, then, is the pattern of relations existing among our cognitive acts and their proportionate objects. Explicit metaphysics conceives, affirms, and implements the understanding of this pattern of relations.

The way in which Lonergan conceives integral heuristic structure implies certain views on the basic philosophic issues of knowing, being, and objectivity. For this reason, he did not proceed with this fourteenth chapter until after those basic issues were clarified. Other philosophies have their views on these basic issues. An enrichment and clarification of Lonergan's views on knowing, being, and objectivity can be achieved by comparing and contrasting his views with those of other philosophies. Every philosophy contains, implicitly or explicitly, views on the relations among the knower, its knowing, and the known. Those views, in Lonergan's account, are either basic positions or basic counter-positions. He writes:

> It will be a basic position (1) if the real is the concrete universe of being and not a subdivision of the "already out there now;" (2) if the subject becomes known when it affirms itself intelligently and reasonably and so is not known yet in any prior "existential" state; and (3) if objectivity is conceived as a consequence of intelligent inquiry and critical reflection, and not as a property of vital anticipation, extroversion, and satisfaction. On the other hand, it will be a basic counterposition, if it contradicts one or more of the basic positions.[83]

By enriching integral heuristic structure with the views of other philosophies, insofar as they are consistent with basic positions,[84] our apprehension of the basic form of human cognitional process could be deepened. By reversing the basic counter-positions of various philosophies, we could deepen our understanding of the root of intellectual aberration.

Lonergan provides an initial implementation of his understanding of explicit metaphysics by enriching it with an analysis of the historical succession of philosophic accounts of knowing, being, and objectivity. However, before integral heuristic structure could be fully implemented, it would have to be integrated with the fields of science and common sense. In the early chapters of *Insight,* scientific and common sense procedures were analyzed as examples of intelligent inquiry and critical reflection. Both scientists and people of common sense seek insights and pause to reflect whether their understanding is correct or mistaken. Still, neither science nor common sense, as it actually exists, is purely and simply the product of the pure desire to know. Lonergan cautions:

> While, then, science and common sense are to be accepted, the acceptance is not to be uncritical. There are precise manners in which common sense can be expected to go wrong; there are definite issues on which science is prone to issue extrascientific opinions; and the reorientation demanded and effected by

the self-knowledge of the subject is a steadily exerted pressure against the common nonsense that tries to pass for common sense and against the uncritical philosophy that pretends to be a scientific conclusion.[85]

Before they can be integrated into a unified viewpoint, science and common sense must be reoriented. The basic procedure for reorientation is reversal of the views which are inconsistent with the basic positions on knowing, being and ojectivity, and which result from confusion over the polymorphism of consciousness.[86] Just as the formal component, integral heuristic structure, is enriched and clarified by the development of positions and the reversal of counter-positions, so too, the material component, science and common sense, is transformed by reversing elements which are inconsistent with the basic positions. In this manner, common sense and science become the transformed materials to be integrated.

The final phase of explicit metaphysics is the integration of the formal principle and the materials to be integrated. Lonergan writes that explicit metaphysics is "formally dependent on cognitional theory and materially dependent on the science and on common sense."[87] With the incompatible counter-positions removed, common sense and science can reveal their complementarity and coherence. The integral heuristic structure which underlies, penetrates, and transforms science and common sense can reveal its unifying capacity. Further, as integral heuristic structure unifies science and common sense, the development of new methods in the fields of common sense and science can be expected to add further enrichment to metaphysical method.

Besides the formal principle of integration, and the materials to be integrated, there is an actual component to metaphysical method. We began by pointing out that human consciousness is the starting point, the guiding agent, and the terminal goal of the metaphysical method. Lonergan adds: "Metaphysics, then, is not something in a book but something in a mind."[88] The integration of the final phase of metaphysics can only occur in the metaphysician's mind. Further, it occurs not as a static concept but as the act of reflective understanding. In one sweep of reflection, the metaphysician's reflective understanding grasps its unified viewpoint as virtually unconditioned. It grasps that cognitional structure is the normative and integrating structure of proportionate being (the conditioned). It understands the way in which its understanding cognitional structure emerges from its analysis of the procedures of mathematicians, empirical scientists, and people of common sense (the link between the conditioned and its conditions). It understands the way in which the combination of human progress and decline is linked to the combination of human insights and oversights (the experiential fulfillment of conditions). Metaphysics is actually the metaphysician's reflective understanding of the integrating potentialities of reflective understanding.[89]

FIGURE 2

Metaphysics and Cognitional Structure

Experience: the existential subject as existing in a bewildering tension between the pure desire to know and other concerns.

Understanding: the grasp and affirmation of the pure desire to know both as intending being and as imposing a normative structure on the subject's cognitional acts.

Judgment: the reflective grasp of the way in which the pure desire to know and its normative structure emerges from an analysis of common sense and science, and in turn, imposes a normative and integrating structure upon them.

Intellectual Conversion

The concept of intellectual conversion appeared in Lonergan's work several years after the completion of *Insight*. It was closely related to the principle of self-appropriation. Still, intellectual conversion added an existential dimension to *Insight*'s discussion of the terms "self-appropriation" and "self-affirmation."

Self-appropriation stands to self-affirmation as the whole to the part. Lonergan writes of self-appropriation:

> First of all, self-appropriation is advertence—advertence to oneself as experiencing, understanding, and judging. Secondly, it is understanding oneself as expe-

> riencing, understanding, and judging. Thirdly, it is af-
> firming oneself as experiencing, understanding, and
> judging.[90]

Hence, self-affirmation is the goal of the process of self-appropriation. Our experience and understanding of self becomes
self-knowledge only with the act of self-affirmation. Conversely, the wider one's experience and the deeper one's understanding, the more meaningful is the act of self-affirmation.

Self-appropriation is paradoxical. It proceeds easily once the
subject recognizes the reflective grasp of the virtually unconditioned and the rationally proceeding judgment to be the criterion of reality. Again, self-appropriation proceeds naturally and
spontaneously as long as one allows the pure desire to know to
dominate and as long as one operates within the intellectual
pattern of experience. But the concrete subject develops over
time. First, the person develops physically; only later does he
or she develop intellectually and rationally. The concrete subject has been successfully dealing with the situations of daily
living long before he or she asks the reflective question, how do
I know? The concrete subject has concerns other than the pure
desire to know; he or she operates in patterns other than the
intellectual. In these other patterns, the standards and criteria
of the subject's performance are less elaborate than the reflective grasp of the virtually unconditioned. One does not have to
inquire, formulate, or judge in order to move out of the path of
oncoming traffic; inasmuch as we are animals, we intuitively
sense danger. Consequently, there is an existential problem to
self-appropriation. The concrete subject has been successfully
living with his or her own standards and criteria long before he
or she reflectively raises questions about the criterion for judging reality. Intellectual conversion pertains to the existential
problem of self-appropriation.

Lonergan first used the notion of conversion, in an intellectual context, in the article "Insight: Preface to a Discussion" in
1958.[91] *Insight* itself had been completed in 1953. In this article, he distinguishes between two worlds: one's private real
world and the universe of being.

> To each of us his own real world is very real indeed.
> Spontaneously it lays claim to being the one real

world, the standard, the criterion, the absolute, by which everything else is judged, measured, evaluated. That claim, I should insist, is not to be admitted. There is one standard, one criterion, one absolute, and that is true judgment. Insofar as ones private real world does not meet that standard, it is some dubious product of animal faith and human error. On the other hand, insofar as one's private real world is submitted constantly and sedulously to the corrections made by true judgment, necessarily it is brought into conformity with the universe of being.[92]

One's private real world is defined in terms of one's interests and concerns. For example, one carefully reads through entire sections of the newspaper and skips over other sections. The ignored areas are outside the scope of one's interest. Again, one's private real world is limited by one's ability to grow and develop, as well as one's success in dealing with dread and anxiety. On the other hand, the universe of being is defined in terms of "what is to be known by the totality of true judgments and not without true judgments."[93]

Intellectual conversion is a matter of shifting one's criterion of reality. The key difference between one's private world and the universe of being is not a difference in particular things. For example, it is not a case of mistaking a stranger for an old acquaintance, or a picture for the real thing. Rather, the key difference between one's private world and the universe of being is the criterion of the true judgment. One's private real world becomes a problem because one uses one's private concerns and interests to determine, not only its content, but also its criterion. Conversely, the criterion of the true judgment leaves the content of the universe of being indeterminate; it only fixes the manner in which that content is to be determined. The content of one's private world is determinate enough and it can be real. But as long as that content is organized around one's private interests as a standard, one needs intellectual conversion. Intellectual conversion, then, is a shift in the principle around which one organizes one's world.

One can recognize the standard of the true judgment and still be involved in error. The process of moving one's private real world into conformity with the universe of being is gradual. It is a matter of continually applying the criterion and constantly and sedulously submitting to its demand. It is a matter of a kind of self-abnegation in which one demotes one's private interests and concerns from the status of absolute standard to the status of relativized content. Lonergan writes:

> I am inclined to believe, however, that the constant and sedulous correction does not occur without a specifi-cally philosophic conversion from the "homo sen-sibilibus immersus" to "homo maxime est mens hominis" (Sum. Theol., 1–2, q. 29, a. 4c.) This existen-tial aspect of our knowing is the fundamental factor in the differentiation of the philosophies in *Insight*.[94]

The constant and sedulous correction, however, is the effect, rather than the cause of philosophic conversion. There is a long task, a lifelong task, of learning and self-correction. But phi-losophic or intellectual conversion itself is a shift in one's criterion of reality. It is a shift from private concerns to the pure desire to know; it is a shift from the person who is immersed in the sensible to the person whose mind is ascendant.

In 1958, Lonergan also conducted a seminar on *Insight* at St. Mary's University in Halifax, Nova Scotia. There, he related the notion of intellectual conversion to the finality of the sub-ject.

> There is, finally, a third aspect to the problem of objec-tivity, the cognitional problem of fact. What is true? What do we know? The conversion, on the intellectual side, is effected by the study of the facts. Whether one adverts to it or not, the finality of the subject is operative; but through the study of the facts one can bring the subject to a fruitful advertence to the conflict between what he holds and what he does in actual knowing and practice.[95]

The phrase "finality of the subject" refers, I believe, to the same reality which *Verbum* referred to as the potential infinity of the intellect, and which *Insight* variously referred to as the pure desire to know, the notion of being, and the universal intention of being. In other words, the cognitional operations are purposive. Ultimately, we experience in order to understand; we understand in order to judge; we judge in order to know beings; we know particular beings in order to know being in general. This is a description of the dynamism of the subject formulated at the end of a long study. The subject can hold a different view of cognitional activity. Intellectual conversion, however, is effected by grasping that dynamic finality. Moreover, although that dynamism spontaneously and naturally operates, intellectual conversion is effected by grasping that dynamic finality. Moreover, although that dynamism spontaneously and naturally operates, intellectual conversion is likely to occur as the realization of the striking contrast between one's spontaneous and natural operations and one's conventional but inadequate cognitional theory.

Finally, in 1964, Lonergan pointed out the need for intellectual conversion in an article entitled "Cognitional Structure." He wrote:

> There exists, then, something like a forgetfulness of being. There exists in man a need for an intellectual conversion "exumbris et imaginibus in veritatem."[96]

In this article, Lonergan sharply contrasts both the naive realist and the idealist, on the one hand, with the critical realist, on the other. We have already discussed the problematic position of the subject who organizes his or her world around private interests and concerns as a standard. Now, Lonergan criticizes philosophies which similarly employ their own inadequate standards of reality. For the critical realist, the one criterion of reality is the true judgment. For the critical realist, the world is the universe of being and "the original relationship of cognitional activity to the universe of being must lie in the intention of being."[97] However, for the naive realist and the idealist, the subject is related to his or her world in terms of an intuition or a look. For the naive realist or the idealist, the world is not the universe of being but rather a kind of picture world. Lonergan writes "it is in looking that the naive realist finds revealed the essence of objectivity, and it is in *Anschauung* that the critical idealist places the immediate relation of cognitional activity to objects."[98] The issue is ultimately a matter of cognitional fact. Do we know being by intuition or by the discursive process of raising and answering intelligent and rational questions?

Intellectual conversion is the realization that our desire to know is a desire to know being. Prior to understanding, we are immediately related to sensible objects. We know them as sensible data, but we do not know them as being. Prior to judgment, we are intuitively present to our thoughts. We know them as suppositions or hypotheses, but we do not know them as expressing being. It is only in the act of judgment that we know the being of the data whose intelligibility we have conceived. Moreover, it is only by reflection on the discursive aspect of our knowing and on the decisive role played by judgment, that we can clearly and precisely know how we know being. Without judgment, we can experience data, or understand ideas, but we do not know being. Intellectual conversion, then, overcomes the forgetfulness of being by affirming the standard of truth over the standard of the intuition.

To summarize, in "*Insight:* Preface to a Discussion," philosophic conversion was spoken of as a shift from the world of sense to the world of the mind. It was a shift which involved the recognition of the true judgment as the one criterion of reality. In the Halifax lectures, intellectual conversion was effected by reflection on the dynamic finality of the cognitional subject. In the article "Cognitional Structure," intellectual conversion was a shift from the forgetfulness of being to the realization that our desire to know is a desire to know being.

Moral Conversion

At the 1958 seminar in Nova Scotia, Lonergan also introduced the notion of moral conversion. In *Insight* he distinguished three levels of the good. Analogous to cognitional structure, but pertaining to the realm of human choice, was the level of objects of desire, the level of the good of order, and the level of the good of value. Similarly, as Lonergan spoke of the self-appropriation of our cognitional selves—the structure of experiencing, understanding and judging—; so also he spoke of the self-appropriation of our moral selves—an intelligent and rational self-consciousness. In the moral realm, rational consciousness becomes rational self-consciousness and the subject encounters the inner demand for consistency between his or her knowing and his or her doing. However, *Insight* had not introduced the notion of moral conversion.

Moral conversion, according to the Halifax lectures, is a shift in the criterion of one's choices. Parallel to the intellectual subject, the moral subject initially is underdeveloped. Further, it is through one's choices that one will make oneself into a morally good or bad person. What criterion of the good is one to employ? Lonergan writes:

> Positively, to do good is to become good oneself, to move from organization on the level of objects of appetite, just as one moves from knowledge organized about intuition, to a self that is in harmony with what is objectively good. There are two types of organization giving rise to two types of questions: What's in it for me? What ought I do?[99]

Moral conversion, then, is a shift in the standard around which one organizes the moral self. As intellectual conversion implies a kind of self-abnegation in which one demotes one's private concerns from their absolute status, so too moral conversion implies a transcendence of the self as individual towards a universal willingness parallel to the pure desire to know.

In conclusion, I would say that Lonergan's notion of moral conversion closely paralleled his notion of intellectual conversion. Still, *Insight* invited one to self-appropriation primarily within the intellectual pattern of experience. Accordingly, reflection on intellectual conversion emerged from a fully developed context. However, Lonergan's reflection on moral conversion was not yet mature. *Insight* devoted a single chapter to the moral context and that chapter only sought to establish the possibility of ethics. In this middle period, reflection on the existential dimension in which one makes oneself was only the beginning.

Lonergan's Development in the Middle Period

The problem of integration chiefly determined the character of this middle period. In order to adequately address this problem, Lonergan had to move beyond the context of historical-hermeneutical research into Aquinas. St. Thomas had handled problems of integration in his own day, but the emergence of the empirical human sciences created an essentially new problem which Aquinas never had to face. I have already characterized the chief development of the early period as the movement from the realm of theory towards the realm of interiority. I would characterize the chief development of the middle period as deepened reflection on the realm of interiority preparatory to meeting the methodological exigence.[100]

The realm of cognitional interiority was the primary concern of the first part of *Insight*. "Insight as Activity" showed that Lonergan's understanding of cognitional procedure had both broadened and deepened.[101] He built on Aquinas' principle: "The human soul understands itself by its understanding, which is its proper act, perfectly demonstrating its power and nature."[102] He moved beyond Aquinas' application of that principle, however. The modern development of mathematics, the natural sciences, and the human sciences provided an as yet unexplored cognitional resource. This new resource provided an opportunity for a fuller, more nuanced grasp of the act of human understanding.

There was another significant move beyond Aquinas as well. While the modern sciences provided new material, Lonergan also underwent development on the formal level of principles. In *Verbum* he had treated the intellect, in Thomist terms, as a *potens omnia facere et fieri*, a potential omnipotence. In *Insight* he treated intellect, in his own terms, as a pure desire to know. The key difference was the shift from metaphysical categories to cognitional categories.[103] Both a potential omnipotence and a pure desire to know are infinite. The former, however, is the potency of a human soul; the latter is an intention of the human subject. Some years later, Lonergan remarked about his procedure in *Insight*: "While I still spoke in terms of faculty psychology, in reality I had moved out of its influence and was conducting an intentionality analysis."[104] Accordingly, the formal principle, or the viewpoint from which the individual issues are regarded, has shifted. Earlier Lonergan had sought to interpret certain aspects of Aquinas' thought. In *Insight* he sought to facilitate self-appropriation.

The general deepening comprehension of cognitional interiority was clearly manifested in the developed treatment of the
notion of judgment in *Insight*.[105] Judgment still proceeded
from the act of reflective understanding, but now the general
form of reflective understanding was characterized as a grasp of
the virtually unconditioned. This represented an important development beyond the strictly Thomist analysis of judgment. In
Verbum Lonergan had discussed judgment in terms of intellectual light: "Hence, the reflective activity whence judgment
results in a return from the syntheses effected by developing
insight to their sources in sense and intellectual light."[106]
Again, he writes:

> Now we have seen that the inner word, whether defini-
> tion or judgment, is the self-expression of the self-
> possessed act of understanding: the definition is the
> expression both of and by an insight into phantasm;
> the judgment is the expression both of and by the
> reflective act of understanding. On the division en-
> ounced above, these two types of expression have their
> grounds respectively in two elements of determination
> and light found in the act of understanding.[107]

In the terms of *Insight*'s analysis, "the syntheses effected by
developing insight" became the conditioned of reflective understanding; the return to sources "in sense and intellectual light"
became the "fulfillment of the conditions" and "a link between
the conditioned and its conditions."[108] I believe the most significant development here was the transformation of *Verbum*'s
intellectual light into *Insight's* link between the conditioned
and its conditions.

Within this general transformation, there are two important
points to be grasped. First, in the case of concrete judgments of
fact, Lonergan identifies the link with cognitional structure
itself. He writes:

> The link between the conditioned and the fulfilling
> conditions is a structure immanent and operative
> within cognitional process. It is not a judgment. It is
> not a formulated set of concepts, such as definition. It

is simply a way of doing things, a procedure within the cognitional field.[109]

The link, then, is a "structure immanent and operative," "a way of doing things," and a "procedure within the cognitional field." The identification of a structure with a procedure causes a problem if we are thinking on an analogy with bodies, but not if we are thinking on an analogy with spiritual things. The key point is that what *Verbum* treated in terms of intellectual light, *Insight* has transformed into cognitional procedure.

Secondly, in the case of judgment on the correctness of insights[110] and in the case of probable judgments,[111] Lonergan identifies the link with the absence of further, pertinent questions. There is a sufficient link between our experiencing and our thinking if all the pertinent questions have been raised and answered. In *Verbum,* every judgment involved a measure of self-knowledge. Intellectual light returned to itself insofar as reflective understanding "returned from the syntheses effected by developing insight to their sources in sense and in intellectual light." In *Insight,* this feature of judgment is expressed in terms of the rational apprehension that one has raised and answered all the relevant questions. The key point is that when *Verbum* treated in terms of the return of intellectual light to itself, *Insight* has transformed into the rational procedure of raising further, pertinent questions.

In summary, *Verbum*'s intellectual light became *Insight*'s cognitional procedure of raising and answering questions. Lonergan moved beyond *Verbum*'s ontology of knowledge to an analysis of what we do when we know. Specifically, in the analysis of judgment, the notion of intellectual light returning to itself has been replaced by the reflective act of understanding which grasps its own capacity to judge in the absence of further, pertinent questions.

There is a theological dimension to the analysis of judgment. According to *Verbum* the human intellect is a participated likeness of the one Uncreated Light.[112] We have a spark of the divine. Although we do not see God in this life, when intellect judges on the basis of its own intellectual light, it is judging on the basis of its participation in the Divine Intellect. *Insight* reaffirms this identity but conceives it in different categories.

The immanent basis of judgment is the reflective grasp of the virtually unconditioned. Accordingly, *Verbum* speaks of a unity between Creator and creature in terms of intellectual light; *Insight* posits a unity between Creator and creature in terms of the technical concepts of a formally and virtually unconditioned.

Insight defines being as the objective of the pure desire to know. In any single instance of our knowing, the pure desire to know reaches its terminal object in the judgment. In the full dynamic orientation of our knowing in general, the pure desire to know reaches its final object in the total context of true judgments. We have a detached, disinterested, and unrestricted desire to know everything.

At the heart of the problem with which *Insight* is dealing is a question of cognitional fact: do we know by intuition or by discursive reason?[113] If it is by discursive reason, by raising and answering questions; then we have the foundations of a general method proportionate to the problem of integration. If we know by asking one question and then another, by asking questions for intelligence and then questions for reflection, by adding answer to answer until we reach a higher context, then the relevance of method is clear.

There is a great distance between the creature and the Creator. There is a great distance between the pure desire to know and its unrestricted objective. That distance includes unexplored territory. Although we may have understood and affirmed the integral heuristic structure of proportionate being, it does not follow that the unexplored territory merely includes repetition of what we already know. To continue the metaphor, we cannot cross that territory by mere looking, mere imagining, or mere intuiting. They have their place, but that place pertains to our animal nature. We cannot cross that territory by any means analogous to merely sensitive living. We can only cross by intellectual labor. We can only travel the road across the expanse of the unknown by intelligent and rational procedure, by raising and answering questions.

Human progress toward the knowledge of being, then, is discursive. It is with reference to this fact that we must understand the notion of intellectual conversion. If our knowing is a process, then surely the key event along the way is the discovery of the norms of that process. That key event is intellectual conversion.

NOTES

[1] *Insight: A Study of Human Understanding,* (London: Longmans, Green and Co.; New York: Philosophical Library, 1957).

[2] *Collection.* I have included the first eight articles of this work in the early period. I include articles nine through fourteen in this middle period. They are: 9. "Isomorphism of Thomist and Scientific Thought" (1955), 10. "*Insight:* Preface to a Discussion" (1958), 11. "Christ as Subject: A Reply" (1959), 12. "Openness and Religious Experience" (1960), 13. "Metaphysics as Horizon" (1963), and 14. "Cognitional Structure" (1964).

[3] Lonergan writes: "After spending many years reaching up to the mind of Aquinas, I came to a twofold conclusion. On the one hand, that reaching has changed me profoundly. On the other hand, that change was the essential benefit. For not only did it make me capable of grasping what, in the light of my conclusions, the *vetera* really were, but also it opened challenging vistas on what the *nova* could be." *Insight,* p. 748.

[4] Ibid.

[5] My distinction between a basic problematic and derivative particular problems is based on an observation by Fr. Frederick Crowe: "Already philosophers distinguish between a 'problematic' and a 'problem,' making a noun of the former and using it in the sense of a confused matrix out of which particular 'problems' arise." Frederick E. Crowe, *The Lonergan Enterprise* (Cambridge, Massachusetts: Cowley Publications, 1980), p. 115, n. 1.

[6] On the movement from common sense notions to technical theorems, see above, chapter one, pp. 18–24.

[7] *Insight,* p. 295.

[8] Ibid., pp. 148–60.

[9] Ibid., pp. 743–44.

[10] Lonergan writes: "No less than the physicists, the human scientist has to learn the inadequacy of mechanist determinism." Ibid., p. 746.

[11] Bernard J. F. Lonergan, *Understanding and Being: An Introduction and Companion to Insight,* ed. Elizabeth A. Morelli and Mark D. Morelli (New York and Toronto: The Edwin Mellen Press, 1980), pp. 113–19.

[12] Lonergan has repeatedly insisted on the need for a detailed account of knowing. It must be considered a key motive behind *Insight.* See, for example, *Insight,* p. xxvii; "Theology and Under-

standing," and *"Insight:* Preface to a Discussion" in *Col.*, pp. 142 and 155; as well as *Understanding and Being*, p. 125.

[13] *Understanding and Being*, p. 125.

[14] "Isomorphism of Thomist and Scientific Thought" in *Col.*, p. 147.

[15] Some twenty years later, Lonergan pointed out the continuity between *Insight* and his theological concerns: "Now, with regard to the business of *Insight, Insight* happened this way: my original intention was method in theology. *Insight* was an exploration of methods in other fields, prior to trying to do method in theology." "An Interview With Fr. Bernard Lonergan, S. J.," in *2nd Col.*, p. 213.

[16] "Theology and Understanding," in *Col.*, p. 139.

[17] *Insight*, pp. 743–47.

[18] *Summa Theologiae* I, q. 12; I–II, q. 3, a. 8; *C. Gent.*, 25–63. Also see *Insight*, pp. 369–70.

[19] Although *Insight* basically explores the philosophic dimensions of the problem of integration, Lonergan clearly regards it as a theological problem as well. He writes: "The fundamental theological problem at the present time is a problem of integration." *Understanding and Being*, p. 117.

[20] *Insight*, p. xii.

[21] Ibid., p. xvii.

[22] Ibid., p. xxi.

[23] Ibid., p. xxiii.

[24] Ibid., p. xxvi.

[25] Ibid., pp. xxviii and 748.

[26] *Understanding and Being*, p. 1.

[27] *Insight* p. 274.

[28] Lonergan writes about the canon of relevance: "There is, then, an intelligibility immanent in the immediate data of sense; it resides in the relations of things, not to our sense, but to one another . . . [it] might be named more briefly formal causality, or rather, perhaps, a species of formal causality." Ibid., p. 78.

[29] Lonergan writes about the field of common sense: "There exists a determinate domain of ordinary description. Its defining or formal viewpoint is the thing related to us, and it enters into the concerns of men." Ibid., p. 292.

[30] Ibid., p. 179.

[31] Ibid., pp. 280–281.

[32] Ibid., p. 281.

[33] This chapter examines the conditions of the possibility of a cognitional act—the judgment. Lonergan clarifies his intent by contrasting his analysis with Kant's analysis: "Kant asked the *a priori* conditions of the possibility of experience in the sense of knowing the object . . . Hence we ask, not for the condition of knowing an object, but the conditions of the possible occurrence of a judgment of fact. We have asked for the conditions of an absolute rational 'Yes' or 'No'

viewed simply as an act." Ibid., p. 339. Strictly speaking, then, Lonergan is asking, not about the object of cognitional acts, nor about the subject of cognitional acts; the terms 'subject' and 'object' are not explicitly introduced until chapter thirteen. He is asking about the condition of the possibility of the occurrence of a certain kind of act—the correct judgment.

34 The following quotation illustrates the three relevant facets of the virtually unconditioned: "The virtually unconditioned . . . has conditions (sec. 1); it itself is among the conditions of other instances of the conditioned (sec. 3); still its conditions are fulfilled: it is a *de facto* absolute (sec. 2)." Ibid., p. 378.

35 Ibid., pp. 280–319.

36 Ibid., p. 319.

37 Ibid., p. 326.

38 Ibid., pp. 326–27.

39 Ibid., p. 319.

40 Lonergan notes the importance of self-appropriation as the experiential factor in *Insight*'s development: "Having the materials required for the verification is the point to our beginning by insisting upon self-appropriation. In the measure that one has achieved self-appropriation, one is capable of verifying grasps the unconditioned, and judges." *Understanding and Being*, p. 165.

41 *Insight*, p. 329.

42 Ibid.

43 Lonergan offers an alternative formulation of the incoherence of skepticism: "In other words, while it is a contingent fact that I am a knower, still *de facto*, I am, and if I talk as though I am not, I am involved in a contradiction. The contradiction is between what explicitly I say and, on the other hand, what implicitly I am." *Understanding and Being*, p. 173.

44 *Insight*, p. 378.

45 Ibid., pp. 338–39.

46 Ibid., p. 342.

47 Ibid., p. 361.

48 *Insight*, p. 378.

49 Lonergan characterizes the pure desire to know in a variety of ways. From a psychological point of view, he calls it an appetite, a tendency, a drive to know. From a metaphysical point of view, he characterizes this dynamic aspect of cognitional process as teleology or finality. For a discussion of these aspects, see *Understanding and Being*, pp. 184–85.

50 Being can be anything that is the objective of the pure desire to know and it can be everything that is the objective of the pure desire to know. Lonergan distinguishes between the two: "Distributively, one talks about beings; collectively, one talks about the totality of everything that is." Ibid., p. 182.

51 There is an important distinction to be recognized between intellect as actually infinite and as potentially infinite. Lonergan writes:

"There is no past instance by which we can show that the actual achievement of knowing was unlimited . . . In the sense of radical potency, radical finality, I think it can be shown that our knowing is unlimited." Ibid., p. 180. Our intellects are potentially infinite and God's intellect is actually infinite.

52 *Insight,* p. 350.

53 Ibid., p. 348.

54 Ibid., p. 349.

55 Ibid., p. 358.

56 Ibid.

57 Ibid.

58 After this series of negations, we can conclude that, by being, Lonergan means nothing less than the concrete universal. Further, we have his explicit statement on the matter: "Again, being is completely concrete and completely universal. It is completely concrete; over and above the being of anything there is nothing more of that thing. It is completely universal; apart from the realm of being there is simply nothing." Ibid., p. 350.

59 Ibid.

60 Ibid., pp. 371–72.

61 Ibid., p. 361.

62 Although in *Insight* Lonergan explains the various notions of objectivity in terms of the pure desire to know and the levels of cognitional process, in other contexts he has explained different senses of the word "object" in terms of metaphysics. "One can speak of objects," he writes, "metaphysically, and then one distinguishes three types of objects: the agent object, the terminal object, and the final object." *Understanding and Being,* p. 178.

63 *Insight,* p. 377.

64 Ibid.

65 There is a tendency to consider knowledge of the subject as so simple a matter that it is present even before one comes to judge. Conversely, there is a complementary tendency to consider knowledge of the object so difficult a matter that it is not present even after one comes to judge.For Lonergan, being is always and only reached, whether the being of the subject or of the object, in the correct judgment.

66 Ibid., p. 378.

67 Ibid., p. 401.

68 Ibid.

69 Lonergan writes: "Metaphysics, then, is conceived in terms of the totality of knowing and the totality of the object of knowing." *Understanding and Being,* pp. 232–33. Again, "Metaphysics, then is the whole in knowledge, but not the whole of knowledge." *Insight,* p. 391.

70 Lonergan contrasts empirical scientific method with philosophic method. "The basic difference is that scientific method is prior to scientific work and independent of particular scientific results, but

philosophic method is coincident with philosophic work and so stands or falls with the success or failure of a particular philosophy." *Insight,* p. 425.

71 Ibid., p. 397.

72 Lonergan points out that Aquinas was aware of this problem. He writes: "Again, Aristotle and Aquinas offered self-evident principles that resulted from the definition of their terms. But Aquinas, at least, has a further requirement; it was not enough for the principles to result necessarily from any terms whatever; the terms themselves needed some validation, and this office was attributed to the judicial habit or virtue named wisdom." *Insight,* p. 407. *Insight* and *Verbum* both affirm this point. Both seek to generate the wisdom which is capable of validating the partial terms of metaphysical principles. Both seek the cognitional ground from whence metaphysics arises.

73 Ibid., pp. 181–91.

74 Metaphysics proceeds in two phases. The initial phase is guided by the goal of bringing the cognitional subject to knowledge of its acts of understanding: direct, inverse, and reflective. This initial phase presupposes that the pure desire to know exists and is operative. The second phase is guided by the cognitional subject. In this phase, the cognitional subject explicates the normative and integrating structure of its understanding. This second phase presupposes that the pure desire to know has been conceived and affirmed, that is, that the pure desire to know has been appropriated.

75 Lonergan draws attention to the tension present in the self-appropriated subject. He writes: "Metaphysics rests upon self-appropriation of the subject in which the self-appropriated subject discovers that, besides the man that he is, there is also the man he is committed to being. The subject is fundamentally a tension between what he is and what he ought to be. . . . There is an ideal component in man. It is this tension that the existentialists emphasize a great deal. . . . In an empirical sense, we already are men, but there is also the man that we have to be. While this tension, on the moral level is familiar, it exists equally on the cognitional level." *Understanding and Being,* pp. 234–35.

76 *Insight.* p. 396

77 Ibid., p. xviii.

78 "Gratia Operans," p. 12.

79 Lonergan makes the same point, not specifically with regard to cognitional structure as the formal principle of metaphysics, but with regard to metaphysics in general: "Moreover, the various empirical sciences and the myriad instances of common sense aim at no more than knowing what in fact is so; but metaphysics is this unification; as a principle, it precedes them; but as attainment, it follows upon them, emerges from them, depends upon them, and so, like them, it too will be factual." *Insight,* p. 393.

80 For a detailed discussion of the complementarity of classical and statistical investigations, see *Insight,* pp. 105–15.

81 Ibid., p. 392.

82 Ibid., p. 391.

83 Ibid., p. 388.

84 The formulation of variouis philosophies will not, of course, be homogeneous. All that is required is that formulated positions of knowing, being, and objectivity be consistent with the actual cognitional performance of intelligent inquiry and critical reflection. The basic inconsistency of counterpositions is that as formulated they contradict actual cognitional practice. Ibid., pp. 388–89.

85 Ibid., p. 399.

86 The source of aberration is identified generally with a confusion over the polymorphism of consciousness. More specifically, Lonergan identifies confusion over the distinction and natures of elementary knowing and fully human knowing. He writes: "The two knowings must be distinguished and kept apart; and it is failure to keep them apart that originates the component of aberration in our dialectic of philosophy." Ibid., p. 423.

87 Ibid., p. 396.

88 Lonergan writes: "Philosophy is the flowering of the individual's rational consciousness in its coming to know and take possession of itself. To that event, its traditional schools, its treatises, and its history are but contributions; and without that event they are stripped of real significance. Ibid., p. 429.

89 Lonergan emphasizes the grasp of potentiality as as essential factor in metaphysics. Insofar as metaphysics rests upon self-appropriation, it finds its ground in the intellectual act which grasps intellectual potentiality (as infinite). Hence, the foundation of metaphysics is not the understanding of everything about everything, but rather the grasp of the actual form through which the understanding of everything about everything will be realized. See *Understanding and Being*, pp. 234–35.

90 *Understanding and Being*, p. 37.

91 "Insight: Preface to a Discussion" in *Col.*, pp. 152–63.

92 Ibid., p. 158.

93 Ibid.

94 Ibid., p. 158, n. 10.

95 *Understanding and Being*, p. 223.

96 "Cognitional Structure" in *Col.*, p. 236.

97 Ibid.

98 Ibid.

99 *Understanding and Being*, p. 288.

100 I use the notion of realms of meaning as an interpretive key to the overall development of Lonergan's notion of conversion. For the application of this interpretive key to the early period, see above, chapter one, n. 6.

101 Lonergan broadened his understanding of cognitional procedure by integrating it with the field of common sense and the sciences. He deepened it by revealing more fruitfully its transforming power to unify the sciences.

102 *Summa Theologiae*, I, q. 88, a. 2, ad 3m.

103 Lonergan writes: "The most shocking aspect of the book, *Insight,* is the primacy it accords to knowledge. In the writings of St. Thomas cognitional theory is expressed in metaphysical terms and established by metaphysical principles. In *Insight,* metaphysics is expressed in cognitional terms as established by cognitional principles." *"Insight:* Preface to a Discussion," in *Col.,* p. 152.

104 *"Insight* Revisited," in *2nd Col.,* p. 277.

105 In Fr. Frederick Crowe's opinion, this entire period can be roughly understood in terms of Lonergan's deepening apprehension of the cognitional level of judgment. Fr. Crowe writes: "For example, we will have a roughly sketched context for interpreting him if we say that the *Verbum* articles record and exploit his discovery of insight, the book *Insight* records and exploits his discovery of reasonable affirmation and the book *Method* records and exploits his discovery of the existential aspects of human consciousness." Crowe, *The Lonergan Enterprise,* p. 52.

106 *Verbum,* pp. 64–65.

107 Ibid., pp. 82–83.

108 On the general form of reflective insight, see *Insight,* p. 280.

109 Ibid., p. 282.

110 Ibid., pp. 283–87.

111 Ibid., pp. 299–304.

112 *Verbum,* pp. 87, 90.

113 *"Insight* Revisited," in *2nd Col.,* pp. 268–69.

CHAPTER THREE

THE LATER PERIOD: THEOLOGY AND THE METHODICAL EXIGENCE

> Just as unrestricted questioning is our capacity for self-transcendence, so being in love in an unrestricted fashion is the proper fulfillment of that capacity (p. 106). . . . It is this other-worldly love, not as this or that act, not as a series of acts, but as a dynamic state whence proceed the acts, that constitutes in a methodical theology what in a theoretical theology is named sanctifying grace. (p. 289)
>
> Bernard Lonergan, *Method in Theology*

The General Context of the Later Period

This third chapter examines the later period of Lonergan's career. This period spans the years from 1964 to his death in 1984. I have chosen to begin from the year 1964 because of the occurrence of a crucial shift in Lonergan's thought evident at that time. Fr. Ryan and Fr. Tyrrell, in their introduction to *A Second Collection* (1974),[1] mention this crucial shift and locate it in the appearance of two papers: "Existenz and Aggiornamento" (1964) and "Dimensions of Meaning" (1965).[2] These two papers introduce certain themes whose development, interpenetration, and mutual clarification dominate the later period. I would identify these themes as: the constitutive role of meaning in human living, the emergence of modern historical consciousness, and the theological task of *aggiornamento*. The single most important achievement of the later period is

Method in Theology (1972).[3] It is a great synthesis, not only of these three basic themes, but also of much of Lonergan's earlier thought. It truly is a culminating work. Consequently, my analysis in this third chapter will emphasize *Method in Theology*. In this first section, however, I will briefly discuss the basic themes which constitute the general context of the later period.

The first of the basic themes is the constitutive role of meaning in human living.[4] Lonergan expands on this basic theme by deriving three notions from the constitutive role of meaning: personal existence, community, and history.[5]

First, the notion of existing as a person can be contrasted with the individual who merely drifts through life. To be a person is to exist within a field of meaning, to be oriented towards values, to operate consciously and intentionally. Each of us is an individual inasmuch as he or she is merely alive. Each of us becomes a person inasmuch as his or her living realizes and incarnates some meaning.

Secondly, the notion of community can be contrasted with a mere aggregate of individuals. A community of persons share a common meaning and common set of values. Several individuals waiting for the bus are not a community. Several persons with common experiences, common understanding, common judgments, and common values constitute a full-fledged community.

Thirdly, the notion of history can be contrasted with a mere sequence of events. History is a matter of developing the possibilities for human living. People are born, mature, beget children of their own, and eventually die. Such a sequence is recurrent; it is the realization of the same possibility over and over again. History pertains more to the developing understanding of what such a sequence means and the new possibilities for living which result. In *Method in Theology*, Lonergan emphasizes the peculiarity of the field of historical investigation:

> Now the peculiarity of this field resides in the nature of individual and group action. It has both a conscious and an unconscious side. Apart from neurosis and psychosis the conscious side is in control. But the conscious side consists in the flow of conscious and

intentional acts that we have been speaking of since
our first chapter. What differentiates each of these acts
from the others lies in the manifold meanings of meaning set forth in Chapter Three. Meaning, then, is a
constitutive element in the conscious flow that is the
normally controlling side of human action. It is this
constitutive role of meaning in the controlling side of
human action that grounds the peculiarity of the historical field of investigation.[6]

Thus, history has more to do with the meaning of events than
with their mere sequence.

In summary, the constitutive role of meaning adds the properly human dimension to living. Without meaning, we have
individuals, but not yet human persons. We have an aggregate
of individuals, but not yet human community. We have se-
quences of events but not yet human history.

The second of the basic themes is the emergence of modern
historical consciousness. It is a broad and difficult theme, but a
few key features can be identified. First, historical consciousness is aware that meaning functions in a context.[7] Lonergan illustrates this awareness by the principle of the
hermeneutical circle.

For instance, one grasps the meaning of a sentence
by understanding the words, but one understands the
words properly only in the light of the sentence as a
whole. Sentences stand in a similar relationship to
paragraphs, paragraphs to chapters, chapters to
books, books to an author's situation and intentions.[8]

On a level higher than the properly hermeneutical level, as
Lonergan understands that term,[9] the lives and thoughts of
authors must be understood within their historical contexts,
including the social and cultural movements of their times.

Modern historical reflection has learned, not only that meaning functions within a context, but also that contexts themselves shift. For example, when St. Augustine developed his
ideas on grace and freedom, he was meeting a crisis within the
Church. When St. Thomas developed his ideas on grace and
freedom—not only did he have St. Augustine's earlier efforts to
reflect upon—but he also had available a developed and de-

veloping theoretical framework.[10] In the centuries from St. Augustine to St. Thomas, theology had shifted from a basically non-technical, common sense context into a predominantly theoretical context. Again, Lonergan refers to Herbert Butterfield's analysis of the emergence of modern sciences. Although discoveries which were to be included within modern science were recurrent since the fourteenth century, the most significant modern scientific achievement was the shift out of the older Aristotelian cultural context and into a newer empirically oriented context. "In brief, Professor Butterfield distinguished between new ideas and the context or horizon within which they were expressed, developed, related."[11] Thus, historical reflection has discovered that meaning and its concomitant contexts are not simply given. They are created by persons, communities, and history.

Modern culture is invented by people. Lonergan contrasts modern culture with its classical predecessor.

> The classicist notion of culture was normative: at least *de jure* there was but one culture and that was both universal and permanent; to its norms and ideals might aspire the uncultured, whether they were the young or the people or the natives or the barbarians. Besides the classicist, there is also the empirical notion of culture. It is the set of meanings and values that informs a way of life. It may remain unchanged for ages. It may be in process of slow development or rapid dissolution.[12]

Modern culture is empirical rather than normative. It is aware that it has, not universal validity, but the validity of meeting concrete circumstances and exigencies. It is, not static, but a process of self-constitution. It is, not necessary, but the result of human decisions and human actions. Historical consciousness is aware that human cultures are constituted by human meaning and it is up to human beings to decide what human living is going to mean.

A third theme is the theological task of *aggiornamento*. It is a term coined by Pope John XXIII and introduced at the Second Vatican Council. It means bringing things up to date. However, ". . . *aggiornamento* is not some simple-minded rejection of all that is old and some breezy acceptance of everything new. Rather it is a disengagement from a culture that no longer exists and an involvement in a distinct culture that has replaced it!"[13] Again, *aggiornamento* does not mean that there is a new revelation, a new faith, or a new religion. Rather, there is a new cultural situation. Since it is the task of theology to mediate "between a cultural matrix and the significance and role of a religion in that matrix,"[14] theology must make every attempt to speak to the people within their contemporary context. It must address the particularly contemporary issues and the challenges they present.

Although the challenge to theology comes not from a new faith, but from a new cultural situation; nevertheless the challenge is serious indeed. Paraphrasing Cardinal Newman's statement, Lonergan remarks that "ten thousand difficulties do not make a doubt; the ten thousand difficulties are in the superstructure, but doubt is in one's personal life."[15] However, theology and religion form a unity, and a threat to the superstructure is truly a threat to the unity. "There are real theological problems, real issues that, if burked, threaten the very existence of Christianity."[16] Modern empirical methods pursue complete understanding of their data. Still, modern science and scholarship are modest; they do not claim to possess absolute truth; they claim only to be the best available opinion and ever open to future revision. Such an approach, backed by thorough familiarity with available data, can easily appear to undermine any claim to authority and normativity based on the Scriptures and tradition.[17]

The emergence of modern hermeneutics and critical history has a twofold significance. First, they have greatly enriched our knowledge and appreciation of the past. They have produced penetrating studies of Greek and Roman cultures, and of Old and New Testament civilizations. Secondly, they have apparently disillusioned us of any claim within modern culture to permanence, universality, or necessity. Lonergan writes:

> It is the development of modern hermeneutics and history that has forced Catholic theology out of the manualist tradition. The old style dogmatic theologian was expected to establish a series of propositions, theses, from the Old Testament and the New, from patristic writings and the consensus of theologians, and from the *ratio theologica*. But modern scholarship set up an endless array of specialists between the

> dogmatic theologian and his sources. With the spe-
> cialists the dogmatic theologian just could not com-
> pete. Without an appeal to his sources the dogmatic
> theologian had nothing to say. Such has been a basic
> and, as well, a most palapable element in the crisis of
> contemporary Roman Catholic theology. Along with
> changes in the notion of science and the notion of
> philosophy, it has been my motive in devoting years to
> working out a *Method in Theology*.[18]

The chasm between the dogmatic theologian and the sources
needs to be bridged. On the one hand, the positive wealth of
information developed by hermeneutical and historical investigations promises to be a profound resource for foundational, doctrinal, and systematic reflection. On the other hand,
its sheer volume and variety call for a principle of selection and
integration which can transform the babel into meaningful dialogue. What is needed is an ordered process from data to
results. Accordingly, Lonergan seeks a method for theology
which could bring the various kinds of theological investigations within "a framework for collaborative creativity."[19]

There is a still more profound need for *aggiornamento*. Modern culture is a human invention and it has its problems. Besides creativity, modernity has a great propensity for
destruction. Briefly, modernity is in trouble and cannot save
itself. But God has entered history; he has entered the process
whereby cultures flourish and decay; his Word has entered into
the world. Lonergan writes:

> . . . however trifling the uses to which words may be
> put, still they are the vehicles of meaning, and meaning
> is the stuff of man's making of man. So it is that a
> divine revelation is God's entry and his taking part in
> man's making man. It is God's claim to have a say in the
> aims and purposes, the direction and development of
> human lives, human societies, human cultures, human
> history.[20]

Thus, theology is but a part of the basic and more profound
mission of the Church to preach the gospel to all nations. God's
word must be communicated to all cultures and to all levels of
culture, to common sense communities, as well as to the scien-

tific and scholarly communities. Nevertheless, it is not to be preached in the same way to everyone. When St. Peter addressed the crowd in Jerusalem on the first Pentecost, he recalled the words of the patriarch David and the prophet Joel (Acts 2:14–36). When St. Paul spoke before the council at Athens, he referred to their poets and writers (Acts 17:16–34). Thus, both men preached the crucified and risen Lord; but they did not put unnecessary obstacles in the way. They used the resources and thought forms of the communities to whom they spoke. Similarly, modern theology must be adapted to modern thought forms, and, in turn, like St. Peter and St. Paul, adapt those same thought forms to its own high purposes.

In conclusion, *Method in Theology* seeks to employ to the greatest possible advantage the developments in modern sciences, in modern philosophy, and in modern scholarship. In large part, they represent valuable developments of the human spirit. Human initiative is not in competition with divine providence because God has bidden us to be fruitful and to fill the earth and to subdue it (Gen. 1:28). Human excellence is not in competition with God's glory because "the glory of the Father is the excellence of the Son, and the excellence of the adoptive sons."[21] Nevertheless, modern science, modern philosophy, and modern scholarship do not evidence any significant awareness that the question of God is implicit in all human questioning and that the desire for God is implicit in all human seeking. Modernity needs to be awakened to the truth about itself and its own deepest intentions. "Long ago St. Augustine exclaimed that God had made us for himself and that our hearts are restless till they rest in Him. What that restlessness is, we see all about us in the mountainous discontents, hatreds and terrors of the twentieth century."[22] Whether theology will develop the categories to speak convincingly to modernity remains to be seen. Whether modernity will be able to recognize in its own empirical unrest a desire for the transcendent may depend on the occurrence of some type of conversion.

The Transcendental Notions

We turn now from the general context of this later period to its most significant achievement, *Method in Theology* (1972).

The first chapter, entitled "Method," is a clarification of transcendental method. Transcendental method provides the basic anthropological component of theological method. Lonergan writes:

> Transcendental method is not the intrusion into theology of alien matter from an alien source. Its function is to advert to the fact that theologies are produced by theologians, that theologians have minds and use them, that their doing so should not be ignored or passed over but explicitly acknowledged in itself and in its implications.[23]

The transcendental notions are the realities which underpin, penetrate, and reach beyond the operations of transcendental method. It is not possible to understand Lonergan's view of theological method, nor his understanding of conversion, without first clarifying what is meant by the transcendental notions. Consequently, it is useful to elucidate as fully as possible the significance of these basic notions.

At once, we can distinguish three functions of the transcendental notions. Consider Lonergan's explanation:

> The transcendental notions are the dynamism of conscious intentionality. They promote the subject from lower to higher levels of consciousness, from the experiential to the intellectual, from the intellectual to the rational, from the rational to the existential. Again, with respect to objects, they are the intermediaries between ignorance and knowledge; . . .
>
> Not only do the transcendental notions promote the subject to full consciousness and direct him to his goals. They also provide the criteria that reveal whether the goals are being reached.[24]

Accordingly, we can identify three functions: the transcendental notions intend objects; they promote the subject to higher levels of consciousness; they provide the criteria which reveal whether goals are being reached. Each of these functions calls for comment.

First, the transcendental notions intend objects. Lonergan distinguishes two basic modes of intending: categorical and transcendental.[25] Determinate questions anticipate categorical answers or objects. Determinate questions are not, of course, answers; but neither are they pure ignorance. Rather, determinate questions presuppose some object which is not yet known but is nevertheless anticipated. On the other hand, transcendental intending is not the intending of a particular question, but rather the condition of the possibility of any questioning at all. Thus, for example, the transcendental notion of the intelligible is the radical intention of the object which would be known by the totality of intelligent answers. Again, the transcendental notion of the true and the real is the radical intention of the object which would be known by the totality of reasonable answers. Finally, the transcendental notion of value and the truly good is the radical intention of the object which would be known and realized by the totality of responsible answers and consequent deeds.

Does one at any particular time actually intend such transcendent objects? That answer is threefold. Commonly, I would say, no. In two special cases, I would say, yes. Commonly one intends this or that particular object on a proportionate level of consciousness. One does not actually desire to know all intelligibility at any given time, but instead one seeks the answer to a particular question. Again, one does not actually seek the absolute good beyond all criticism at any given time, but rather one pursues the good according to the opportunities present in one's external circumstances. There is, however, a special intermediate case. As animals, we are confined to the here and now, but as rational creatures, we can transcend particular places, particular times, and particular instances. We can reflect upon a plurality of instances of understanding or a plurality of instances of valuing. In those pluralities we can discern a dynamism towards an unrestricted goal. Will our intelligent questioning ever dry up? Will we ever be satisfied with any determinate good? Thus, we can discover within ourselves an infinite potentiality to question, a pure desire to know, and a pure desire for value. These are the transcendental notions. Finally, there is a second special case. What we discover by reflection, the mystic discovers by experience.[26] As the mystic withdraws into the cloud of unknowing, his or her interest is dropped in what can be discovered via question and answer. Even though the inquiring mode is dropped, however, subjectivity still reaches for its transcendental goal. Thus, we can find in the mystic this same unrestricted intending. In summary, the transcendental notions commonly are not the actual mode of our intending. We actually intend in a determinate mode. Instead, the transcendental notions are the infinite potentialities, of which our actual intentions are but the partial actuation. In the special case of the mystic, however, the transcendental notions are the actual mode in which intending occurs.

Secondly, the transcendental notions promote the subject to higher levels of consciousness. They promote the subject from the experiential to the intellectual, to the rational, and to the existential levels of consciousness. Lonergan writes:

> What promotes the subject from experiential to intellectual consciousness is the desire to understand, the intention of intelligibility. What next promotes him from intellectual to rational consciousness, is a fuller unfolding of the same intention: for the desire to understand, once understanding is reached, becomes the desire to understand correctly; in other words, the intention of the intelligibility, once an intelligible is reached, becomes the intention of the right intelligible, of the true, and through truth, of reality. Finally, the intention of the intelligible, the true, the real, becomes also the intention of the good, the question of value, of what is worthwhile, when the already acting subject confronts his world and adverts to his own acting in it.[27]

In another context, Lonergan refers to the various levels of consciousness and intentional operations—experiencing, understanding, judging, and deciding—and points out that what promotes the subject from a lower level of operation to a higher level is "the operator."[28] The operator is the ability to question. There are three types of operator: questions for intelligence, questions for reflection, and questions for deliberation. Thus, if one is trying to pinpoint the agent which principally effects the movement from a lower level to a higher level, one should focus upon the role of questioning.

Just how does the ability to question function as the operator or the principle which promotes the subject to a higher level of consciousness? As an example, let us consider the movement from experiential to intelligent consciousness within the intellectual pattern of experience. R. G. Collingwood contrasted two types of historian. "Scissors and paste historians," as he characterized the first type, assemble all the data they can find within a limited range and hope that something emerges from the assembly. Scientific historians, as he characterized the second type, ask questions. Their questions presuppose that they have already done a good deal of thinking. Thus, they do not merely assemble data; they gather evidence. In this context, evidence is data which has a good chance of being significant from an already determined intellectual perspective. Again, Professor Collingwood approved of the scorn which the detective Monsieur Hercules Poirot poured upon the " 'human blood hound' who crawls about the floor trying to collect everything, no matter what, which might conceivably turn out to be a clue . . ." and concurred with M. Poirot's insistence that "detection was to use what, with possibly wearisome iteration, he called 'the little grey cells.' "[29] The single point of these two examples is that there is a difference between chronological order and intentional order.

Chronologically, we must experience before we can understand. Intentionally, however, experience will begin to flow in certain channels, and will begin to reveal certain patterns, and will anticipate the emergence of the higher level of organization, when the subject already has an intelligent question. More generally, lower levels begin to anticipate the emergence of higher levels of organization once the higher level operator has emerged. It is the transcendental notions which ground these intelligent, reasonable, and responsible questions or operators.

Thirdly, the transcendental notions provide the criteria that reveal whether the subject's goals are being reached. They are normative. It is on the basis of the transcendental notions that the cognitive subject anticipates intelligibility and it is on the basis of them that the subject reflects on whether sufficient intelligibility has been reached. Have all the further, pertinent questions been asked and answered? It is on the basis of the transcendental notions that the moral subject anticipates value and it is on the basis of them that he or she deliberates on whether sufficient self-transcendence has been attained. In each case it is the dynamic orientation beyond partial attainment and towards totality—the dynamism of self-transcendence—which provides the actual criterion for our performance. In each case it is the transcendental notions which underpin, penetrate, and transform consciousness and promote it toward its intended objectives.

In actual practice, the normativity of the transcendental notions does not ofttimes prevail. We are sinners: the will is weak and the intellect darkened. Still, insofar as we desire to understand correctly, to appreciate and pursue the truly good, it is the transcendental notions which guide us. Again, we can be misguided by the cognitional myth that knowing is approximately like looking; nevertheless, we spontaneously ask questions which are answered by our thinking and doing and not simply by more looking. We can be restricted by egotistic or group biases, but feelings spontaneously relate us to a world beyond ourselves, our group, and our merely practical living. The transcendental notions operate but their operation does not automatically eliminate all aberration. Still, to know that they operate provides us with a powerful advantage. To advert to the pure desire to know, or to the pure desire for value, focuses consciousness on the principles from which all progress comes. In actual practice as long as questioning is allowed to seek its unrestricted objectives, the transcendental notions will assert their normativity.

In conclusion, we can characterize the transcendental notions as intentional, conscious, and normative. They intend objects; they promote the subject to higher levels of consciousness; they provide the principles which can guide and criticize actual operation. In practice, they exist in tension with other dynamisms. Still, they can be distinguished from those other dynamisms by their unrestricted orientation.

Finality

The notion of finality is complementary to the transcendental notions. Since in this later period Lonergan has moved into a context where metaphysics is secondary and derivative while intentionality analysis is basic,[30] the notion of finality can be overlooked. Finality is still, however, an important notion. If intentionality is characteristic of the basic dynamism from lower to higher levels of consciousness, finality is characteristic of the basic dynamism from lower to higher levels of being. Lonergan had written in *Insight:*

> Just as intellectually patterned experience heads towards insights and judgments, so potency heads towards forms and acts. Just as cognitional activity mounts through accumulations of insights to higher viewpoints, so objective process involves the information and actuation of prime potency only to uncover a residue of coincidental manifolds and so mount through successive levels of higher systematization. . . . Indeed, since cognitional activity is itself but a part of this universe, so its heading to being is but the particular instance in which universal striving towards being becomes conscious and intelligent and reasonable.[31]

Accordingly, finality is the dynamism of objective process correlative to the dynamism of subjective process.

Lonergan distinguishes three types of finality: absolute, horizontal, and vertical.[32] Absolute finality was a basic principle of Aquinas' theology and Lonergan retains its primacy in his own work. The basic principle is: all things seek God.[33] In *Insight,* he noted that the pure desire to know "is a key instance of the universal law that *omnia Deus appetunt*."[34]

Horizontal finality is movement to the end that is proportionate to the essence of a given being. If we can say that all creatures seek God simply from the fact that they exist, nevertheless, all creatures have a horizontal finality determined by their respective natures. In other words, while all things seek God, they do not seek Him in the same manner. The mode of seeking is determined by the nature of the creature. This translates into cognitional terms as: intelligence seeks God under the aspect of absolute intelligence and intelligibility; reason seeks God under the aspect of absolute truth and being. Accordingly, the general principle of horizontal finality is: "There are many grades of being, each with its defining essence and its consequent and commensurate mode of appetition and process."[35]

Vertical finality presupposes absolute and horizontal finality.

Besides the movement by which all things seek God, and the proportionate manner in which they do, there is a more complex movement whereby beings of lower levels are taken up into a higher level. Lonergan writes:

> Vertical finality is to an end higher than the proportionate end. It supposes a hierarchy of entities and ends. It supposes a subordination of the lower to the higher. Such subordination may be merely instrumental, or participative, or both, inasmuch as the lower merely serves the higher, or enters into its being and functioning, or under one aspect serves and under another participates.
>
> The classicist view of the universe acknowledges hierarchy and the instrumental type of vertical finality. An evolutionary view adds the participative type: subatomic particles somehow enter into the elements of the periodic table; chemical elements enter into chemical compounds, compounds into cells, cells in myriad combinations and configurations into the constitution of plant and animal life.[36]

In the language of *Method in Theology,* each of the lower levels can be sublated by the higher levels. Vertical finality is not found in a lower level entity simply as an individual existent; nor is it found in the members of lower species as limited by essence; rather vertical finality is found in the coincidental manifold, in their conjoined plurality. Thus, it takes combinations of combinations of sensitive experiences to lead to a scientific insight. It takes a large number of judgments before one can begin to discern the pattern which constitutes the basic cognitional process of objectivity. Finally, "only when and where the higher rational culture emerged did God acknowledge the fullness of time permitting the Word to become flesh and the mystical body to begin its intussusception of human personalities and its leavening of human history."[37]

To conceive vertical finality in its full generality is to envisage the whole universe. It is to conceive an upthrust beginning with subatomic particles and moving through chemical and biological processes. And no less, it includes the human dimension. We develop biologically to develop psychically; we develop cognitionally to develop morally and religiously. Still, in the human person there is reached a critical point: in human consciousness vertical finality can become conscious of itself.

The Transcendental Notions and Vertical Finality

Lonergan has also formulated the transcendental notions in terms of various natures. He relies on Aristotle's understanding of a nature as an immanent principle of movement and or rest.[38] Thus, the transcendental notion of the intelligible is a nature or immanent principle which sets the subject in motion by questioning and brings the subject to rest when answers are satisfactory. Likewise, the transcendental notions of being and of value are natures which initiate an inquiring movement in the subject and sustain that movement until the goals are satisfactorily reached. Accordingly, each nature, on each level, is an immanent principle of movement, by initiating questions, and an immanent principle of rest, by finding satisfactory answers.

There is a deeper dimension to this analysis. Although each level of conscious and intentional operation is a nature, a principle of movement and of rest, the human person is a unity. Thus, each level, and the dynamism which promotes the subject from one level to the next, is only a part of the unfolding of a single transcendental intending of interchangeable objectives.[39] Each is only a single aspect of a deeper and more comprehensive principle, "a tidal movement that begins before consciousness, unfolds through sensitivity, intelligence, rational reflection, responsible deliberation, only to find its rest beyond all of these."[40] That deeper principle is the dynamic state of being in love.[41] This is the deepest unifying principle which underpins, penetrates, and promotes all levels of conscious and intentional operation. As a principle of movement, it immerses the subject in a process both purgative and illuminating. As a principle of rest, it dissolves the subject's restlessness in the fulfilling union of love.

The dynamism of vertical finality and the dynamism of self-transcendence are complementary notions. The former is characteristic of world process as conceived within an evolutionary world view. The latter is characteristic of cognitional and volitional processes. Vertical finality permeates world process and self-transcendence in the human person which does not exist without self-knowledge and self-determination.

It is at this point that we can begin to discern the relevance of conversion vis-a-vis the transcendental notions. In conversion, vertical finality and self-transcendence enter into the realm of human personhood.[42] The human person is called to self-knowledge. In intellectual conversion, the person is affirmed to be a knower. The person conceives and rationally affirms the dynamic orientation to truth and being which constitutes the central thrust of cognitional intentionality. Again, the human person is called to self-determination. In moral conversion, the person decides to be a person who makes his or her own decisions. The person decides in favor of the desire for goodness which constitutes the heart of his or her existence. Finally, the person is called to become a person within a community: local, global, and cosmic. In religious conversion, the person finds his or her self surrounded by a cosmic dimension of love. In summary, at these higher levels, the transcendental notions reveal the horizon within which one becomes a person.

Method in Theology and Conversion

The notion of conversion pervades Lonergan's entire elucidation of method in theology. There is hardly a functional specialty in which it does not play some role. "It can have its occasion in interpretation, in doing history, in the confrontation of dialectic; but it does not constitute an explicit, established, universally recognized criterion of proper procedure in these specialties."[43] In the second phase of theology, in foundations, doctrines, systematics, and communications, it does constitute such a criterion of proper procedure. Hence, conversion has a broad relevance to every aspect of theological method. More specifically, Lonergan discusses religious, moral, and intellectual conversions, and their interrelations in the tenth chapter on the functional specialty, *Dialectic*. He discusses the point to which conversion is inserted into theological method in the eleventh chapter on the functional specialty, *Foundations*. Accordingly, first I shall discuss each of the three types of conversion as they relate to theological method in general;

secondly, I shall discuss the role of conversion in *Dialectic* and in *Foundations.*

Intellectual Conversion

The discussion of intellectual conversion in *Method in Theology* is fundamentally consistent with the treatment of that notion in the middle period. There is, however, a difference of emphasis that is important to note. The discussion of intellectual conversion in the middle period emphasized the personal nature of the event; the later period, I would say, emphasizes its communal and historical features. In *Insight:* "The crucial issue is an experimental issue, and the experiment will be performed not publicly but privately."[44] However, Lonergan immediately adds that in spite of the personal nature of the act, self-appropriation has antecedents and consequences which are public. Nevertheless, *Insight* stresses what we can experience for ourselves; what is called immanently generated knowledge. All of this is consistent with the concern of the middle period for interiority. The later period is concerned with method, with "a framework for collaborative creativity."[45] Now, intellectual conversion is understood in terms of human community and human history.

Intellectual conversion is a discovery of the self-transcendence proper to knowing.[46] This is equivalent to *Insight's* treatment of the notion. Through the process of experiencing, understanding, and judging, we come to know a world independent of merely private concerns. Now, however, Lonergan draws attention to a further feature of cognitional operations: they are both immediate and mediate.[47] For example, immediate operations such as seeing, hearing, and touching make immediately present what is seen, heard, and touched. There are, however, more complex operations; they operate in both an immediate and a mediate manner. For example, by thinking we are immediately present to our thoughts and mediately present to what is thought about. By speaking, we are immediately present to language and mediately present to what is spoken about. This mediated reality is not confined to the here and now. It also includes the past and the future, the actual, and also the ideal. By our cognitional operations, then, we are operating in both manners simultaneously. Questions relate the subject immediately to the intended object. "What was that noise?" Answers relate the subject mediately to the intended object. "A cat knocked over a flower pot in the garden." Answers, then, mediate objects because they are answers to questions.

There is a world beyond the world of sensitive intuitions which is opened up by our mediating operations. Because we can understand, judge, and decide, we live in a fuller world than do mere animals. Because we can act meaningfully, we can construct and participate in a world which transcends nature. This world is the world mediated by meaning.

The infant's world of immediacy is the totality of what can be sensed and perceived. But it is no larger than the nursery and mother's arms. The larger world mediated by meaning is made up of the memories of people, the investigations of scientists and historians, the reflections of philosophers and theologians, the communal fund of tested insights and knowledge. Each of us, as adults, participates in this larger world by our mediating operations. Nevertheless, it is a precarious world. It is constituted by meaning and meaning is on the move. It develops, but it also goes astray; there is both progress and decline. Still, for good or ill, meaning is the stuff of our historical and communal self-constitution.

The confusion between the world of immediacy and the world mediated by meaning is the source of the critical problem for philosophers. The naive realists know the world mediated by meaning but think they know it by looking. What is a dog? It is out there now capable of being looked at. What is an historical fact? It is what one would have seen if one was on the scene. The idealists realize that human knowing is not a matter of simply looking; it also includes some understanding. What is a dog? It is something beyond the aggregate of sensible data which one has available from simple observation.[48] What are historical facts? "They are mental constructions carefully based on data recorded in documents."[49] The idealists retain the naive realists' sense of reality but consider the world opened up by understanding as ideal. For the critical realist the world mediated by meaning is the real world. "For the world mediated by meaning is a world known not by the sense experience of the individual but by the external and internal experience of a cultural community, and by the continuously checked and rechecked judgments of the community."[50] Consequently, our knowing involves a process of continual self-correction which is both historical and communal.

Belief is more intimately connected to intellectual conversion in this later period. Our judgments rest on a communal and historical fund of tested insights. Neither scientists nor people of common sense, neither scholars nor saints, go around directly testing each of their presuppositions. If there are oversights and errors they are expected to emerge within the communal process of reflection. Lonergan writes:

> But you can have an entirely different world—the world mediated by meaning—the world that is most known through belief. Ninety-eight percent of what a genius knows, he believes. It isn't personally independently acquired knowledge. Human knowledge is an acquisition that goes on over centuries and centuries, and if we want to accept nothing, that we don't find out for ourselves, we revert to the paleozoic age. At that period they found out for themselves everything they knew.[51]

Consequently, to appropriate the structure of our knowing, the way in which we actually operate, will mean to recognize and to appreciate the considerable role of belief.

Belief plays an important role in all areas of knowledge. Religious belief, however, plays a special role in the promotion of intellectual conversion. Lonergan notes that moral conversion opens the subject to the world of values. Amongst the values discerned by the eye of love is the value of believing the truths taught by religious tradition. It is within these religious truths that we find the seeds of intellectual conversion.[52]

In the later period, the treatment of intellectual conversion has been expanded. I think we should distinguish, however, between the material and formal aspects of this expansion. *Insight* relied heavily upon analysis of the field of the natural sciences. There Lonergan contrasted the viewpoint of ordinary description and the viewpoint of explanation. The principle, however, which grounded and criticized these two viewpoints and the principle which met the critical problem was judgment. Whether from the viewpoint of natural sciences or from the viewpoint of daily living, the real is what can be rationally affirmed. Our knowledge of the real is grounded in a reflective grasp of the virtually unconditioned.

This later period adds a consideration of the realm of scholarship. Meaning emerges as a central concern. Now Lonergan moves beyond the world we simply know about, the physical universe, to the worlds we make, our communities and our traditions. He contrasts the world of immediacy and the world mediated by meaning. The critical problem is conceived in terms of the contrast between these two worlds. Is this a material or formal difference between the middle and later periods? I believe it is a material difference. The criterion for reality, in both the world of immediacy and the world mediated by meaning, is still the true judgment.

There is, however, a formal development beyond the middle period. Lonergan indicates it while describing intellectual conversion. "The criteria for objectivity are not just the criteria of ocular vision; they are the compound criteria of experiencing, of understanding, of judging, and of believing."[53] The addition of belief to this sequence is a formal advance over the earlier treatment. *Insight* had transposed the *Verbum* account of reflective self-knowledge into the performance of raising and answering further, pertinent questions. Intellectual light had become the process of this questioning. Now, in the later period, this personal dynamism of questioning is sublated into the concrete historical and communal process of self-constitution. One comes to awareness and understanding of what intelligence, reasonableness, and responsibility are, to a knowledge of what could be meant by authentic existence, not by oneself alone, but by appropriating one's social, cultural, and religious heritage. A basic tendency of this later period is to move the notion of reflective self-possession, that is, of intellectual conversion, into the concrete and sublating context of community and history.

The Development of the Notion
of Judgments of Value

The analysis of judgments of value in *Method in Theology* grew out of Lonergan's earlier treatments of the notion of judgment in *Verbum* and *Insight*. There is, to be sure, a development beyond those earlier treatments. Earlier treatments confined themselves to judgment on the third or rational level of consciousness; the analysis of judgments of value expands to the fourth or existential level of consciousness. However, consider Lonergan's concise statement: "Judgments of value differ in content but not in structure from judgments of fact."[54] Accordingly, there is continuity in the analysis of the structure of judgment but judgments of value pertain to a different type of content.

Let us begin with the structure of judgments of value. Lonergan compares and contrasts judgments of value and judgments of fact:

> They do not differ in structure, inasmuch as in both there is the distinction between criterion and meaning. In both, the criterion is the self-transcendence of the subject, which, however, is only cognitive in judgments of fact but heading towards moral self-transcendence in judgments of value. In both, the meaning is or claims to be independent of the subject: judgments of fact state or purport to state what is or is not so; judgments of value state or purport to state what is or is not truly good or really better.[55]

The key distinction here, in *Method in Theology*, is between criterion and meaning. The significance of this distinction, however, can be appreciated more fully when set against the background of the analyses of judgment in *Verbum* and *Insight*.

In *Verbum*, the judgment is an inner word which rationally proceeds from the act of reflective understanding. In the act of reflective understanding, we can distinguish two elements: an element of determination and an element of light. For example: "Hence the reflective activity whence judgment results is a return from the syntheses effected by developing insight to their sources in sense and intellectual light."[56] On the one hand, our understanding has a source in an element of determination because we are human persons—composites of body and soul. But in this case, I am focusing on the bodily aspect: our understanding begins in our senses. No matter how reflective it may become, our understanding is always an act of understanding something; it is never a pure act but always an act with respect to some particular matter. On the other hand, our understanding has a source in an element of light because we are rational; we are intelligences capable of reflecting upon our acts of understanding, upon the validity of our intelligent and rational procedure and upon the native infinity of our intellects. Indeed, the human intellect, as intellectual light, is a participated likeness in the divine Light.

In *Insight,* the judgment is an answer, a "Yes" or a "No," to a reflective type of question, e.g., Is it so? Is such and such the case? Lonergan moves beyond the general notion of judgment to distinguish concrete judgments of fact, common sense judgments, scientific judgments, and mathematical judgments. These analyses greatly enrich his earlier treatment of judgment. Still, *Insight*'s basic analysis of judgment is in terms of a virtually unconditioned, which involves three elements, namely:

(1) a conditioned
(2) a link between the conditioned and its conditions, and
(3) the fulfillment of conditions.[57]

First, a conditioned is the product of direct understanding; it is what *Verbum* calls "the syntheses effected by developing insight." It is a conditioned because it is hypothetical: it stands in need of evidence. Direct understanding has proposed the conditioned, but reflective understanding has now to consider the question, Is it so? Secondly, the fulfillment of conditions is given different ways in different contexts. Basically it is a return to the level of presentations, to the element of determination. Can the data, whether they be sensible, perceptual, imaginary, or merely hypothetical, support our ideas and conceptions? Finally, the link between the conditioned and its conditions also will differ from context to context. It differs, for example, for scientific and for common sense judgments. Nevertheless, it is based on the ability of the rational subject to grasp the sufficiency of its own intelligent and rational procedure. Have I given intelligence and rationality free play? Have I pursued the issue far enough? In brief, the key question is, have I raised, considered, and sufficiently answered all the further, pertinent questions? Accordingly, what *Verbum* discusses in terms of the reflective nature of intellectual light, *Insight* has cast into the form of raising further, pertinent questions.

This brings us to the analysis of judgments of value in *Method in Theology*. As we have seen, Lonergan distinguishes between criterion and meaning. The criterion for a judgment of value is the self-transcendence of the subject. It is the transcendental notion of value which accounts for the moral subject's ability to achieve self-transcendence. While this is Lonergan's basic position, there are three aspects which must be distinguished. First, the transcendental notion of value lifts the subject out of the merely cognitive context and places him or her in a practical and existential world in which he or she must decide and act. That is, the transcendental notion of value promotes the subject from the rational to the responsible level of consciousness. Secondly, the transcendental notion of value directs the responsible subject to his or her goals. To begin with, the subject does not know what is truly good and so he or she must question and deliberate, evaluate, and then decide. On the basis of his or her decisions, the subject can act. Still, all the while it was the transcendental notion of value which was guiding the subject's responsible procedure from questioning to action. Thirdly, the transcendental notion of value provides the criterion that reveals whether goals are being reached. Ultimately, we shall never be satisfied until we can rest in a goodness absolutely beyond criticism. The transcendental notion of value grounds self-criticism, the dissatisfaction with partial answers, and the disenchantment with human failure and mediocrity. Accordingly, it is the transcendental notion of value which initially raises the question about value and goodness and which subsequently keeps the moral subject discontent until he or she has satisfactorily responded to the question.

The transcendental notion of value is a technical expression. It is one of the transcendental notions; other examples are: the transcendental notion of the intelligible, the true, and the real. They provide the foundations for transcendental method. Lonergan prefers to use this type of technical expression because he wants to break from a metaphysical system based on faculty psychology and move into a method based on intentionality analysis. Thus, for example, Lonergan contrasts his formulation of the transcendental notions with the metaphysical psychology of earlier theology:

> If one wishes to transpose this analysis into metaphysical terms, then the active potencies are the transcendental notions revealed in questions for intelligence, questions for reflection, questions for deliberation. The passive potencies are the lower levels as presupposed and complemented by the higher.[58]

With specific reference to the transcendental notion of value:

> The fourth level, which presupposes, complements, and sublates the other three, is the level of freedom and responsibility, of moral self-transcendence and in that sense of existence, of self-direction and self-control. Its failure to function properly is the uneasy or the bad conscience. Its success is marked by the satisfying feeling that one's duty has been done.[59]

In summary, the transcendental notion of value can be understood, in the technical language of an earlier theology, as an active potency; in the interiority language of transcendental method, as the guiding principle which raises moral questions and directs the moral subject towards the answers; and in the common sense language of everyday living, as the conscience. Simply stated, it is the conscience which provides the criterion for judgments of value.

When Socrates addressed the jury at his trial, he referred to a spiritual voice which he ofttimes heard. Explaining why he did not seek public office, Socrates said:

> Perhaps it may seem odd that although I go about and give all this advice privately, quite a busybody, yet I dare not appear before your public assembly and advise the state. The reason for this is one which you

have often heard me giving in many places, that something divine and spiritual comes to me. . . . This has
been about me since my boyhood, a voice, which when
it comes always turns me away from doing something I
am intending to do, but never urges me on.[60]

Socrates continues on, confiding that although he is facing a
death sentence, he has no regrets for the way he has lived; for
even now he says:

This that has happened to me is good, and it is impossible that any of us conceives it aright who thinks it is an
evil thing to die. A strong proof of this has been given
to me; for my usual signal would certainly have opposed me, unless I was about to do something good.[61]

Socrates' voice opposes him when he is about to do something
wrong and encourages him, but only by its silence, when he is
about to do something good. I think it is possible to discern an
analogy between the transcendental notion of the truth or
intellectual light, on the one hand, and the transcendental notion of value or Socrates' spiritual voice, on the other hand.
Thus, it is not the task of reflective understanding to suggest
possible lines of intellectual development. Direct understanding is the operation that suggests, supposes, hypothesizes;
reflective understanding is the operation that scrutinizes,
raises critical questions, and grasps the adequacy of direct
understanding in its own absence of further, pertinent questions. Analogously, it is not the task of the transcendental
notion of value, or conscience, to positively conceive lines of
responsible and free development. Rather like Socrates' spiritual voice, it guides by troubling us when we are wrong and
allowing us to peacefully rest when we have done our duty.
Lonergan makes a related point:

It is because the determination of the good is the work
of freedom that ethical systems can catalogue sins in
almost endless genera and species yet remain rather
vague about the good. They urge us to do good as well
as to avoid evil, but what it is to do good does not get
much beyond the golden rule, the precept of universal
charity, and the like.[62]

Accordingly, the criterion of judgments of value can be formulated as the moral subject's grasp of his or her own successful self-transcendence in the peace and quiet of an easy conscience.

Verbum contrasted the element of light and the element of determination. *Insight* contrasted the link between the conditioned and its conditions and the fulfillment of conditions. *Method in Theology* contrasts the structure and the content of judgments of value. The judgment of value and the judgment of fact have the same structure but pertain to different types of content. The key factor which allowed Lonergan to move beyond the merely factual and into the realm of human values was the analysis of feelings.

An elementary distinction within the whole range of human feelings is between feelings which have a merely vital basis and feelings which have an intentional basis. Feelings with a vital basis operate prior to the subject's apprehension of any object. For example, hunger and thirst, fatigue and anxiety. "One first feels tired and, perhaps belatedly, one discovers that what one needs is a rest."[63] Feelings with an intentional basis arise out of the conscious apprehension of some object. For example, the arrival of the beloved floods the lover with joy. "We have feelings about other persons, we feel for them, we feel with them."[64] The world mediated by meaning, that is, the reality opened up by the thought of philosophers and theologians, by the creations of artists and builders, by religion, culture, and social living—is a world which is permeated by feeling. It is intentionally based feelings which orient the subject in this world, which channel his or her living and pervade his or her consciousness. Roughly stated, feelings with a vital basis arise from our animal nature and orient us within a physical environment. Feelings with an intentional basis arise from our self-conscious nature and orient us within a world mediated by meaning.

Another distinction, this time within the range of intentionally based feelings, is between feelings which are merely self-regarding and feelings which are responses to values, to that which is really good. Lonergan states the distinction in the following way: "Feelings that are intentional responses regard two main classes of objects: on the one hand, the agreeable or disagreeable, the satisfying or dissatisfying; on the other hand, values, whether the ontic value of persons or the qualitative value of beauty, understanding, truth, virtuous acts, noble deeds."[65] For example, one may find someone personally disagreeable but admit that he is an honorable man. Again, one may be attracted to certain foods, but regret that they really are unhealthy.

Lonergan also points out that feelings and the values to which they respond do not exist in isolation, but subordinate one another in a scale of preference. He lists, in ascending order: vital values, social values, cultural values, personal values, and, at the summit of human feeling, religious values. Such an order is, of course, ideal. In the concrete, one is apt to find some distortion in the scale of values.

Verbum and *Insight* emphasized the development of understanding. *Method in Theology* points out that feelings develop as well. Initially, feelings arise quite spontaneously. However, feelings can be tutored by an educational process. Lonergan remarks: ". . .feelings are enriched and refined by attentive study of the wealth and variety of the objects that arouse them, and so no small part of education lies in fostering and developing a climate of discernment and taste, of discriminating praise and carefully worded disapproval, that will conspire with the pupil's or student's own capacities and tendencies, enlarge and deepen his apprehension of values, and help him towards self-transcendence."[66] The development of feelings can be conceived analogously to the self-correcting process of learning described in *Insight*.[67] Mathematicians pondering images arrive at insights, which they express in terms of new symbols, which in turn, provide the basis from which new mathematical insights can arise. People of common sense, expressing their understanding, as well as their oversights, in word and deed, provide for each other the evidence in which they can discern the need for self-correction. Similarly, by our speaking, writing, and doing, we reveal our feelings. Individually and collectively we can reflect on those feelings to encourage and strengthen them where they are appropriate, to adjust them where they are aberrant, and to control them according to some scale of preference where they are disordered. As there is an individual, communal, and historical self-correcting process of cognitive learning; so too there exists an individual, communal, and historical self-correcting process of affective learning. There is a process of the development and refinement of human feelings. Such a process provides the content for our judgments of value.

To conclude, the key statement on which we have been reflecting is: "Judgments of value differ in content but not in structure from judgments of fact."[68] *Verbum* contrasted the element of determination and the element of light. *Insight* contrasted the fulfilling conditions and link between conditioned and conditions. *Method in Theology* contrasts feelings that are intentional responses to values and the transcendental notion of value. Feelings are the element of determination and the conditions in which our judgments of value are to be verified. The transcendental notion of value is the element of reflective light—in the moral context instead of characterizing this reflective quality as self-knowledge we might characterize it as self-control and self-direction—and the principle which does the verifying. Lonergan has retained the structure of his earlier analysis of judgment but broadened that analysis to encompass feelings.

Moral Conversion

Moral conversion is a decision for the transcendental notion of value. There are two sentences in Lonergan's discussion of this type of conversion which are key:

> So we move to the existential moment when we dis-
> cover for ourselves that our choosing affects ourselves
> no less than the chosen or rejected objects, and that it
> is up to each of us to decide for himself what he is to
> make of himself. Then is the time for the exercise of
> vertical freedom and then moral conversion consists in
> opting for the truly good, even for value against satis-
> faction when value and satisfaction conflict.[69]

Moral conversion consists in opting for the truly good, for value. Since conversion is a movement which sets up a whole new horizon, we can conclude that moral conversion is a decision, not simply for this or that value, but for the transcendental notion of value. Such a conclusion is supported by an analogous understanding of intellectual conversion which is a movement into the horizon set up by the transcendental notion of being.

The function of the transcendental notion of value is fourfold. First, it promotes the subject to the existential level of consciousness. The transcendental notion of value grounds the question: Is it worthwhile? Is it truly or only apparently good? These questions promote the subject to the level of responsible living. Secondly, it directs the subject to its goals. As the transcendental notion of value raises responsible questions, so too through the process of questioning it guides the subject to answers, and indeed, the answers that can guide living towards its goals. Thirdly, it provides the criterion that reveals whether the goals are being reached. That criterion is the absence of further, pertinent questions, the success of self-transcendence bearing fruit in a peaceful conscience. Fourthly, it is the transcendental notion of value which promotes the subject beyond any categorical good, and beyond any finite achievement towards the good. It keeps us restless, in this life, pursuing an absolute goodness which lies beyond our powers of criticism. Consequently, to decide for the transcendental notion of value is to opt for an open and dynamic orientation which ever presses us beyond our present moral achievement.

Once moral conversion occurs, it becomes the first principle of the subject's moral living. It becomes the source of ever further development because it is transcendent in orientation. However, besides the developments which flow from moral conversion, are the developments which constitute the preconditions for its initial occurrence. There are three types of development which should be considered as the conditions of the possibility of moral conversion.

First, before the moral subject can be converted he or she must be developed. The transcendental notions, which ground a person's basic orientation and authentic existence, are experienced by the moral subject as an ever present possibility. "Still, this possibility and exigence become effective only through development."[70] It takes time to develop knowledge of what might be meant by such an elusive notion. It takes time to develop and tutor the feelings which respond to one's inner pull towards authenticity. It takes time to develop the willingness which withstands the attraction of less valuable objects and keeps one on the right path. In *Insight,* Lonergan described the basic difficulty for the developing moral subject.

> For complete self-development is a long and difficult process. During that process one has to live and make decisions in the light of one's undeveloped intelligence and under the guidance of one's incomplete willingness.[71]

Given the lesser criteria actually used by the subject in day to day living, it is a radical breakthrough to discover within consciousness an intention of absolute goodness. This discovery sets up a whole new horizon of evaluating, deciding, and acting; if the subject decides to operate according to that radical intention. Consequently, moral conversion presupposes a certain amount of personal development.

Secondly, persons are born into families and soon enter into larger and mutually interacting communities. By a community Lonergan means a group of persons with common experiences, understanding, judgments, and values. Thus when we noted that the moral subject must develop knowledge and feelings and self-control, it is within the community that such development takes place. We learn; we are socialized; we become cultured. All of this occurs because persons live within communities. Communities are constituted by a common meaning and regulated by common value. When liberty, personal authenticity, and self-transcendence are common values, then the subject has a great advantage. The moral subject is surrounded by examples in which he or she can begin to discern what is meant by the transcendental notion of value. The moral subject is supported in his or her own personal search for authenticity. On the other hand, when the ideals of the community include some form of ideology which alienates the subject from his or her need to be attentive, intelligent, rational, responsible, and loving—then the moral subject is at a distinct disadvantage.

Thirdly, historical development is a factor in the subject's moral maturity. When communities exist over time, their common meanings and values develop. The development can constitute either progress or decline; traditions can grow and flourish or decay and wither:

> . . . the words are repeated, but the meaning is gone. The chair was still the chair of Moses but it was occupied by the scribes and Pharisees. The theology was still scholastic, but the scholasticism was decadent. The religious orders still read out the rules, but one wonders whether the home fires were still burning. The sacred name of science may still be invoked but, as Edmund Husserl has argued, all significant scientific ideals can vanish to be replaced by the conventions of a clique.[72]

Thus one may decide for the transcendental notion of value, but the meaning is more or less distorted. Since the tradition has watered down what it means to pursue the good, one is unable to find powerful examples. Contemporary persons stand in a complex relationship to tradition. While the total rejection of tradition is no answer, neither is the uncritical acceptance of the archaic. Still, one can find within one's tradition, perhaps, the very seeds of liberation and the challenge to moral conversion. "Repent, the kingdom of God is at hand" (Matt. 3:2).

Moral conversion is a high achievement. It demands that moral subjects commit themselves to the ever open dynamism of the transcendental notions and the exigences of developed personal consciences. Still, for all its personal decisiveness, moral conversion has historical and communal preconditions. If moral subjects decide that their achievement of moral conversion is a good thing, then surely they must value the tradition and community which led them to that achievement. They must revere the very preconditions of their own personhood. Now the moral subject is capable of full moral self-transcendence; now the moral subject is capable of "benevolence, beneficence, of honest collaboration and of true love, of swinging completely out of the habitat of an animal and of becoming a person in human society."[73] Further, there is the question of responsibility to future generations. By one's decisions and actions one makes the world which they will inherit. Will that world make the achievement of moral conversion and moral maturity more accessible or more difficult?

Religious Conversion

Lonergan's discussion of religious conversion is deceptive in its simplicity. In fact, he subsumes a wealth of material under this topic. The notion of religious conversion as expounded in *Method in Theology* integrates elements from the realms of common sense, theory, interiority, and transcendence. Religious conversion is the response to God's gift of love and love is a reality simple enough to be appreciated by an infant and complex enough to evade intellectual analysis. Since Lonergan's approach to theological method involves the complex use of rather simple notions, it is instructive to review the treatment of religious conversion in each of its diverse contexts lest we mistake his methodical style for simple-mindedness.

Lonergan expresses a basic understanding of religious conversion with common sense notions. From the scriptures he reminds us that it is "God's love flooding our hearts through the Holy Spirit given to us" (Rom. 5:5). Again, it is the replacement of a heart of stone with a heart of flesh. And again, it is a spiritual transformation which bears fruit in a spirit filled with love, joy, patience, kindness, goodness, trustfulness, gentleness, and self control (Gal. 5:22). He emphasizes the unity of this love with other kinds of love.[74] There is the domestic love among parents and children. There is the patriotic love of one's country. There is the philanthropic love of mankind. I do not think that Lonergan is making any technical, philosophical or theological point; he is merely adverting to the fact that we can experience many types of love and religious conversion initiates us into a love similar to these other types of love.

In *Grace and Freedom* Lonergan studied theology within the medieval theoretical context. Religious conversion was part of that theoretical framework. Aquinas' use of Aristotle included a metaphysical psychology with its own nest of terms and relations: "the essence of soul, its potencies, habits, and acts."[75] This represented the order of nature and since Philip the Chancellor, a theoretical frame of reference divided the order of nature from the order of the supernatural.[76] Religious conversion, then, is a grace, a gift from beyond the order of nature. Radicated in the essence of the soul, it perfects and sanctifies nature.

Further theoretical distinctions can be drawn. Religious conversion is an operative grace. Aquinas writes: "God moves man's will, as the Universal Mover, to the universal object of the will, which is the good."[77] Conversion is a special case because an operative grace initiates a special movement towards God as a special end. Conversion as a special movement can require prevenient graces to prepare the soul and subsequent graces to help the soul persevere. Recalling this early work, Lonergan writes in *Method in Theology:* "Operative grace is religious conversion. Cooperative grace is the effectiveness of conversion, the gradual movement towards full and complete transformation of the whole of one's living and feeling, one's thoughts, words, deeds and omissions."[78] Within the theoretical context, religious conversion is an operative grace that changes the radical orientation of the will.

In *Method in Theology* religious conversion reveals an added meaning within the realm of interiority. In the theoretical context "souls are differentiated by their potencies; potencies are known by their acts; acts are specified by objects."[79] However, objects are not understood in terms of the consciousness that intends them, but in terms of causality. One and the same nest of terms and relations can be applied to the analysis of plants, animals, and intelligences. "Now to effect the transition from theoretical to methodical theology one must start, not from metaphysical psychology, but from intentionality analysis and, indeed, from transcendental method."[80] In the realm of interiority religious conversion is understood in terms of human consciousness and intentionality.[81]

The transcendental notions are our capacity for self-transcendence. They are the grounds of unrestricted questioning. They underpin, penetrate, and promote the various levels of consciousness toward their cumulative and interdependent goals. Lonergan writes: "Just as unrestricted questioning is our capacity for self-transcendence, so being-in-love in an unrestricted fashion is the proper fulfillment of that capacity."[82] When we are in love we spontaneously function, not for ourselves alone, but also for others. Religious conversion is to an unrestricted love and, as a result, it spontaneously relates us to an other-worldly realm.

In the context of interiority, religious conversion initiates the subject into a dynamic state of other-worldly love. This dynamic state is "prior to and principle of subsequent acts."[83] The subject becomes a subject in love and all its living and feeling, speaking, and thinking proceed from and participate in this prior state of love. "It is this otherworldly love, not as this or that act, not as a series of acts, but as a dynamic state whence proceeds the acts, that constitutes in a methodical theology what in a theoretical theology is named sanctifying grace."[84] From an anthropological point of view, we can say that people seek self-transcendence.[85] Religious conversion, then, initiates us into the dynamic state of love which both fundamentally satisfies that desire and makes further acts of self-transcendence more efficacious, more secure, and more gracious.

Religious conversion initiates us into the realm in which God is known and loved. This is the realm of transcendence. However, Lonergan agrees with Fr. Karl Rahner's description of "consolation without a cause."[86] Religious experience has content but there is no intellectually apprehended object. Still, Lonergan distinguishes between experience and knowledge. While one can experience the dynamic state of love, it takes tradition, learning, and revelation to know that this is the Holy Spirit poured into our hearts. Our response to this gift "both constitutes religious conversion and leads to moral and even intellectual conversion."[87] In itself, however, the gift of the Holy Spirit is the actuation of our potential orientation to transcendent mystery. It releases our ability to love in an unrestricted fashion. Through the Holy Spirit flooding our hearts and through the resultant release of our own native potency to love, we are invited to participate in the very life of God. We become temples of the Holy Spirit and God's adoptive children.

Besides the invisible gift of the Holy Spirit is the visible mission of the Son. The Spirit orients us towards mystery; but the life, death, and resurrection of Jesus Christ add a determination to the transcendent orientation. Lonergan writes:

> Without the visible mission of the Word, the gift of the
> Spirit is a being-in-love without a proper object; it
> remains simply an orientation to mystery that awaits
> its interpretation. Without the invisible mission of the

Spirit, the Word enters into his own, but his own re-
ceive him not.[88]

Therefore, God communicates to us, not only by flooding our
hearts with his love, but also by entering into history himself.
As the Word, God entered into a particular historical setting to
personally communicate his message and himself to us. That
message and self-communication can be distinguished into distinct levels. First, it is a range of data. Secondly, it constitutes a
dimension of meaning. Thirdly, it enters history at a determinate time and place. Fourthly, it demands an existential response from us.[89] The mission of the Word encounters and
challenges us on the successively deeper levels of experiencing, understanding, judging, and deliberating.[90] Hence, we encounter the Word initially in the pages of scripture but
eventually as a totally involving invitation: "Repent! The kingdom of heaven is close at hand" (Matt. 4:17). The Word pre-
pares us for conversion.

Besides the mission of the Son and the gift of the Holy Spirit
is the drawing by the Father. It is Jesus who tells us: "No one
can come to me unless he is drawn by the Father who sent me"
(Jn. 6:44). To Simon Peter's profession of faith at Caesarea
Philippi, Jesus responds: "Simon, son of Jonah, you are a
happy man! Because it was not flesh and blood that revealed
this to you but my Father in heaven" (Matt. 6:17). Lonergan
quotes Eric Voegelin's interpretation of this episode:

> . . .nobody can recognize the movement of the divine
> presence in the Son, unless he is prepared for such
> recognition by the presence of the divine Father in
> himself. The divine Sonship is not revealed through
> information tendered by Jesus, but through man's re-
> sponse to the full presence in Jesus of the same Un-
> known God by whose presence he is inchoatively
> moved in his own existence.[91]

To listen to the unrest in one's own heart, to learn from the
longing in one's own intellectual, rational, and moral consciousness: this is to be drawn by the Father. Not that one has
apprehended any intellectual object, for nobody has seen the
Father except the Son (Jn. 6:46). Yet, in the language of the

Johannine Jesus, to "be taught by God, and to hear the teaching of the Father, and to learn from it, is to come to me" (Jn. 6:45). Accordingly, the recognition of the movement of the Father in one's soul is the precondition for the recognition of the significance and value of the Son. Finally, it is the Father and Son together who send the Holy Spirit down upon the members of the Mystical Body.

Religious conversion is a fecund notion. It is a transformation in and through God's love. In the common sense notions of scripture, it is evidenced in St. Paul's change of heart on the way to Damascus. In the theoretical framework of St. Thomas, it is a grace that moves our will towards God as a special end. In the realm of interiority, it is a dynamic state of love which grounds and penetrates the proceeding acts of the converted subject. In the realm of transcendence, it is the Holy Spirit flooding our hearts.

Conversion, Dialectic, and Foundations

We turn now from the consideration of conversion vis-a-vis theological method in general to the consideration of the point within theological method where conversion makes its explicit entry. That point lies between the functional specialty, *Dialectic* and the functional specialty, *Foundations*. This is also the point where theological method pivots from its first phase of operations to its second phase of operations, from theology "*in oratione obliqua* that tells what Paul and John, Augustine and Aquinas, and anyone else had to say about God and the economy of salvation" to theology "*in oratione recta* in which the theologian, enlightened by the past, confronts the problems of his own day."[92] In order to understand more precisely how conversion functions within theological method, it is necessary to accurately conceive this pivotal point which is located between *Dialectic* and *Foundations*.

The Functional Specialty Dialectic

The fourth functional specialty is dialectic. Dialectic focuses on conflicts. There are conflicts in the Christian movements of

the past; there are conflicts in the interpretation of those movements; there are conflicts between opposed classes of scholars.
Dialectic seeks to methodically address these conflicts and to
discover their roots in the light of conversion.

Conversion occurs on the fourth level of conscious and intentional operation—the existential level. The functional specialties interpretation and history operate on the intelligent and
reasonable levels respectively. Consequently, by raising the
issue of conversion, dialectic moves the results of interpretive
and historical investigations on to a higher level. Lonergan
remarks that there are two deficiencies in the prior levels of
investigation which dialectical method seeks to remedy.[93]

First, neither interpretation nor history methodically address
the issue of human values. Interpretive investigations intend to
determine what was meant; but dialectic "adds to the interpretation that understands further interpretation that appreciates."[94] Historical investigations intend to determine what in
fact was going forward in the past; but dialectic adds "a history
that evaluates achievements, that discerns good and evil."[95]
Accordingly, dialectic raises interpretive and historical inquiry
on to the level of responsible questioning—the existential level.

Secondly, the attempt to evaluate the past raises the issue of
an interpreter's standpoint and an historian's horizon. In the
chapter on interpretation, Lonergan sketches the operations by
which an interpreter approaches the meaning of a text. He
notes that every interpretive inquiry includes the standpoint of
the interpreter. That standpoint may or may not be sufficiently
developed. For example: "The major texts, the classics, in
religion, letters, philosophy, theology, not only are beyond the
initial horizon of their interpreters but also may demand an
intellectual, moral, religious conversion of the interpreter over
and above the broadening of his horizon."[96]

Similarly, in the chapters on history, Lonergan offers an
account of the procedures of critical historical investigation.
He notes that such procedures head towards univocal results
only if historians begin from similar horizons. But historians
operate from differing and even opposing horizons. This leads
to conflicting results, for example:

> What are historical facts? For the empiricist they are
> what was out there and was capable of being looked at.

> For the idealist they are mental constructions carefully
> based on data recorded in documents. For the critical
> realist they are events in the world mediated by true
> acts of meaning.[97]

The functional specialty interpretation raises the issue of conflicting interpretive standpoints but it does not provide a proper
method for dealing with that issue. Again, the functional specialty history raises the issue of conflicting historical horizons,
but it does not methodically address that problem. By raising
the results of these two specialties to the evaluative level,
dialectic directly confronts the issue of radical conflicts. By
insisting on the need for conversion, it points the way towards a
methodical solution.

The type of method needed to confront the issue of radical
conflicts will differ from the type of method employed in the
empirical sciences. Natural sciences properly use empirical
methods. They restrict their questioning to what "can be settled through appeal to observation and experiment;"[98] they
investigate data in which value judgments have no constitutive
role. Human sciences properly use empirical methods also. But
they are less successful in methodically avoiding the issue of
human values. Their data can include problems which are
constituted by conflicting value judgments. Still less can theology evade such a radical issue. If it is to be methodical,
theology must directly confront the issue of conflicting values
and opposed horizons. It must develop the means to handle
these problems.

To address these problems, Lonergan offers a dialectical
method. The method proceeds through the integration of two
levels: a material level and a formal level. On the material level
are the conflicts of Christian living, with their opposed interpretations and their opposed histories. Dialectic seeks to discover the underlying reasons for these conflicts. Under the
guidance of transcendental method, it seeks these reasons in
the presence or absence of conversion. On the formal level,
there are principles according to which basic conflicts are
evaluated. These principles are twofold: to develop positions
and to reverse counter-positions.

> Positions are statements compatible with intellectual,
> moral, and religious conversion; they are developed by

being integrated with fresh data and further discovery. Counter positions are statements incompatible with intellectual, moral, and religious conversion; they are reversed when the incompatible elements are removed.[99]

These two precepts—develop positions and reverse counterpositions—are the formal aspect under which the materials of the past are evaluated.

Through the procedures of dialectic, the subjectivities of the various investigators are objectified. There is an initial objectification when investigators distinguish positions and counterpositions implicit within the tradition. There is a further revelation of their subjectivities when they develop what they take to be positions and reverse what they take to be counterpositions. Finally, the activity of the investigators themselves can become the material of dialectic. Then, dialectic proceeds within a communal self-correcting process of learning.

There is, however, an ambiguity in dialectical method. The operation of dialectic presumes that one can distinguish between positions and counter-positions. No doubt, positions and counter-positions exist within various traditions but more immediately they exist as the actual tensions within the performance of present day investigators. In the operation of dialectic, unconverted persons will mistake positions for counterpositions and vice versa.

Still, the efficacy of dialectical method resides, not in peoples' ability to be certain, but in their ability to learn. We learn about ourselves through an encounter with the persons and values of the past. Reciprocally, we judge the past according to our present self-understanding and our present horizon. Again, it is our past which has made us what we are and it is in the light of our present that we come to know what that past has been. However, we are not trapped in a vicious circle. Our present standpoints are not completely constituted by the past. They are also constituted by a possibility that is ever present: a possibility that was part of our past, is part of our present, and will be part of our future. That possibility is self-transcendence. It is our ability to learn more than we presently know. It is our ability to develop beyond our present level of achievement. It is our ability to be in love. Lonergan comments: "Now it is only through the movement towards cognitional and moral self-transcendence, in which the theologian overcomes his own conflicts, that he can hope to discern the ambivalence at work in others and the measure in which they resolved their problems."[100] The actual basis from which we may understand the past and the present is a reality: the movement of self-transcendence. It is self-transcendence which is the actual norm of dialectical method.

The Functional Specialty Foundations

The fifth functional specialty is foundations. It is the task of this specialty to provide foundations, however, only in a special sense. Lonergan distinguishes different types of theological foundations:

> Accordingly, we are seeking the foundations, not of the whole of theology, but of the three last specialties, doctrines, systematics, and communications. We are seeking not the whole foundations of these specialties—for they obviously will depend on research, interpretation, history, and dialectic—but just the added foundations needed to move from the indirect discourse that sets forth the convictions and opinions of others to the direct discourse that states what is so.[101]

Thus, we can identify three types of foundations. First, the dependence of the last three specialties on the first phase of theology. Secondly, the foundations of the whole of theology. Thirdly, the foundations needed to move from indirect discourse to direct discourse. For the sake of exposition, I believe it is helpful to designate these three types of foundations as material, formal, and actual. The functional specialty foundations is concerned with foundations of the actual type. We can best understand, however, what is meant by this by reflecting first on the material and formal foundations of theology.

The first phase of theological method provides the material foundations. The specialties research, interpretation, history, and dialectic correspond to the successive levels of conscious and intentional operation—experiencing, understanding, judging, and deciding. Consequently, as the movement to higher and more complex levels of consciousness reveals a concomitantly more complex object; so too the movement from research to interpretation, from interpretation to history, from history to dialectic, reveals a continuously unfolding and ever more complex object. Nevertheless, however complex the object may become, we can think of it as a material object.

Research, interpretation, history, and dialectic are examples of field specialization. They are distinguished from one another on the basis of the material objects they investigate. Scholars have had to accept field specialization because of the increase in the data available. One does well to master even the most limited range of data. Old Testament studies divide into the Law, the Prophets, and the Writings. As research makes more data available, fields divide and subdivide. One must specialize in order to do justice to one's material.

There is much to be gained from careful attention to a limited range of data. The interpreter spirals into the meaning of a text. Paralleling the common sense pattern of learning, the interpreter accumulates a core of insights.[102] Initially, there need not be much formulation; interpretation begins by going over the same material again and again. As inquiry proceeds and insights begin to accumulate, one moves nearer and nearer to the interests, questions, and horizon of the interpreted author. Eventually there begins to emerge a topic around which an interlocking and interwoven set of questions and answers forms. The topic can be expressed in a few phrases; but the questions and answers, the subtopics, and issues which flow from it can be numerous and complex. Lonergan describes the procedure as "the interlocking of questions and answers and the eventual enclosure of the interrelated multiplicity within a higher limited unity."[103] Historians employ a similar procedure of question and answer, forming ever higher intelligible unities. Further, these interwoven sets of question and answers, and these higher intelligible unities, are criticized, purified, and verified by a continuous and self-correcting process of "reaching results by an appeal to the data."[104] Hence, the first phase of theology proceeds by building up successive and more complex interlocking unities of questions and answers. Each step in the process must ultimately rest on an appeal to the data, where the data is provided by the results of lower level specialties.

For all its excellence, scholarship has its limitations. The field of data over which any one person can attain such a thorough mastery is limited. Scholars can immerse themselves in the details and lose sight of the larger picture. The general result is a bewildering maze of unrelated facts. Further, scholars in diverse fields must communicate with one another and with others outside the field of scholarship. There is needed a common ground. There is needed a common structure and a common point of reference so that scholars can relate their own investigations to larger inquiries and can communicate their results to larger communities.

To introduce method into this situation is to order these otherwise disparate investigations. By correlating functional specialties with the levels of conscious and intentional operation, we have a principle for such an ordering. Thus, research settles what was written. Interpretation moves beyond the written word. It investigates the intended meaning. History moves beyond what any particular person meant. It investigates what was going forward. A particular text or a particular person's deed will participate in and be revelatory of deeper historical currents. For the most part, however, contemporaries' apprehension of the historical trends of their own time will be partial and vague. Dialectic moves beyond the narrative account of the unfolding of some historical current. Dialectic finds its material object in the conflicts, opposition, and tensions which inform Christian living, its history, and its diverse theological interpretations.[105]

At the level of dialectic, we have moved beyond the horizon of both the empiricist and the idealist. Lonergan writes:

> What are historical facts? For the empiricist they are what was out there and was capable of being looked at. For the idealist they are mental constructions carefully based on data recorded in documents. For the critical realist they are events in the world mediated by true acts of meaning.[106]

Dialectic investigates these events as they existed in interconnection in the field of concrete tension and conflict. That field cannot consistently be an object for the empiricist or the idealist. The tensions are not now, nor were they ever, out there capable of being looked at. Nor are they mere mental constructions. While the concrete tensions are only discovered by the difficult mental labor of scholarship; and while they are only brought to light through interpretive reconstructions; nevertheless, as they existed and operated in the past, they were palpable and prereflectively influential. Dialectic investigates these tensions which have informed the human spirit. Accordingly, while the human spirit cannot be an object of investigation for the empiricist or the idealist; its basic conflicts and tensions are the object of investigation for the critical realist operating in dialectic.

The basic form or conflict is between human authenticity and human unauthenticity. It is a battle which rages in the hearts of people at all times and places. Still, the proper object of the first phase of theology is not to accumulate increasing evidence to prove such a generality. Instead, its proper object is to delineate as clearly as possible the actual historical dimensions and details of the basic conflict. Lonergan writes:

> When things turn out unexpectedly, pious people say, "Man proposes but God disposes." The historian is concerned to see how God disposed the matter, not by theological speculation, not by some world-historical dialectic, but through particular human agents.[107]

In other words, the basic form of human conflict may be between human authenticity and human unauthenticity, but the proper object of the first phase of theology is a material one. What are the details? What are the concrete and particular spatio-temporal circumstances? What features of human tension and conflict can be precisely and fully determined? In this manner the first phase of theological method provides the material foundations.

Transcendental method provides the formal foundations for theological method. To state at once what is meant by transcendental method, let us recall Lonergan's definition of method:

> A method is a normative pattern of recurrent and related operations yielding cumulative and progressive

results. There is a method, then, where there are distinct operations, where each operation is related to the
others, where the set of relations forms a pattern,
where the pattern is described as the right way of doing
the job, where operations in accord with the pattern
may be repeated indefinitely, and where the fruits of
such repetition are not repetitious, but cumulative and
progressive.[108]

This is a general definition of method, but the method we are
concerned with now is transcendental method. The relevant
operations proceed from an unrestricted intending. The pattern
in which the operations occur is formally dynamic—that is,
self-assembling, with each operation calling forth the next.
Because the operations and the dynamic pattern are rooted in
and actuation of an unrestricted questioning, they can provide
for their own normativity. Finally, because the method is transcendental, it extends to an unrestricted field of objects, and
even to objects which lie outside the field of human experience.

Transcendental method provides the basic anthropological
component of theological method. It is relevant to all fields in
which the human mind operates and it derives its efficacy from
the fact that different materials do not radically alter the fundamental operations of experiencing, understanding, judging, and
deciding. Lonergan writes:

However true it is that one attends, understands,
judges, decides differently in the natural sciences, in
the human sciences, and in theology, still these differences in no way imply or suggest a transition from
attention to inattention, from intelligence to stupidity,
from reasonableness to silliness, from responsibility to
irresponsibility.[109]

Since theology is produced by theologians, and since theologians must proceed by the laborious process of question and
answer—in other words, by exploiting the potentialities of
human intelligence, rationality, and responsibility—the relevance of transcendental method is clear.

Transcendental method is related to the operations of scholarly research as form is related to matter. Again, transcendental
method stands to the operations of all eight of the functional

specialties as soul stands to body. Let us recall some of Lonergan's earliest reflections on theological method:

> Thus the content of speculative theology is the content of a pure form. It is not something by itself but the intelligible arrangement of something else. It is not systematic theology but the system in systematic theology.[110]

And again, with respect to Aquinas' ordering of theorems in his theology of grace:

> This fact of synthesis cannot perhaps be expressed, for synthesis in a field of data is like the soul in the body, everywhere at once, totally in each part and yet distinct from every part. But to be certain of the fact of synthesis is as easy as to be certain of the fact of the soul. One has only to remove this or that vital organ and watch the whole structure tumble into ruin; the old unity and harmony will disappear, and in its place will arise the irreconcilable opposition of a multiplicity.[111]

Similarly, transcendental method is a pure form, an intelligible arrangement of something else: it is like the soul in the body, everywhere at once.

The pattern of operations, the dynamic structure in which they operate, and the dynamism which underpins, penetrates, and reaches beyond it all: this is the basic form. When I use this term, the basic form, I am thinking of this basic nest of terms and relations which thematizes the reality of transcendental method.[112] It not only embraces theology as a whole; it also penetrates each part. First, the pattern of operations is present in each of the levels. Theologians doing research, interpretation, history, dialectic, foundations, doctrines, systematics or communications all proceed by experiencing, understanding, judging, and deciding. Secondly, the dynamic structure of operation pertains to both phases. In the first phase the results of lower levels of investigation provide the data for higher level investigations; in the second phase, the results of doctrines, for example, provide the truths upon which systematic theologians reflect. Finally, the basic dynamism which underpins and penetrates both phases of theological operation and all eight of the specialties proceeds from and terminates in the religious life of the church. It is the task of the first phase to determine the factors which have led to the present religious situation; it is the task of the second phase to improve the religious situation in the present and for the future. Accordingly, one must not take an extrinsic view of transcendental method. It only underscores the most basic pattern of relations which can be verified in all facets of theological inquiry.

Transcendental method provides the formal foundations for theological method. It is not a foreign import. It makes systematic what is authentic to theological procedure in each of the functional specialties. However, it is intrinsic to theological procedure because, more fundamentally, it is intrinsic to human procedure. Similarly, it is fundamental to human procedure because it is grounded in human subjectivity. If we could speak of a basic human form—that is, what one would understand if one grasped what was most significant about human beings and the way they operate—then transcendental method would be that basic human form as it relates to the intellectual pattern of experience. Theology in the middle ages affirmed: "*Agere sequitur esse:* perfection in the dynamic field of operation is radically one with perfection in the static order of being."[113] Transcendental method, then, simultaneously clarifies the basic form of human existing, and on the basis of that radical clarification, proceeds to an efficacious ordering of human operations. From the enlightened grasp of the basic human form proceeds strengthened acts of decision, judgment, understanding, and communication. Accordingly, transcendental method provides the formal principle of theological method because it is based on an understanding and implementation of the basic form of human existing.

The actual foundations for theological method are provided by conversion. The functional specialty foundations is most concerned with this type of foundations. Lonergan writes: "As conversion is basic to Christian living, so an objectification of conversion provides theology with its foundations."[114] And again, "Inasmuch as conversion itself is make thematic and explicitly objectified, there emerges the fifth functional specialty, foundations."[115] Properly speaking, then, it is an objectification of conversion that provides theology with its fifth functional specialty, foundations. Again, conversion is basic to Christian living but it is the objectification of conversion that is basic to theological method.

The objectification of conversion is not a simple matter. It involves a complex movement. Conversion is not an already-out-there type of reality capable of being looked at. Neither is it to be found within oneself, if one conceives introspection in terms of inward looking. Instead, conversion is the type of reality that emerges from the interaction of material and formal principles. Conversion occurs in one's actual living and within the tension and conflict between one's transcendental end and one's empirical conditionality. It is an event which does not strictly pertain to the body or to the soul, but to the concrete person who is a compound of body and soul, matter and form, limitation and transcendence. Hence, to objectify conversion is to objectify the interaction between two principles.

Dialectic focuses on the tensions of the past. While it aims at a simplifying grasp of those tensions, dialectic is not simple-minded. It wants to understand them in their full historical and social reality. The functional specialty foundations brings "to light the opposite poles of a conflict in personal history."[116] Do dialectic and foundations investigate the same tensions? It is the same tension if one regards it from the viewpoint that all human beings need to develop; that human development proceeds within the tension between authenticity and unauthenticity; and that human authenticity is a matter of being faithful to the precepts: be attentive, be intelligent, be reasonable, be responsible, be in love. It is not the same tension if one regards it from the viewpoint that human development occurs under diverse historical conditions and with varying opportunities and hindrances. Further, while the basic human conflict is between authenticity and unauthenticity, certainly not every person has explicitly understood himself or herself in those terms. And again, one can respond to the transcendental precepts if one is free, but concrete psychological, economic, sociological, and political pressures can severely threaten one's effective freedom.

I would say that the key point is that the conflicts investigated by dialectic and the conflicts objectified by foundations are analogous. First, there is an identity. Whether one under-

stands it or not, authenticity is a most valued human achievement, and so its pull is felt by everyone. Secondly, there is a
non-identity. The particular opportunities and hindrances of
one person's life are never the same as those of another person's life. Finally, there is a unity. The conflicts of personal life
and those found in the communal and historical past form a
whole, in the sense that the person we are considering is not
the abstract subject of pure reason, but the concrete subject
incarnated in history. The person lives off the past and the past
lives on in the person. Consequently, we can think of the
conflicts of dialectic and foundations analogously.

In general, Lonergan conceives theological method to proceed on two interacting levels. He writes:

> In this fashion there is set up a scissors movement with
> an upper blade in the categories and a lower blade in
> the data. Just as the principles and laws of physics are
> neither mathematics nor data but the fruit of an inter-
> action between mathematics and data, so too a the-
> ology can be neither purely *a priori* nor purely *a
> posteriori* but only the fruit of an ongoing process that
> has one foot in a transcultural base and the other on
> increasingly organized data.[117]

While the upper blade of theological method is constituted by
the theological categories which one derives from the structure
and dynamism of conscious intentionality; and while these
realities are transcultural—that is, they are the principles
which are observed when cultures flourish and the principles
which are violated when cultures decline; nevertheless our
grasp of the upper blade, the base of theological categories, this
transcultural reality, is insecure. One can define the basic tension in human living as the conflict between authenticity and
unauthenticity, and this is true. However, one's grasp of what is
precisely meant by those key terms is uncertain. Similarly, the
lower blade of theological operation can also be a bewildering
maze. Interpreters offer conflicting interpretation; historians
work out of a variety of perspectives; more radically, philosophies tend to deepen these oppositions and give them a kind of
permanence. Nevertheless, all of this vagueness and pluralism
receives a precision and unity under the rule of theological
method.

Theological method takes its stance on the self-correcting process of learning. Our personal grasp of what is precisely meant by authenticity and unauthenticity, by attention, intelligence, reasonableness, and responsibility may be vague; but we have "a vast multitude of individuals in whom such basic nest of terms and relations can be verified: for they too attend, understand, judge and decide. Moreover, they do so not in isolation but in social groups, and as such groups develop and progress and also decline, there is not only society but also history."[118] Thus, the data from which we can derive an understanding of human operation and human authenticity and to which we can return to criticize and verify our ideas is rich and extensive. Conversely, the array of philosophic positions and counter-positions, and of interpretive and historical styles of investigation, is awesome, but there exists simple human demands for attention, intelligence, rationality, and responsibility to which they all must pay heed. In other words, our social and historical situation provides us with a plurality of examples in which we can discern what is meant by authenticity and unauthenticity; reciprocally, our personal grasp of the radical human realities can be criticized and purified in interaction with the data.[119]

In the self-correcting process of learning, we must distinguish between the materials to be operated on and the operator. History can teach us what is meant by human wisdom and human folly, but the subject must be docile. History contains not only the examples from which we can learn, but also the oversights, biases, and sins which prevent our learning. The secure basis from which to decide which are examples of folly and which are examples of wisdom resides on the upper blade, with the operator. Specifically, it lies in the operator's ability to put its pure desire for truth and value into action by raising questions and continuing to raise them until that desire is satisfied. Consequently, in the interaction between lower and upper blade, between *a posteriori* data and *a priori* form, it is the latter which occupies the superior and normative role. It is with the operator rather than the materials that we are to locate normativity.[120]

The operator's self-possession can be incipient, mature, or receding. From the viewpoint of the functional specialty dialectic, it is the task of the operator to develop positions and reverse counter-positions. The functional specialty, foundations, takes a complementary view. Besides the development which the operator effects, there is the development of the operator itself. The operator of dialectic need not be a converted subject because all that is required is the ability to recognize radically opposed statements. However, the operator of foundations needs to be converted because it needs to operate on the basis of an act of self-appropriation.

The act of self-appropriation is an act of heightening consciousness. It is not a matter of reading books. It is not a matter of belonging to a special group. Basically, conversion is an event. One can perhaps remember the exact date; recall the precise place; pinpoint it in one's personal history. But, although conversion emerges from such an empirical matrix, it transcends its material conditions. It unfolds its significance throughout a lifetime. Conversion is a heightened grasp of the form of human existing.[121] It is a radical clarification of one's own nature. This does not mean that one is now in possession of an irrevisible definition of one's existence. What one possesses is, not a formulation, but the reality which admits of many different formulations. Conversion is a grasp of one's preconceptual form. Certainly, the more one has read, the more history one knows, the more authentic the groups to which one belongs, the more materials one has at one's disposal which favor the emergence of the event of conversion. Nevertheless, conversion occurs as the heightened possession of one's self, and perhaps it occurs as the realization: how could I have been so alienated from my deepest, most abiding intentions?

Conversion must be understood as located between the material and formal principles of theological method. In conversion, a basic form—the human being as attentive, intelligent, reasonable, responsible—emerges from its coexistence and confusion with other material elements of human living, from the polymorphism of consciousness, into a distinct and distinguishable status. Conversion is, not the basic form, nor the material conditions from whence it emerges, but the emergence itself as an event. As the functional specialty, foundations, is concerned to objectify the "immanent and operative set of norms that guides each forward step in the process"[122] of theological method, so conversion is that same process of objectification transposed into the context of Christian living. Again, as theological method seeks to thematize the basic normative pattern of our conscious and intentional relations, so conversion is the emergence of that basic form on the prereflective level. Conversely, as Christian living, with its call to repentance, promotes the emergence into consciousness of our basic nature before God, so theology is a heightening and clarification of that prior process of emergence.

We cannot be either an empiricist or an idealist and consistently affirm the reality of an event like conversion. For the empiricist, reality must be confined to the level of presentations. But the basic form is never a datum. It is always the intelligible and intelligent arrangement of something else. For the idealist, one can clarify one's subjectivity but such a clarification is never an event that could be located alongside other events in objective history. Nevertheless, something happened to Saul of Tarsus, for example, on his way to Damascus and that event has had enormous historical consequences. In the event of conversion, the empirical and the transcendental converge in a unique way.

Conversion provides the actual foundations for theological method. It also provides the foundations which are the basis of the more personal stance of the second phase of theology. I think we can find the actual and the personal component of theological foundations in the movement of self-transcendence; I think we can find it in the act of the emergence of the basic form. Such an act is extremely personal. First, it is personal in the sense that the particular circumstances of anyone's self-discovery are unique. Nor would it do us any good to travel on the road St. Paul took to Damascus. Each of us is, as it were, confined to our own individuality. Discovering ourselves, then, will have uniquely personal overtones. Secondly, the act of emergence of the basic form is personal in a deeper sense. The event occurs as an invitation: this is what you could be and should be if you truly wanted it. The dark side of the experience is that there resides in us the inertial tendencies to fail in attention, intelligence, reasonableness, responsibility; there is a tendency to drag our feet against the pull of vertical finality. Consequently, the emergence of the basic form is personal in the sense that it presents us with a challenge to become persons. It invites us to overcome our limitations and to "surrender to the demands of the human spirit."[123]

The act of emergence of the basic form provides the actual foundations for theological method because it is the act of self-transcendence par excellence. It provides the basic model on which to judge our other acts of self-transcendence. Lonergan writes:

> The derivation of the categories is a matter of the human and the Christian subject effecting self-appropriation and then employing this heightened consciousness both as a basis for methodical control in doing theology, and, as well, as an *a priori* whence he can understand other men, their social relations, their history, their religion, their rituals, their destiny.[124]

We should distinguish here between the basic form as content and the basic form as act. As content, it can serve as the *a priori* whence we can understand others. But the emergence of the basic form as act is an extremely reflective, liberating, and loving experience. It is this emergence, as an act, which provides the actual methodical control in doing theology. Again, conversion as content provides an *a priori*, a type of preunderstanding we can bring to the appreciation of interpretive and historical investigations. However, it is conversion as an act that is most significant. When one has experienced conversion as an act, then one finds oneself in love. One finds oneself committed to the act of self-transcendence. Then one has at one's disposal an extremely enlightening and strengthening norm. It is conversion as act that provides the actual foundation of theology. It is an event which is at once personal and yet capable of grounding and criticizing the operations of the various functional specialties.

In summary, the material foundations of theological method are located in the functional specialties of the first phase. This phase promotes the emergence of a complex material object: an object which in the context of the functional specialty dialectic is characterized by the tension between human authenticity and unauthenticity. The formal foundations of theology are located in transcendental method. However, these foundations are provided by transcendental method, not as it is formulated, but as it underpins, penetrates, and reaches beyond all of the eight functional specialties and both of the phases of theological method. Finally, actual theological foundations are provided by conversion. On the level of religious living, conversion is the emergence into consciousness of the preconceptual form of human existing. Theological method both reflects and reflects upon this event. Thus, the actual foundations are provided by the fruit of the interaction of the material and formal foundations.

Lonergan's Development in the Later Period

As in the middle period, the problem of integration continued to engage Lonergan's interest.[125] In *Insight* Lonergan had sought to provide an integral heuristic structure for common sense and the natural sciences. In *Method in Theology* the problem of integration still asserts its influence but it is differently conceived. There is a new challenge. "The new challenge came from the *Geisteswissenschaften,* from the problems of hermeneutics and critical history, from the need of integrating nineteenth-century achievement in this field with the teachings of Catholic religion and Catholic theology."[126] Lonergan seeks to accomplish this new integration via method: "a framework for collaborative creativity."[127] Accordingly, we can understand this later period as the sustained effort to integrate the realm of scholarship and the realm of transcendence.

Lonergan's response to the task of integration produced developments on several related levels. First, he moved on from his analysis of mathematics, natural science, and common sense to an analysis of the procedures of modern scholarship. Secondly, he expanded his analysis of cognitional structure into an account of transcendental method. Thirdly, he shifted his concern for cognitional self-appropriation to the fuller context of conversion. Each of these levels of development calls for some elaboration.

First, Lonergan shifted his attention from the developments in modern mathematics and modern science to the contemporary developments in scholarship.[128] As we have seen, contemporary hermeneutics and critical history disconnected the old style dogmatic theologian from his sources.[129] The German Historical School initiated a movement away from what it saw as the *a priori* idealist construction of the meaning of history.[130] However, the movement away from the admixture of philosophic speculation and historical research became a movement towards a style of empirical research permeated by a steadily more pronounced positivism.[131] As scholars attended every more assiduously to their data, they increasingly relied upon some type of cognitional myth.

Lonergan's response to this situation was to raise again the question he so effectively posed in *Insight:* What am I doing when I am knowing? Now the question takes newer forms: what do interpreters do when they are understanding a text? And what do historians do when they are reconstructing the historical facts? *Insight* had dealt with the truth of interpretation in a systematic fashion. *Method in Theology* provides "an orderly set of direction on what is to be done" in interpretive and historical investigation.[132]

The key to Lonergan's account of scholarly procedure is the way in which a series of questions and answers interweave and interlock into higher levels of intelligibility. It is a parallel process to the common sense procedure of accumulating insights into concrete situations. The criterion for the correctness of these types of judgments is the absence of further, pertinent questions. Thus, to the predominantly empirical approach to interpretive and historical investigations, Lonergan adds an *a priori*. It is not, however, an *a priori* determination of what a text must mean or of how history must have been. Rather, the *a priori* is an anticipatory structure, fixing the broad lines of how scholars are to proceed if they are to be faithful to the exigencies of human inquiry. Accordingly, Lonergan takes Albert Einstein's advice: "pay very little attention to what scientists say and a great deal to what they do,"[133] and applies it to an analysis of contemporary scholars and their procedure.

Secondly, Lonergan expands his account of cognitional structure into an account of transcendental method. The most obvious development is the emergence of a distinct fourth level of consciousness, the existential. The existential level is the level of evaluation and deliberation, of responsible decision, of the notion of value and good, the level of personal, communal, and historical self-constitution. The emergence of this fourth level of consciousness has the effect, not only of adding a new dimension to Lonergan's analysis of interiority, but also providing a new explicit principle on which to integrate each of the previous levels—intentionality.

Intentionality analysis unifies the cognitional and volitional levels of consciousness. Cognitional processes are conceived in terms of conscious and intentional operations. Moral deliberation reflects upon feelings which are intentional responses to values. Gone is the separation between the faculty of reason and the faculty of will. It is replaced by successively sublating levels of conscious and intentional operation. Lonergan writes:

> The dethronement of speculative intellect has been a general trend in modern philosophy . . .
> I am far from thinking that this tendency is to be deplored. What once was named speculative reason today is simply the operations of the first three levels of consciousness—the operations of experiencing and inquiring, understanding and formulation, checking and judging. There operations occur under the rule and guidance of the fourth level, the level of deliberating, evaluating, deciding. Philosophers and scientists recognize this fact when they deliberate about the proper method to be followed in their work.[134]

Thus, Lonergan will be able to integrate scholarship and Catholic teaching because he has an integrated view of the successive levels of conscious and intentional operations.

Theological method provides a framework for collaborative creativity. It provides an integrated structure within which theologians can locate their own interests, relate them to other theological enterprises, and to the task of theology as a whole. *Insight* emphasized immanently generated knowledge and personal appropriation of cognitional structure; *Method in Theology,* on the other hand, emphasizes critically controlled belief; it stresses the ordering of many different types of operation in a process from data to results and within a community of investigators. The emphasis of *Insight* and the emphasis of *Method of Theology* are, of course, not opposed; rather, they presuppose and mutually support one another. Individuals only become persons within communities and communities are constituted and enriched by persons. Nevertheless, there is a development from the middle period to the later period. *Insight* emphasized "the personally appropriated structure of one's own experiencing, one's own intelligent inquiry and insights, one's own critical reflection and judging and deciding."[135] *Method in Theology* builds on that structure and expands it into a methodically ordered pattern of operations yielding cumulative and progressive results.

Thirdly, Lonergan places his notion of intellectual conversion within the fuller context of threefold conversion.[136] Intellectual conversion is set alongside moral conversion and religious conversion. Further, all three conversions are related to one another in terms of sublation. Lonergan writes:

> Because intellectual, moral, and religious conversions all have to do with self-transcendence, it is possible, when all three occur within a single consciousness, to conceive their relations in terms of sublation. I would use this notion in Karl Rahner's sense rather than Hegel's to mean that what sublates goes beyond what is sublated, introduces something new and distinct, puts everything on a new basis, yet so far from interfering with the sublated or destroying it, on the contrary needs it, includes it, preserves all its proper features and properties, and carries them forward to a fuller realization within a richer context.[137]

Thus, intellectual conversion is sublated by moral conversion; intellectual and moral conversion are sublated by religious conversion. Religious conversion transforms the subject into a subject in love. The subject is not automatically cured of all sin and all bias, but the state of love is an habitual actuation of one's capacity for self-transcendence.[138] The subject's apprehension and response to values is more secure because he or she is a subject in love. The subject's desire for truth and being is more efficacious because it is included within the richer context of the pursuit of all value.

Theology needs intellectual conversion because it reflects on religion.[139] Reflection itself, however, is a matter of conscious and intentional operation, of raising fruitful and penetrating questions, and of sustaining inquiry until sufficient evidence has been gathered and satisfactory answers have been reached. Reflection itself is the pursuit of a value, namely truth. That pursuit is guided, not only by the exigencies of logic, but also by the imperatives of responsible performance. Consequently, intellectual conversion calls for and is filled out by a moral conversion which sets the subject within the concrete communal and historical quest for values.

Moral conversion calls for and is filled out by religious conversion. The transcendental notions are our capacity for self-transcendence. They are the ground of unrestricted questioning, of the questions we have asked, the questions we will ask, and the questions we could ask. They are our capacity to learn more than we presently know and to become more than we presently are. However, that capacity for self-transcendence reaches a basic fulfillment when the subject is transformed by religious conversion. It is not a fulfillment that puts an end to all questioning, like an anesthetic that deadens the spirit. Rather, it is a fulfillment that quickens the spirit, like a lover, who even while embracing the beloved, is filled with a still deeper longing for communion. Religious conversion fulfills the dynamism of human effort because that dynamism seeks its term, not in righteousness, but in a dynamic state of love. Religious conversion fills us with God's love which fulfills, and at the same time, beckons us ever on. It finds an echo in Pascal's remark: "Take comfort, you were not seeking me if you had not already found me."[140]

Insight investigates the subject's pursuit of being. That pursuit proceeds according to the norms of empirical, intellectual, and rational consciousness. *Method in Theology* reveals the subject's pursuit of being as a part of its more fundamental pursuit of goodness and value. Finally, the pursuit of all value is placed within the context of a dynamic state of being in love.

In summary, the problem of integrating contemporary scholarship with Catholic theology and Catholic religion dominates the later period.[141] In order to address this problem Lonergan develops an account of cognitional procedure within the realm of scholarship; he expands his analysis of cognitional structure into a framework for collaborative creativity; he integrates his account of intellectual conversion within the fuller context of moral and religious conversion.

NOTES

[1] William F. J. Ryan, S.J. and Bernard J. Tyrrell, S.J., Introduction to *A Second Collection,* (Philadelphia: The Westminster Press, 1974).

[2] Lonergan, "Existenz and Aggiornamento," pp. 240–51; "Dimensions of Meaning," pp. 252–67 in *Collection,* ed. F. E. Crowe (New York: Herder and Herder, 1967).

[3] Bernard J. F. Lonergan, S.J., *Method in Theology* (New York: Herder and Herder, 1972).

[4] Lonergan distinguishes three different functions of meaning in his article "Dimensions of Meaning." Meaning mediates reality, guides the transformation of human society and is partially constitutive of human living. He writes: ". . .as the child develops into a man, the world of immediacy shrinks into an inconspicuous and not too important corner of the real world, which is a world we know only through the mediation of meaning. Further, there is man's transformation of his environment, a transformation that is effected through the intentional acts that envisage ends, select means, secure collaborators, direct operations. Finally, besides the transformation of nature, there is man's transformation of man himself; and in this second transformation the role of meaning is not merely directive but also constitutive." p. 255.

[5] *M.i.T.,* pp. 79–81.

[6] Ibid., pp. 177–78.

[7] Although Lonergan maintains that meaning is contextual, he is not a relativist. He maintains our ability to attain objective knowledge; however, historical realities are complex. He writes: ". . .note that truths that are not eternal are relative, not to a place and time, but to the context of a place and time; but such contexts are related to one another; history includes the study of such relations; in the light of history it becomes possible to transpose from one context to another; by such transpositions one reaches a truth that extends over places and times." Lonergan, "Philosophy and Theology," in *A Second Collection* (Philadelphia: The Westminster Press, 1974) pp. 207–08.

[8] *M.i.T.,* pp. 208–09.

[9] Lonergan correlates hermeneutical investigation with the objective of the level of intelligence operation, that is, with the development of direct understanding. He correlates historical investigation with the objective of rational operation, that is, with the development of reflective understanding. Lonergan criticizes the leading figures in the German hermeneutical discussion, e.g., Schleiermacher, Dilthey, and

Heidegger, for not sufficiently appreciating the distinction. "There is an insufficient awareness of this third level of cognitional activity in the authors we have been mentioning and a resultant failure to break away cleanly and coherently from both empiricism and idealism." *M.i.T.,* p. 213.

[10] In his dissertation Lonergan maintained that the thought of St. Augustine is chiefly within the realm of common sense. "The division of grace into operative and co-operative arose not from a detached love of systematization but to meet the exigencies of a controversy." *Grace and Freedom,* p. 2. In Aquinas, the context is chiefly theoretical and the concern is for the development of speculative theology.

[11] "Theology in Its New Context," *2nd Col.,* p. 56.

[12] As early as 1930 Lonergan had already begun to question the adequacy of what he later was to call the classicist notion of culture. "Christopher Dawson's *The Age of the Gods* introduced me to the anthropological notion of culture and so began the correction of my hitherto normative or classicist notion." *"Insight* Revisited," *2nd Col.,* p. 264.

[13] "The Absence of God in Modern Culture," *2nd Col.,* p. 113.

[14] *M.i.T.,* p. xi.

[15] "Belief: Today's Issue," *2nd Col.,* p. 97.

[16] *M.i.T.* p. 140.

[17] Thus, the empirical investigations of such a notable scholar as Rudolf Bultmann are able to reconstruct the process by which the synoptic gospels were formed. This type of scholarly work possesses an authoritativeness of its own. Nevertheless, it does not presuppose belief in the evangelist's statements nor any special validity to the tradition which they founded. That tradition also possesses an authoritativeness. Lonergan is concerned to work out a framework whereby these two types of authority can be related. See *M.i.T.* p. 186.

[18] Lonergan, *Philosophy of God and Theology* (Philadelphia: The Westminster Press, 1973) p. 32.

[19] *M.i.T.,* p. xi.

[20] "Theology in its New Context," *2nd Col.,* pp. 61–62.

[21] "Existenz and Aggiornamento," in *Col.,* p. 249.

[22] "Theology and Man's Future," in *2nd Col.,* p. 146.

[23] *M.i.T.,* pp. 24–25.

[24] Ibid., pp. 34–35.

[25] Ibid., p. 11.

[26] Lonergan writes: "When finally the mystic withdraws into the *ultima solitude,* he drops the constructs of culture and the whole complicated mass of mediating operations to return to a new, mediated immediacy of his subjectivity reaching for God." Ibid., p. 29.

[27] "The Subject," in *2nd Col.,* p. 81.

[28] Lonergan, "Mission and the Spirit" in *Experience of the Spirit,* eds. Peter Huizing and William Bassett (New York: Seabury Press, 1976) pp. 73–75.

29 R. G. Collingwood, *The Idea of History* (Clarendon Press, 1946; Reprint edition Oxford University Press, 1974) p. 281.

30 Lonergan writes: Without the explicit formulations that later were possible, metaphysics had ceased for me to be what Fr. Coreth named the *Gesamt—und Grundwissenschaft*. The empirical sciences were allowed to work out their basic terms and relations apart from any consideration of metaphysics. The basic inquiry was cognitional theory and, while I still spoke in terms of a faculty psychology, in reality I had moved out of its influence and was conducting an intentionality analysis." *"Insight* Revisited," *2nd Col.*, pp. 276–77.

31 *Insight,* pp. 444–45.

32 "Mission and the Spirit," in *Experience of the Spirit*, p. 70.

33 Lonergan points out that for Aquinas: ". . .man and, as well, all creatures according to their mode naturally love God above all things. And, of course, this love of God above all is only a particular case of the general theorem that absolutely all finality is to God." "Finality, Love, Marriage," in *Col.*, p. 25.

34 *Insight,* p. 746.

35 "Finality, Love, Marriage," in *Col.*, p. 19.

36 Mission and the Spirit," p. 70.

37 Finality, Love, Marriage," in *Col.*, p. 21.

38 American Catholic Philosophical Association, *Proceedings* 51 (1977). "Natural Right and Historical Mindedness," p. 134.

39 "The Subject," in *2nd Col.*, p. 81, n. 13. Lonergan remarks: "These objectives are approximately the scholastic transcendentals, *ens, unum, verum, bonum,* and they are interchangeable in the sense of mutual predication, of *convertuntur.*"

40 "Natural Right and Historical Mindedness," p. 136.

41 Lonergan writes: "For self-transcendence reaches its term not in righteousness but in love and, when we fall in love, then life begins anew. A new principle takes over and, as long as it lasts, we are lifted above ourselves and carried along as parts within an ever more intimate yet ever more liberating dynamic whole." Ibid., p. 137.

42 If vertical finality is an upthrust towards higher levels of being, and if human consciousness is a realization of this upthrust and a reflection on its significance, value, and end; then human personhood consists in a special relation to God as end of the universe. Human personhood is more than the realization that objective process is cognate to subjective process; more than the realization that we are truly at home in the universe; it is more than the realization that vertical finality and self-transcendence are related in origin. Human personhood involves an acceptance of an invitation to participate in the life of God. The Johannine Jesus tells us: "You are my friends if you do what I command. I shall not call you servants any more, because a servant does not know his master's business; I call you friends because I have made known to you everything I have learned from my Father" (John 15:15). To be involved in the general movement

of vertical finality, to effect a self-transcendence within oneself; this is truly to be busy at the Father's business.

43 *M.i.T.,* p. 268.

44 *Insight,* p. xi.

45 *M.i.T.,* p. xi.

46 Lonergan writes: "Only the critical realist can acknowledge the facts of human knowing and pronounce the world mediated by meaning to be the real world; and he can do so only inasmuch as he shows that the process of experiencing, understanding, and judging is a process of self-transcendence." Ibid., p. 239. It is the notion of self-transcendence which grounds the essential unity of the three types of conversion. "As intellectual and moral conversion, so also religious conversion is a modality of self-transcendence." Ibid., p. 241. On the other hand, Lonergan complains: "Now this unity of the human spirit, this continuity in its operations, the cumulative character in their results, seem very little understood by those that endeavor to separate and compartmentalize and isolate the intellectual, the moral, and the religious." "Natural Knowledge of God," in *2nd Col.,* p. 128.

47 For Lonergan's discussion of the notion of mediation, see *M.i.T.,* pp. 27–30.

48 Lonergan writes: "The difference between the world of immediacy and the world mediated by meaning is the source of the critical problem of philosophers. The world mediated by meaning is for the naive realist just an abstraction; for the idealist it is the only world we know intelligently and rationally, and it is not real but ideal; for the critical realist it is the world we know intelligently and rationally, and it is not ideal but real. The world of immediacy is only a fragment of the real world." "Existenz and Aggiormanento," in *Col.,* pp. 243–44.

49 *M.i.T.,* p. 239.

50 Ibid., p. 238.

51 "An Interview with Fr. Bernard Lonergan, S.J.," in *2nd Col.,* p. 219.

52 I believe that intellectual conversion can be mediated not only to a Christian tradition, but even to a Christian reflecting upon the truths of other religious traditions. I believe that one will find the seeds of intellectual conversion, for example, in the Zen koan.

53 *M.i.T.,* p. 238.

54 Ibid., p. 37.

55 Ibid.

56 *Verbum,* pp. 64–65. Also see chapter one, above, and chapter two.

57 *Insight,* p. 280.

58 *M.i.T.,* p. 120.

59 Ibid., p. 121.

60 Plato, *Great Dialogues of Plato: The Apology* eds. Erich H. Warmington and Philip G. Rouse, trans. W. H. D. Rouse (New York: The New American Library, 1956; A Mentor Book), p. 437.

61 Ibid., p. 445.

62 "The Subject," in *2nd Col.*, p. 83.

63 *M.i.T.*, p. 30.

64 Ibid., p. 31.

65 Ibid.

66 Ibid., p. 32.

67 *Insight,* pp. 174–75, 286–87, 289–91.

68 *M.i.T.*, p. 37.

69 Ibid., p. 240.

70 Ibid., p. 51.

71 *Insight,* p. 627.

72 *M.i.T.*, p. 80.

73 Ibid., p. 104.

74 During this period, Lonergan consistently writes about a three-fold conversion. It was in *Doctrinal Pluralism,* the 1971 Pere Marquette Theology Lecture at Marquette University, that conversion was first distinguished into religious, moral and intellectual. However, he distinguishes conversion into slightly different categories some eight years later. He writes: "Again, as always, emancipation has its roots in self-transcendence as includes an intellectual, moral and affective conversion . . . as affective, it is commitment to love in the home, loyalty in the community, and faith in the destiny of man." "Natural Right and Historical Mindedness," p. 70. The category of religious conversion has been broadened to include the transformation of the subject by love; but now in contexts other than the explicitly religious.

75 *M.i.T.*, p. 288.

76 *Grace and Freedom,* pp. 13–19.

77 *Summa Theologiae* 1–2, q. 9, a. 6, ad. 3m.

78 Lonergan compares the movement to God as the Universal Good with the movement to him as a special end. "Strictly there is not the slightest incompatibility; grace moves the will to God, who is determinate indeed but also the *bonum universale* (q. 9, a. 6) beyond all limitation or classification; further, grace moves the will to God not by adding potency' in the sense of limitation and contraction, but by being a further actuation and so giving expansion and enlargement. The really free are those who enjoy the freedom of the sons of God; perfect love of God is perfect detachment from created excellence and perfect liberty in choice." *Grace and Freedom,* p. 123, n. 29.

79 *M.i.T.*, p. 341.

80 *Verbum,* Introduction, p. viii.

81 Lonergan distinguishes between the expression of God's gift of love in the realm of theory and in the realm of interiority. He writes: "This gift we have been describing really is sanctifying grace but notionally differs from it. The notional difference arises from different stages of meaning. To speak of sanctifying grace pertains to the stage of meaning when the world of theory and the world of common sense are distinct but, as yet, have not been explicitly distinguished from and

grounded in the world of interiority. To speak of the dynamic state of being in love with God pertains to the stage of meaning when the world of interiority has been made the explicit ground of the worlds of theory and of common sense. It follows that in this stage of meaning the gift of God's love first is described as an experience and only consequently is objectified in theoretical categories." *M.i.T.*, p. 107.

82 Ibid., p. 106.

83 Ibid., p. 240.

84 Ibid., p. 289.

85 As Aquinas maintained that people naturally loved God, so too, in the context of intentionality analysis, we can say that people naturally and spontaneously seek self-transcendence.

88 Lonergan explains: "Fr. Rahner takes 'consolation without a cause' to mean 'consolation with a content but without an object.' " Karl Rahner, *The Dynamic Element in the Church, Quaestiones disputatae* 12 (Montreal: Palm Publishers, 1964) pp. 131ff. *M.i.T.*, p. 106, n. 4.

87 Ibid., p. 327.

88 "Mission and the Spirit," p. 77.

89 *M.i.T.*, p. 135.

90 "Mission and the Spirit," p. 76.

91 Catholic Theological Society of America, *Proceedings of the Thirty-Second Annual Convention* (1977), p. 9.

92 *M.i.T.*, p. 133.

93 Ibid., p. 245.

94 Ibid., p. 246.

95 Ibid.

96 Ibid., p. 161.

97 Ibid., p. 239.

98 Ibid., p. 248.

99 Ibid., p. 249.

100 Ibid., p. 252.

101 Ibid., p. 267.

102 Lonergan describes the scholarly differentiation of consciousness: "The scholarly differentiation of consciousness is that of the linguist, the man of letters, the exegete, the historian. It combines the brand of common sense of its own place and time with a common sense style of understanding that grasps the meanings and intentions in the words and deeds that proceeded from the common sense of another people, another place, or another time." Ibid., p. 274.

103 Ibid., p. 165.

104 Ibid., p. 243.

105 Lonergan writes: "Dialectic finally finds its units in the metamorphoses of what is basically the same conflict, now on the level of religious living, now in opposed histories of the prior events, now in opposed theological interpretations." Ibid., p. 141.

106 Ibid., p. 239.

107 Ibid., p. 179.

108 Ibid., p. 4.

109 Ibid., p. 23.

110 "Gratia Operans," p. 12.

111 *Grace and Freedom*, p. 143.

112 By the term "basic form," I am proposing a term which can provide a common point of reference for the notion of transcendental method and for the general notion of conversion. Lonergan has pointed out that the central form of a human being is a compound unity that is both intelligible and intelligent. *Insight*, pp. 518–20. In transcendental method, this central or basic form is objectified in concepts, propositions and words. In conversion, this central or basic form emerges in an act of self-possession and self-expression. It is one and the same basic form which emerges in the event of conversion and which is objectified as the basic pattern of operations in transcendental method.

113 *Grace and Freedom*, p. 42.

114 *M.i.T.*, p. 130.

115 Ibid., p. 131.

116 Ibid., p. 144.

117 Ibid., p. 286.

118 Ibid., p. 286.

119 Ibid., p. 293.

120 Although the formal principle provides the normativity in a way in which the material principle does not, Lonergan cautions about the need for proper openness to the material principle of theological method. "There is, perhaps, inevitably, a dependence of the first phase on the second. But the greatest care must be taken that this influence from the second phase does not destroy either the proper openness of the first phase to all the relevant data or its proper function of reaching its results by an appeal to the data." *M.i.T.*, p. 143.

121 See note 113 above.

122 *M.i.T.*, p. 270.

123 Ibid., p. 268.

124 Ibid., p. 292.

125 The problem of integration which dominated the middle period was the emergence of the modern natural sciences and their relation to and impact upon the world of common sense. The problem of integration which dominates the later period is related to this earlier problem but also different in important ways. In the later period, Lonergan seeks to integrate the emergent scholarly differentiation of consciousness with the realms of Catholic theology and religion.

126 "*Insight* Revisited," in *2nd Col.*, p. 277.

127 *M.i.T.*, p. xi.

128 Lonergan writes: "I wish to propose a convention. Let the term, science, be reserved for knowledge that is contained in principles and laws and either is verified universally or else revised. Let the term, scholarship, be employed to denote the learning that consists in a common sense grasp of the common sense thought, speech, action of

distant places and/or times. Men of letters, linguists, exegetes, historians generally would be named, not scientists, but scholars." *M.i.T.,* pp. 233–34.

129 See above, chapter three, section one.

130 *M.i.T.,* p. 208.

131 Lonergan writes: "Modern history is one thing and the philosophic assumptions of historians are another. H. G. Gadamer has examined the assumptions of Schleiermacher, Ranke, Droysen, and Dilthey. In more summary fashion Kurt Fror has stated that the work of historians in the earlier part of the nineteenth century was marked by a mixture of philosophic speculation and empirical research, and that what eliminated the speculation in the later part of the century was an ever more influential positivism." Ibid., pp. 317–18.

132 "*Insight* Revisited," in *2nd Col.,* pp. 275–76.

133 "Isomorphism of Thomist and Scientific Thought," in *Col.,* p. 147.

134 "Revolution in Catholic Theology," in *2nd Col.,* pp. 236–37.

135 *Insight,* p. xviii.

136 As I pointed out above in note 74, the notion of threefold conversion in this later period has evolved from the combination of intellectual, moral and religious conversion to the combination of intellectual, moral and affective conversion.

137 The interrelation of conversions is grounded in the unity of the human spirit. *M.i.T.,* p. 241.

138 Lonergan writes: ". . .a distinction has to be drawn between being in love in an unrestricted manner (1) as it is defined and (2) as it is achieved. As it is defined, it is the habitual actuation of man's capacity for self-transcendence. . . . On the other hand, as it actually is achieved in any human being, the achievement is dialectical." Ibid., pp. 283–84.

139 Lonergan writes: "In both Barth and Bultmann, though in different manners, there is revealed the need for intellectual as well as moral and religious conversion. Only intellectual conversion can remedy Barth's fideism. Only intellectual conversion can remove the secularist notion of scientific exegesis represented by Bultmann. Still intellectual conversion alone is not enough. It has to be made explicit in a philosophic and theological method, and such an explicit method has to include a critique both of the method of science and of the method of scholarship. Ibid., p. 318.

140 Ibid., p. 341, n. 6.

141 While Lonergan is concerned with problems faced by Roman Catholic theology and religion, he also is concerned with problems faced by ecumenical dialogue. Nevertheless, he writes: "The method I indicated is, I think, relevant to more than Roman Catholic theologians. But I must leave it to members of other communions to decide upon the extent to which they may employ the present method." Ibid., p. xii.

CHAPTER FOUR

CONVERSION: SUMMARY AND CRITICISMS

It is not knowledge of religious conversion, awareness of religious conversion, interpretation of the psychological phenomena of conversion, propositions concerning conversion. It is simply the reality of the transformation named conversion.

Bernard Lonergan, *Foundations of Theology,* p. 227.

Conversion and the Realms of Meaning

I have traced the development of Lonergan's notion of conversion through three periods. The early period was concerned with "reaching up to the mind of Aquinas."[1] The middle period was concerned with the modern critical problem—how do we know? The later period investigated the dimensions of meaning, of historicity, and of method. Again, *Grace and Freedom* introduced the notion of religious conversion. In *Verbum* we discerned the seeds of the notion of intellectual conversion, and in *Insight,* the matured fruit. *Method of Theology* differentiated religious, moral, and intellectual conversions and unified them in terms of different modalities of self-transcendence. This represents much intellectual labor and many separate investigations. Consequently, I would like to first present an overview of Lonergan's development of the notion of conversion and then offer my own account of the chief features of religious, moral, and intellectual conversion.

Grace and Freedom investigated the development of St. Thomas' thought on operative grace. Lonergan approached his material from the point of view of a theory of speculative development. Speculative theology has developed, he argued, by generating technical terms from earlier common words; it has developed by moving from common notions to precise theological theorems and by ordering scientifically such theorems into intelligible syntheses. This was the scientific ideal implicit in Aquinas' theological performance.

Earlier, St. Augustine had distinguished between operative grace and cooperative grace. He made this distinction, however, to meet the challenges of controversy. He argued with terms which were the common possession of all. Accordingly, Lonergan placed St. Augustine's reflections within the world of common sense.[2] Nevertheless, St. Augustine revealed "such a penetration of thought and understanding that one must affirm the development of speculative theology already to have begun."[3]

Following St. Augustine, Aquinas also distinguished between operative and cooperative grace. He further distinguished between habitual grace and actual grace. Such distinctions were not drawn to meet an immediate controversy; rather they emerged from and were defined in terms of a theology oriented towards speculative coherence and comprehensiveness. Further, Aquinas met the difficulties involved in reconciling God's initiatives and human liberty with a precise theological tool—the scientific theorem. General theorems subordinated more specific theorems. In this context, the meaning of conversion was fixed in terms of the integration of two theorems. First, according to the theorem of universal instrumentality, God applies all agents to their activities. Secondly, according to a more specific theorem, human volitional activity unfolds in two phases: initially, God alone operates on the human will to make it good and, subsequently, He cooperates with a good will to give it good performance. Consequently, the meaning of conversion was fixed in terms of the relations between theological theorems.

In *Verbum,* Lonergan sought to establish the intellectualism of Aquinas. It was the act of understanding which was central for Aquinas. While it is true that his theological procedure involved the scientific ordering of theorems, still the principle which synthesized the theorems, which held them together in an intelligible unity, was the act of understanding. Again, while it is true that Aquinas turned to the rational soul in order to deepen understanding of the trinitarian processions; and while it is true that Aquinas relied on Aristotelian metaphysics to account for the operations of the soul; nevertheless, the key feature in Aquinas' account of the soul, according to Lonergan, was its self-knowledge through its act of understanding.

What did Aquinas mean by the act of understanding and by intelligible emanation? Lonergan proposed a method to approach this question which was both profound and simple. "A method tinged with positivism would not undertake, a method affected by conceptualist illusion could not conceive, the task of developing one's own understanding so as to understand Aquinas' comprehension of understanding and its intelligibly proceeding inner word."[4] In Lonergan's view, one could develop one's understanding to the point of: 1) grasping what Aquinas meant by understanding; 2) grasping what Lonergan meant by understanding; and 3) grasping what occurs in one's own mind when one understands. This was a reaffirmation of Aquinas' principle that the human soul understands itself through its acts of understanding.[5] In this context, I believe, we can discern the seeds of intellectual conversion in "the act by which intellectual light reflects by intellectual light upon intellectual light to understand itself and pronounce its universal validity."[6] Consequently, although Aquinas employed Aristotle's metaphysical psychology, his account of *verbum* also presupposed that the soul could reflectively understand itself.

In these two works of Thomist interpretation, we can trace Lonergan's developing appreciation of Aquinas. *Grace and Freedom* approaches Aquinas in terms of a theory of speculative development and *Verbum* approaches Aquinas in terms of the interpretive need to develop understanding. The latter approach is more dynamic. Again, *Grace and Freedom* analyzes successively more general theological theorems whose structured synthesis fixes an act of understanding. On the other hand, *Verbum* employs the act of understanding to fix the basic features of successive hermeneutical circles. In the former, the relations between the theorems fix the act of understanding; in the latter, the act of understanding fixes the terms and relations. The movement from *Grace and Freedom* to *Verbum* is the movement from the generation of theological theorems to the generating intellect, from theory to interiority. Consequently, Lonergan's understanding of conversion developed from an element within a theoretical theology to a reflective grasp of cognitional fact.

In *Insight,* Lonergan continued his efforts to clarify cognitional interiority. In this middle period, however, he moved away from the difficulties of Thomist interpretation and into the modern problematic of cognitional theory. The advances in modern science represented both a new problem and a new resource. First, modern science heightened the contrast between what is prior for us and what is prior in itself, between the common sense world in which the sun rises and sets and the world of scientific theory in which the earth moves around the sun. Secondly, modern scientists have provided us with many more acts of understanding and have formulated them within rigorously fixed contexts. Aquinas maintained that we can understand ourselves through our acts of understanding and Lonergan applied that principle to the realm of modern scientific theory. Consequently, in *Insight,* he used modern science as the scaffolding for entry into the realm of cognitional interiority.

The key factor in *Insight* is the self-appropriation of the cognitional subject. It is a matter of

> . . . one's own rational self-consciousness clearly and distinctly taking possession of itself as rational self-consciousness. Up to that decisive achievement, all leads. From it, all follows.[7]

Self-affirmation constitutes a pivotal point in *Insight*. From the understanding of understanding and from the reflective grasp of one's cognitional activity, one proceeds to a knowledge of the broad lines of all that can be known, and thence to a critically based metaphysics. In this context, intellectual conversion is a realization that the sufficient development of understanding is a criterion for the real. In the act of reflective understanding, one has not only the immanent perfection of the cognitional subject but also the sufficient basis from which to affirm knowledge of being. In summary, the intellectually converted subject realizes that it is in the act of judgment that being is known.

In the later period, the key notions are meaning, historicity, and method. While *Insight*'s analysis of the natural sciences was sufficient to provide a preliminary notion of method, theological method demands more. Natural scientists seek insights into ranges of data; however, theologians seek insights into the communities and traditions which have formed their own minds. In the field of the natural sciences, the object can be reduced to experiential conjugates and the subject is an incarnation of scientific disinterestedness—the pure desire to know. In theology, the object is, not simply experiential, but already constituted by human acts of meaning, e.g., texts, historical movements, and theological controversies. The subject is not simply an incarnation of the pure desire to know, but a subject within an historical, communal, and personal process of development. "Indeed, historicity and history are related as object to be known and investigating subject."[8] Accordingly, to introduce method into this situation is to enable the historical subject to fruitfully reflect upon its constituting historicity in order to reflectively guide its making of history.

Besides the conditions of one's historicity, there is the unrestrictedness of one's intentionality. This is a factor which transcends diverse cultures and various historical epochs. In every culture, there are good men and women. In each historical epoch, there are those who search for the truth and seek to live in its light. Further, more significant is the gift of God's love. It is offered to everyone in all times and places. "It is not restricted to any stage or section of human culture but rather is the principle that introduces a dimension of other-worldliness into any culture."[9] Consequently, Lonergan grounds theological method in the unrestricted intending of the transcendental notions.

In the context of method, conversion pertains to the norms of theological procedure. It is a shift into the realm set up by the intentionality of the transcendental notions. Theologians are historical subjects and they need to reflect upon their past in order to understand themselves. However, that self-understanding can transcend history when theologians awaken to their transcendental intentionality. Indeed, the religiously converted subject is a subject in an unrestricted state of love and that state both constitutes his or her inmost being as well as

provides the norms for his or her historical activity. Consequently, in this later period conversion is conceived in terms of
the concrete norms which guide the historical subject.

In summary, conversion has been formulated in several different manners. In *Grace and Freedom* it was conceived in
terms of grace. In *Verbum* it was discerned in the notion of
intellectual light. In *Insight* it was a matter of the reflective self-
appropriation of the subject. In *Method in Theology* it was a
movement into the horizon of the transcendental notions. Accordingly, it remains to begin to draw all of these diverse
approaches into a unified perspective. Therefore, I would like
to present in as elementary terms as possible my view of
religious, moral, and intellectual conversion.

Religious Conversion

Religious conversion is the gift of God's love flooding our
hearts. In our inmost being, we experience the indwelling of
God's unrestricted acceptance and favor. Such an event occurs,
not on the empirical level of the flow of sensible data, nor on
the intelligent level of thinking and supposing, nor again on the
rational level of criticizing and judging. Instead, God's grace is
poured into that part of our consciousness which is concerned
with personal existence. Indeed, the indwelling of God's love
occurs concurrently with our discovery of our true selves. The
true self which we discover is worthwhile and significant. Consequently, I would say that religious conversion is the discovery of ourselves as worthwhile and significant because we exist
in God's love.[10]

The discovery of God's love dwelling at the very heart of our
existence is a gift. We feel immeasurably blessed because God
has chosen to love us. We realize that our lives are important
because God has entered them. Yet, God's love is unmerited.
We are important and valuable because God loves us; God does
not love us because we have first established our significance
and value. God's love does not depend on our achievements, or
on our virtues.[11] God's love is not given because of anything we
have said or done. Rather, like parents beholding their sleeping
child, love is focused upon the very being. Similarly, God's love

is focused upon our being. However, God's love is more than the ground of our meaning and value; it is the ground of our being. Accordingly, in a special sense, God's love is our very being.

God's love floods our hearts and grounds our existence in a dynamic state of being in love. That dynamic state is the principle of subsequent and proceeding acts of love. "We are to love, then, because He loved us first." (I John 4:19). We are to love our neighbors out of God's love overflowing in our hearts. Our particular acts of kindness, goodness, fidelity, gentleness, and self control (Gal. 5:22) flow from that deeper dynamic state. Since God's unrestricted love has convinced us of our worth and significance, there is no felt need to establish our value by diminishing others. Indeed, our inner peace and freedom permit us to more clearly perceive the true and mysterious value of other persons. Consequently, we can actually do the good with ease because we are in love.

Inversely, death is the final and chief fact for the unconverted subject. Most people simply pass from this life and are forgotten. Nor is there comfort in the fact that this lot is shared in common. Nor, again, does the facticity of death confine its significance to the end of one's life. What is the point of pursuing knowledge and what is the meaning of one's pure desire to know, if death cuts short one's existence after a few decades? Again, what is the point to working so hard and what is the good of one's pure desire for value, if one's life is no more than a worthless statistic? Finally, why love and why surrender to the dynamic eros of human living, if the cosmos is merely a silent tomb? Consequently, for the unconverted subject, the brute fact of death not only stands waiting at the end of life but also subverts even partial and interim pretenses of meaning and value.

Death is a fact for both the religiously converted and the religiously unconverted person. For the religiously converted person, however, flooded with God's love, death has been overcome. With St. Paul, we can be certain that nothing, not even death, can come between us and God's love (Rom. 8:38). The religiously converted person is operating within an horizon which subverts the facticity of death; death no longer has an ultimate significance. One can fully surrender to one's desire for unrestricted love. However, if love subverts the ultimacy of death, nevertheless the relevance of death remains. To love one's neighbor means to die to life on the basis of competing egoism. To be open to the inner movements of the Holy Spirit means to die to one's childish fears and wishes. Finally, the religiously converted subject will always need to pray along with Jesus in the garden of Gethsemane: "Nevertheless, Father, not my will but Yours" (Lk. 22:42).

The unrestricted state of being in love is the ultimate principle of the converted person's life. It underpins, penetrates, and promotes forward operations on the successive levels of consciousness.[12] It is a principle which originates prior to consciousness and terminates in a reality beyond consciousness. Thus, when the subject surrenders to God's unrestricted love, he or she is surrendering to a reality which precedes and transcends conscious control. The individual can perceive such a surrender of conscious control as a kind of death. For example, the physical development of the individual had been a matter of gradually gaining control over physical operations. Again, the psychic development of the individual had been a matter of gaining some familiarity and mastery over feelings. Consequently, when the individual is invited to surrender to a principle over which there is no conscious control, this is perceived as an invitation to death.

Religious conversion turns ordinary life upside down. The fearful individual's perception of death is transformed into the loving person's acceptance of the way to new life. Thus Jesus says: "Unless a grain of wheat falls on the ground and dies, it remains only a single grain; but if it dies, it yields a rich harvest" (John 12:24). The religiously unconverted person is dominated by death and has no reason to fully surrender to the dynamism of self-transcendence.

Moral Conversion

Moral conversion is the free response of the moral subject to the transcendental notion of value. The transcendental notion of value is not the notion of any particular good, nor the notions informing the concrete structures which insure the recurrence of particular goods, that is, the good of order.[13] Instead, I would identify the transcendental notion of value with a dynamic state of freedom. It is such a dynamic state, not as a private possession, but rather as a possibility in which all persons are invited to share. Consequently, in moral conversion, the subject freely responds to the dynamic thrust towards freedom for himself or herself and for others.

The thrust of the moral subject towards the transcendental notion of value is concretely actuated in the decision. As transcendental, it is oriented beyond all particular goods and all concrete social and cultural orders. As the immanent thrust of a concrete subject, however, it is realized in the choice of particular goods and in the building and support of some good of order. The act of decision, then, is the realization in the concrete of the person's orientation towards a goodness beyond all criticism and towards an unrestricted freedom. In the act of decision, the moral knowledge and feelings, the deliberation and evaluation, of the person come to fruition. The person operates neither arbitrarily nor compulsively, but within the context of responsible freedom. The act of decision is more, however, than the immanent perfection of the responsible person. With the act of decision begins the real self-transcendence of the person—the transformation of moral intentionality into moral performance. The person transforms the world in the light of his or her responsible decisions. Consequently, through the act of decision, the moral person both constitutes himself or herself as more proximately capable of free activity, as well as constitutes the world as a freer place.

For the morally converted person, the ultimate criterion of moral living is the pure detached desire for freedom. Particular goods can be judged to be truly or only apparently good insofar as they promote freedom. Similarly, the good of order must be judged in terms of its promotion of freedom. However, the morally converted person is not yet a morally perfect person. He or she has yet to apprehend the fullness of human authenticity and freedom; he or she has yet to achieve the spontaneous and "sustained self-transcendence of the virtuous man."[14] The morally converted person has to develop in knowledge and in moral feelings. However, even while learning, the morally converted person already possesses the needed criterion for discernment—that is, the pure detached desire for freedom.

Inversely, satisfaction is the final criterion for the morally unconverted person. From experience, he or she knows the good of particular objects. He or she knows the satisfaction of meeting particular needs—e.g., a good meal or a sound night's sleep. From the development of understanding and feeling, he or she knows the value of the good of order. The morally unconverted person knows the efficacy and the security of a social and economic order that works. On these levels, the morally unconverted person feels secure in identifying the good with that which satisfies.

However, in time the satisfaction of the morally unconverted person can turn to despair. Whether acknowledged or not, the pure and detached desire for freedom underlies, penetrates, and transforms the hierarchy of satisfactions and goods. Freedom cannot be found on the level of particular goods, nor on the level of the good of order. Freedom is to be found only in surrender to the pure and detached desire. The glamour and attractiveness of particular goods can quickly vanish. The feelings of excitement and opportunity at the outset of a marriage, a career, or any new venture can sour. One seeks new opportunities, new challenges, and new stimulation. Yet, because they are on the same level, they are subject to the same unsatisfactoriness. That unsatisfactoriness is grounded in the real yet unacknowledged frustration of the pure and unrestricted desire for freedom.

Liberation lies in surrender to the pure detached desire for freedom. This desire includes the desire for meaning and value because there is no freedom without these dimensions. Both the morally converted person and the morally unconverted person experience this desire. However, only the former has decided to make it normative. The morally unconverted person is dominated by insistent cravings and by contracting fears. For example, to give free reign to one's pure desire to know means withdrawing from the race to accumulate as many consumer goods as possible; it means forsaking one's anxieties about making a mark in the world, or rising in the esteem of one's social group. Again, to exercise one's pure desire for freedom means dying to one's fears concerning the unknown and to one's cravings for security; it means breaking away from one's settled routines. For the morally unconverted person, the potential rewards of such exercises are too distant to outweigh the satisfaction of meeting immediate desires and of calming nagging fears.

Moral conversion reverses the dominance of satisfaction over desire. The morally unconverted person correctly apprehends that goods satisfy. In fact, particular goods and a smoothly operating good of order can be satisfying. However, the criterion for the good is not satisfaction but desire. Unless one surrenders to one's pure desire for value and to one's unrestricted desire for freedom, one ultimately faces despair. By making *de facto* satisfactions normative, the unconverted subject frustrates and degrades the pure desire for freedom. Eventually, even the satisfaction provided by categorical goods is spoiled. In the gospel of St. Luke, Jesus says: "That is why I am telling you not to worry about your life and what you are to eat, nor about your body and how you are to clothe it . . . no, set your hearts on His kingdom, and these other things will be given you as well" (Lk. 12:22,31). Similarly, moral conversion is a matter of setting one's heart on the pursuit of value and of surrendering to the pure detached desire for freedom.

Intellectual Conversion

Intellectual conversion is the discovery of the significance of the pure desire to know. The pure desire to know is the principle which underpins, penetrates, and promotes forward all of our cognitional operations. It is the principle which awakens questioning. It draws the objects, events, and characteristics of ordinary living out of their initial contexts and into the context of elemental wonder. It frees the subject's memory and anticipation, conation and imagination, from the routines of practical living and enlists them in the service of intelligent questioning. Again, it is the pure desire to know which promotes the subject from the level of intelligent formulation to the level of rational judgment. It is the principle which raises and sustains the critical question—is it so? It guides reflective understanding, the marshalling and weighing of evidence, and the rationally proceeding judgment. Finally, it is the pure desire to know which orients us beyond all present cognitional achievements towards the distant goal of the totality of being.

The pure desire to know is an unrestricted intention of being. Aquinas affirmed that man is a potency in the realm of intellectual substances; Lonergan affirms that the pure desire to know is only a desire. If we are to fulfill that unrestricted intention, to actuate that infinite potency, to satisfy that pure desire, we must first turn towards the sensible world. Consequently, the pure desire to know is more than an immanent principle guiding cognitional operations to perfection; it is a principle that leads us from ignorance to knowledge. It is the intention of being.

The intellectually converted subject recognizes in the object of sensation, not what he or she wants to know, but the material basis for what he or she wants to know. The subject regards the sensible object, neither as real nor unreal, neither as a being nor as a non-being. The sensible object is data for understanding, the material for insight. Again, the intellectually converted subject recognizes in the single insight, in the clustering of insights, and in the discoveries of science, not what he or she intends to know, but the intelligibility that might be relevant to what he or she intends to know. The subject regards the idea, the theorem, and the system, neither as true nor false, neither as facts nor as errors. All formulations of direct understanding are merely hypotheses which stand in need of verification. The intellectually converted subject recognizes in the products of understanding, in his or her conditioned formulations, the material basis for the reflective question—is it so?

The unrestricted intention of being reaches a partial but actual fulfillment in the act of judgment. In this life, our acts of understanding are always conditioned. They are always acts with respect to some determinate content. We do not purely and simply understand; we understand something. Thus, one aspect of our rational nature is the fact that we must proceed piecemeal, one step at a time, accumulating and combining individual insights. We understand first one thing, then another, until both insights are integrated in a higher viewpoint. The unrestricted intention of being can provide a criterion or standard for our developing understanding because, although the unrestricted intention is not itself knowledge, it is an anticipation of the act through which knowledge is achieved. It is an anticipation of the act of cognitional self-transcendence. In the act of reflective understanding, the intellectually converted subject actuates that anticipation—whets his or her appetite. In the act of judgment, the intellectually converted subject partially but actually satisfies that unrestricted intention of being.

Intellectual conversion reverses the dominance of the object over intentionality.[15] Initially, the subject is ignorant. The subject knows neither about elementary objects nor about himself or herself. Still, the first order of business is to learn about one's immediate environment. The self-knowledge of the subject is a later development. The subject masters elementary objects and it is through the understanding of elementary objects that the subject can begin to understand himself or herself, his or her acts of understanding, and his or her intentionality. Chronologically speaking, however, knowledge of objects precedes and is the condition for the self-knowledge of subjects.

As intellectual development goes forward, there occurs a reversal or shift in priorities. For example, the interests of the beginning student and the interests of the scholarly exegete are different. "The student reads a text to learn about the objects that as yet he does not know. . . . On the other hand, the exegete may already know all about the objects treated in the text, yet his whole task remains to be performed."[16] The exegete reads the text to learn about the intentions that informed the context within which the text as a whole is to be understood. Thus, the student reads Aquinas to learn about grace; the exegete reads Aquinas to understand his struggle to order scriptural and traditional data in terms of general and specific theological theorems. The former is interested in the objects Aquinas expounded. The latter is interested in the intentions behind Aquinas' manner of proceeding.

Again, critical historical investigation offers a powerful example of the reversal in the dominance of object over intentionality. First, the historian takes as an object "the remains of the past perceptible in the present."[17] The task is to understand these objects. However, the reconstruction of the meaning of scraps of historical data leads, not to historical knowledge, but to historical experience. Secondly, the historian reconstructs from any number of imaginatively reconstructed experiences, the contexts of historical understanding and knowledge. The second historical procedure—from historical experience to historical knowledge—is not guided by a mere second look at the remains of the past. It is primarily guided by the intentionality of the historian. It is guided by the historian's previously acquired historical knowledge, by the cumulative work of other historians bearing on the same topic, and most significantly, by the intelligent and reflective questions which the historian can ask. Indeed, once the historian has understood the right questions to ask, the perceptible objects can be shifted to a broader and richer context. More and more, historical inquiry is dominated by the historians's intentionality, as expressed in questioning, rather than by the initial perceptible objects.

Hermeneutical and historical investigations reveal how human intentionality becomes ascendant over the object. However, exegetes and historians are not cognitional theorists and what is implied by actual scholarly performance need not be explicitly reflected upon. More generally, intellectual conversion is a discovery of the significance of the pure desire to know, that is, the unrestricted intention of being. It is that intention which ultimately determines the contexts within which objects have meaning. Certainly, we must first learn about the objects. Only after some knowledge of the objects can we proceed through the act of understanding to the knowledge of the subject. However, intellectual conversion reverses this priority. It liberates the subject from an infantile fixation on the object, the merely given, the already-out-there-now-real. Intellectual conversion awakens the subject to the pure desire to know. It actuates the unrestricted intention of being. The intellectually converted subject still seeks to understand data and to reach results by appeal to the data; but the contexts within which data are apprehended, understood, and verified are contexts created by a subject who understands precisely what he or she is doing when he or she is knowing.[18]

In summary, the pure desire to know is the unrestricted intention of being. Intellectual conversion grasps the significance of this identity. It is a psychological fact that we desire to know; it is an epistemological fact that what we desire to know is being. Thus, to desire to know is to intend being. The intention of being provides the criterion or standards to which our judgments must measure up. Although the intention of being is not a knowledge of what being must be, it is an anticipation of the act through which knowledge of being is achieved—the act of cognitional self-transcendence. Again, the pure desire to know determines what any particular judgment means;[19] it guides the development of understanding. Through the process of question and answer, it constructs the contexts within which data are understood. Accordingly, intellectual conversion is a grasp of our potential to understand what an object means and to judge whether or not that understanding is correct.

Other Interpretations

I have presented my own views of the notion of conversion in as brief an account as possible. Religious conversion moves the subject into an horizon wherein God's unrestricted love is ascendant over the fact of death. Moral conversion moves the subject into an horizontal wherein the unrestricted desire for freedom is ascendant over mere satisfactions. Intellectual convesion moves the subject into an horizon wherein the pure desire to know and the intention of being are ascendant over the objects of extroverted consciousness. Further aspects of the notion of conversion and its foundational role in theological method can be brought out by contrasting these views with those of other interpreters. Consequently, I shall present and comment upon interpretations offered by Fr. Charles E. Curran, Fr. Karl Rahner, Professor Walter E. Conn, and Fr. David Tracy.

Fr. Charles Curran

In a paper written for the 1970 International Lonergan Congress, Fr. Curran discussed Lonergan's notion of conversion.[20] Positively, he proposed a twofold distinction in the basic notion of conversion: an intellectual conversion and a general existential conversion with moral, religious, and Christian aspects. Negatively, he questioned the reality of the distinction between moral and religious conversion in the concrete order. Accordingly, I shall expand a bit on Fr. Curran's points and suggest responses I believe to be consistent with Lonergan's positions.

Fr. Curran proposed to unite moral, religious, and Christian conversion into a general type of existential conversion. His reasons for this proposal are: 1) an understanding of conversion in terms of a movement away from sin and evil; and 2) an insistence on our need for grace, not only on the level of religious living, but also on the level of moral living. Fr. Curran contends that "sin is not primarily an act but a condition affecting or even severing man's multiple relationships"[21] with God, with his neighbor, with himself, and with the world. He understands moral, religious, and Christian conversions as various aspects of our struggle to overcome this radically sinful condition. Further, Fr. Curran contends that in the abstract, one can distinguish between moral and religious activity; however in the concrete, not only our religious self-transcendence, but even our moral self-transcendence requires God's grace. Consequently, in order to transcend our sinful situation, we need God's grace in the form of an existential conversion with moral, religious, and Christian aspects. Only such a broadly conceived conversion, he argues, is proportionate to the diverse aspect of the problem of human sinfulness.

Lonergan understands the notion of religious conversion differently. He does not understand it chiefly in terms of a movement away from sin. Instead, he emphasizes the positive side of the notion. In his dissertation, he worked out his basic ideas on religious conversion in terms of the relations between God's grace and human freedom. Certainly, we need grace to overcome sinfulness, but more important, we need it to attain our transcendent finality. In the dissertation, Lonergan had reflected on Aquinas' formulation of the issue.

> Hence, in the state of the integrity of nature, man needs a gratuitous strength superadded to natural for one reason, viz., in order to do and will supernatural good; but in the state of corrupted nature he needs it for two reasons, viz., in order to be healed and, furthermore, in order to carry out works of supernatural virtue, which are meritorious. Beyond this, in both states man needs the divine help that he may be moved to act well.[22]

Here we can recall Aquinas' use of various theological theorems: the states of human liberty, the theorem of the supernatural, and the division of graces. While it is true that in our fallen state we need graces in order to be healed and to be restored to our natural perfection; God's grace extends beyond that. As St. Paul says: "The gift itself considerably outweighs the fall" (Rom. 5:15). For Lonergan, religious conversion is God's gift of love, a gift far outweighing the offense of sin. It not only restores us from the state of corrupted nature to the state of the integrity of nature; it further elevates us into true union with God. In *Grace and Freedom*, the meaning of religious conversion is worked out in terms of the distinction between human liberty and divine aid. The underlying unity of this distinction is not the movement from sin, but the movement towards union with God.

Lonergan also understands the distinction between the religious and the moral orders differently. Again, we can recall his work on the development of the theology of grace. Specifically, we should recall the theorem of the supernatural. Lonergan explains:

> About the year 1230 Philip the Chancellor completed a discovery that in the next forty years released a whole series of developments. The discovery was a distinction between two entitatively disproportionate orders: grace was above nature; faith was above reason; charity was above human good will; merit before God was above the good opinion of one's neighbors. This distinction and organization made it possible (1) to discuss the nature of grace without discussing liberty (2) to discuss the nature of liberty without discussing grace and (3) to work out the relations between grace and liberty.[23]

Consequently, as grace is above nature and charity above human good will, so too the religious order is above the moral order. Further, these distinctions pertain to the theoretical theology of Aquinas, but I believe that Lonergan maintains their intention in his methodical approach to theology. In that later context, he distinguishes between, on the one hand, a dimension of holiness characterized by joy and peace, and other-worldly love, and on the other hand, a dimension of self-constitution wherein one makes oneself into a good or a bad person.[24]

Fr. Curran is aware of these distinctions. He contends, however, that in the real, concrete and existential order the moral and religious levels interpenetrate. In the concrete, there is only one important problem—human sinfulness, and in the concrete there is only one adequate solution—God's grace in the form of a general existential conversion. However, Lonergan is also aware of the concrete; he writes:

> In the long term and in the concrete the real alternatives remain charity and cupidity, the elect and the *massa damnata*. But the whole problem lies in the abstract, in human thinking. . . .[25]

Lonergan and Fr. Curran seem to agree: in the concrete the real alternatives are an existential acceptance or rejection of God's grace, conversion or damnation. There is, however, I believe, an ambiguity about terms like "the real," "the concrete," and "the existential."

Lonergan agrees that the distinction between the moral and the religious realm lies in the abstract. However, the abstract is unreal only insofar as one refuses to understand abstraction as grasping what is most significant about the data, the thing, or the situation.[26] Human thinking is unreal only insofar as one overlooks the fact that human thinking is intentional: by our thinking we intend to know some aspect of being. Existential thought is itself an enrichment, as long as one does not simply brush aside more traditional and more technical, philosophic, and theological problems.

Lonergan does not propose to brush aside the gains of earlier theological labors. He wholeheartedly accepts the accomplishments of medieval theoretical theology. It represented an advance over an even earlier theology which was unable to deal with the more technical problems which spontaneously arose. However, given the task of *aggiornamento,* Lonergan has pressed to move beyond the gains of theoretical theology and into the enterprise of a methodological theology. He invites us to do for our age what Aquinas did for his.

Thus Lonergan distinguishes between intellectual, moral, and religious conversion. These are distinctions within his conception of a methodical theology. In daily living, they are not ultimate distinctions. In daily living the primary distinction, I believe, is between converted and unconverted people. Secondarily, we can ask about the degree to which conversion has penetrated into and been integrated with the totality of their living.

Although the threefold distinction of conversion belongs to the context of methodical theology, it is not to be regarded as simply irrelevant to the concrete existential order. From the methodical point of view, the concrete existential order is not some ultimate court of appeal. It is not the standard or criterion of reality. That standard or criterion is still the true judgment. Consequently, theological method begins by reflecting upon the facts from the past which have contributed to constitute the present concrete situation. It continues on, however, to consider what is authentic or unauthentic in the present concrete situation; what needs to be retained and what needs to be transformed. Thus, theological method provides the reflective principle for the Church as a community engaged in a process of self-constitution. Theological method provides the reflective principle which can guide the very transformation of our concrete existential situation.

The distinction between moral and religious conversion is primarily reflective in nature. It was based on the distinction of an earlier theoretical theology but is maintained within the context of methodical theology. Nevertheless, its relevance to the existential order, I believe, will take the form of allowing the human sciences—psychology, sociology, economics, etc.—to work out their own terms and relations. They operate on the moral level of human freedom. Religious conversion will be relevant by pointing out that regardless of what appears, human beings possess potentially infinite intellects, are constituted by freedom and dignity, and exist in a loving relationship with the origin and destiny of the universe. Thus the moral realm is the realm of human self-constitution and an enlightened human science should be part of that enterprise. Nevertheless, God has entered history; he has entered into community with humans, and he has entered into persons' lives. It is only his gift of Himself to mankind which can save it from idolatry and related forms of self-destruction.

In conclusion, I believe Lonergan's distinctions among intellectual, moral and religious conversion must be understood as part of his intention to move ahead to a contemporary method for theology. I believe that Fr. Curran's proposal of a single existential conversion with moral, religious, and Christian aspects would contribute to a less differentiated theological situation. If religious conversion entirely depends on God's grace, as Fr. Curran correctly maintains, and if there is no real distinction between religious and moral conversion, as he incorrectly maintains; then have we not reintroduced the problems which troubled the monks at Hadrumentum in St. Augustine's time: if everything depends on God's grace, what is the point of human freedom and effort?[27]

Fr. Karl Rahner

Fr. Rahner has offered some thoughts[28] on an article by Lonergan entitled "Functional Specialties in Theology."[29] This article contained what is now the fifth chapter in *Method in Theology*. Fr. Rahner contended that if Lonergan's exposition of the functional specialties in theology was supposed to present the method which is uniquely suitable for theological procedure, then it was incomplete. He writes: "Lonergan's theological methodology seems to me to be *so generic that it really fits every science,* and hence is not the methodology of theology as such. . . ."[30] Some aspects of Fr. Rahner's objection were addressed when the full text of *Method in Theology* appeared a few years later. Still, as might be expected, Fr. Rahner's point was incisive and it is fruitful to consider its implications.

Fr. Rahner formulates his reservation concerning Lonergan's notion of theological method in several ways. He is most concerned, however, about the absence of a specifically theological principle. He writes: "The words 'God' and 'Jesus Christ' do indeed appear in his article, but only as designations of the material objects with which the science of theology, as distinct from other sciences is occupied, not as words from whose content the peculiarity of theological method as such must be determined, and which, therefore, designate something like formal objects of theology (or, in the unity of the two, *the* formal object of theology)."[31] Fr. Rahner is looking for the aspect of Lonergan's theological method which reveals its specifically theological and Christological character. The fact that Lonergan's method uses the words "God" and "Jesus Christ" as material for reflection is not good enough. Fr. Rahner insists that the words "God" and "Jesus Christ" must serve not just as the materials reflected upon, but also by somehow informing the mode of reflection. He does not discern this in Lonergan's exposition of the functional specialties in theology.

Lonergan agreed with Fr. Rahner's appraisal of his article on functional specialties. He responded simply: "The incompleteness of the chapter on functional specialties only shows that one is not trying to say in one chapter what one hopes to convey in a dozen."[32] Further, when Fr. Rahner first encountered the article on functional specialties, it was presented as the intended second chapter of *Method in Theology*—the first chapter being on transcendental method in general. Fr. Rahner correctly concluded that, if these two chapters represented Lonergan's basic views on theological method, then Lonergan did not attach much foundational significance to religion. At the First International Lonergan Congress, Lonergan commented: "That chapter on functional specializations is not going to be chapter two (as was said a year and a half ago when I sent the paper to *Gregorianum*), it's chapter five now. The four background chapters are 'Method,' 'The Human Good,' 'Meaning,' and 'Religion.'"[33] It is through those four background chapters that Lonergan links his basic notion of transcendental method to religion.

Lonergan understands religion in terms of conversion. Religion is "conversion in its preparation, in its occurrence, in its development, in its consequent, and also, alas, in its incompleteness, its failures, its breakdowns, its disintegration."[34] More important for the present question, Lonergan understands conversion as the specifically theological principle of theological method. Let us recall the distinctions among the material, the formal, and the actual foundations of theological method. The specifically theological principle is not located on the level of the materials reflected upon: "since the sources to be subjected to research are not specified, they could be the sacred books and tradition of any religion."[35] Again, the specifically theological principle is not located on the level of the formal mode of reflection, e.g., the dynamic structure of the eight functional specialities. Fr. Rahner is quite correct when he reports to have found no specifically theological principle on this level. Lonergan concurs: "Clearly functional specialties as such are not specifically theological. Indeed the eight specialties we have listed would be relevant to any human science that investigated a cultural past to guide its future."[36] Instead, the specifically theological principle is located in religious conversion. Lonergan writes: "It is not knowledge of religious conversion, interpretation of the psychological phenomena of conversion, propositions concerning conversion. It is simply the reality of the transformation named conversion."[37] Moreover, the specifically theological principle for Lonergan is conversion in the sense that theological method and theological reflection are conceived as actual parts of the subject's and the community's historical transformation and movement into God.

Although the specifically theological principle is properly located in the actual foundations of theological method, it is also related to the formal foundations. Lonergan formally grounds theological method in human subjectivity—a subjectivity understood in terms of the intentional dynamism of the transcendental notions. The transcendental notions underpin, guide and promote the subject toward its intended objectives and onto successively higher levels of consciousness. As Lonergan notes, they are principles of movement and of rest: of movement, as arousing the subject out of indifference and into a state of inquiry, reflection and the pursuit of values; of rest, as guiding the subject to answers and goals and providing the criteria that reveal when objectives have been satisfactorily reached. Grounding the successive transcendental notions is an ultimate principle of movement and rest: the dynamic state of other-worldly love. Thus, for example, the transcendental notion of truth guides us to knowledge of being; but why do we want to know being? Because being is good. And again, why is being good? Because it is grounded in God's love and it is through our loving that we are united to that love and at peace with ourselves. Accordingly, the intentional dynamism which grounds the successive transcendental notions is the dynamic state of love.

Lonergan has linked religion and the transcendental notions. However, we should note the nature of the link. He has linked them in an explanatory framework. First, we needed to understand how the single transcendental notion guides the subject and provides the criterion for operation. Secondly, we needed to grasp how the dynamism of the transcendental notions promotes the subject from lower to higher levels of consciousness. Thirdly, we needed to begin to conceive an ultimate dynamic state, both a principle of movement and of rest, which underpins, guides, and promotes the subject towards transcendent mystery. This is the order of exposition. On a similar point, Lonergan remarks:

> In an order of exposition I would prefer to explain first intellectual, then moral, then religious conversion. In order of occurrence I would expect religious commonly but not necessarily to precede moral and both religious and moral to precede intellectual.[38]

As an occurrence, religious conversion is extremely simple. One is filled with love. However, remaining faithful to that love, making it the center of one's life, and integrating it with all of life's various aspects, may demand a certain formation and perhaps reformation. Because it is one's spontaneity that needs to be scrutinized and reordered, one might find oneself engaged in a good deal of intellectual reflection. This is an approximation. I am merely trying to suggest how closely these successive levels of conscious living connect. Consequently, in the order of occurrence, religious conversion and the transcendental notions are linked rather naturally and spontaneously; in the order of exposition, one must successively formulate and integrate ever higher intelligibilities into the integrated whole of a higher viewpoint.

The transcendental notions as the formal foundations of theological method are immediately related to the dynamic state of other-worldly love. They are related as potency to act;

as, for example, general willingness to actual willing. Lonergan defines the dynamic state of love as "the habitual actuation of man's capacity for self-transcendence."[39] It is the first principle of the subject's acts of self-transcendence. In the context of theological method, it is the first principle of theological operations.

Fr. Rahner's question reemerges. Where are the Theological and Christological principles? If the dynamic state of other-worldly love is the actual foundation of Lonergan's theological method, what is its Theological and Christological character? Again, if the dynamic state of other-worldly love grounds, not theological objects, but theological operations, then what are the Theological and Christological characteristics of the operations? Fr. Rahner is asking how Lonergan's method is a specifically Theological and Christological way of proceeding. He is asking, I believe, not for a method of theology, but for a theology of method.

Method in Theology does not specifically address this question. Lonergan's chief concern in that book is with theological method and not with theology proper. While the two realities cannot be separated, neither can one do everything at the same time. Consequently, Lonergan explains in the Introduction, "I am writing not theology but method in theology. I am not concerned with the objects that theologians expound but with the operations that theologians perform."[40] Nevertheless, now that *Method in Theology* has been in print for more than a decade and now that Lonergan's formulation of theological method has come to fruition, may we not begin to reflect on method and ask: if this is a fruitful way for human beings to proceed when pursuing specifically theological answers, what does such a method imply about the kind of universe we live in, about its origin and destiny, and about its properly human dimension of existing?

Before answering this question, let me summarize my analysis thus far. Fr. Rahner asked for the Theological and Christological character of Lonergan's theological method. He did not find it in Lonergan's exposition of the functional specialties. This is understandable because for Lonergan the functional specialties are determinations of the transcendental notions and pertain to the formal foundations of theological method. The specifically theological principle of Lonergan's theological method is located on the level of actual foundations—religious conversion as the transformation of the subject by the dynamic state of other-worldly love. Still, such a principle would need to be reflected upon before we could draw out its Theological and Christological character. Lonergan has done this himself to some extent. I shall indicate what I believe to be some fruitful areas for reflection.

First, there is an analogy between the methodical movement from data to results and Lonergan's notion of the procession of persons in the Trinity. The procession from data to results is a process of coming to understand successive levels of objects and through such successive acts of understanding, coming to understand understanding itself. Upon that heightened possession of itself, theological method pivots to communicate its self-understanding and self-evaluation to successively more determinate levels. Lonergan compares this methodical process to the Trinitarian processions:

> Now in God the origin is the Father, in the New Testament name *Theos,* who is identified with *agape* (1 John 4:18, 16). Such love expresses itself in its Word, its *logos,* its *verbum spirans amorem,* which is a judgment of value. The judgment of value is sincere, and so it grounds the Proceeding Love that is identified with the Holy Spirit.[41]

Thus, Lonergan's entire conception of methodical proceeding is stamped with a Trinitarian character.

Secondly, there is an analogy between the methodical movement from dialectic to foundations and the dramatic movement of the passion, death, and resurrection of Jesus Christ. In the functional specialty dialectic, one focuses on the unresolved conflicts immanent in religious living, opposed histories, and opposed theological interpretations. In the functional specialty foundations, the dialectical tensions are transcended as one moves into the integrating horizon of other-worldly love. Oversimplified as my formulation is, I believe, we can discern in Jesus Christ an acceptance of the sins and evils of the world in order to transcend them and transform them in a loving openness and obedience to transcendent Mystery. As Aquinas maintained that the truths of faith found the apex of their intelligibility in the transcendence of God; Lonergan locates, I believe, the synthetic principle which integrates and unifies theological operations in the paschal mystery immanent in the minds, the souls, and hearts of theologians.

Thirdly, there is an analogy between the guidance provided by the theological principle of conversion and the guidance provided by the Holy Spirit. The functional specialty foundations objectifies the theologian's orientation to mystery. However, the movement of self-transcendence into transcendent Mystery is not an easily isolated element of consciousness. In the marketplace of ideas, there are more attractive and ready to use norms for operation. There are less intractable standards of procedure than conversion—a principle which like the Holy Spirit moves wherever it pleases. I believe that the choice of conversion as the foundation of method is based in a deep rooted faith in the efficacy of the Holy Spirit. The general bias of common sense is a short-sighted practicality; it would mistake for wisdom some more easily manipulated criterion.

In conclusion, Fr. Rahner's response to Lonergan's article on functional specialties is brief. Its implications, however, are extensive. He pointed out the absence of a theological principle on the formal level. This led me to consider a theological principle on the actual level of foundations. It led me to consider how conversion operates as such a principle.

Walter E. Conn

Professor Conn has done important work on Lonergan's notion of moral conversion. In an essay offered for the *Festschrift* in honor of Lonergan's seventy-fifth birthday, Professor Conn compared the notion of moral conversion to Lawrence Kohlberg's theory of moral development.[42] In the course of his essay, he focused on Kohlberg's sixth stage of moral reasoning—the self-chosen universal ethical principle orientation— and discussed how Lonergan's notion of moral conversion could elucidate the properly existential character of this stage.

Professor Conn distinguishes two types of moral conversion. First, critical moral conversion is a shift from the horizon wherein one decides on the basis of values. The key factor which makes such a shift critical is that it originates in the realization that "it is up to each of us to decide for himself what he is to make of himself."[43] In other words, the moral subject must recognize himself or herself, through his or her self-transcending choices of value, as the criterion for the truly good. Second, uncritical moral conversion is also a shift in the criterion for decision. One moves from the standpoint of choosing based on satisfactions to the standpoint of choosing based on values. The key factor which makes such a shift uncritical is that it originates, not in the critical acceptance of oneself as the judge of what is or is not worthwhile, but in the uncritical acceptance of "a *given* set of values, be they given by parents, church, peers, 'society,' or whomever."[44] Professor Conn maintains that such a shift is a real conversion from satisfactions to values but it presupposes no understanding of the role of the subject in establishing values. Accordingly, both critical and uncritical moral conversion involves shifts from satisfactions to values, but the former presupposes insight into the importance of self-chosen values while the latter does not.

On my interpretation of moral conversion, it is a shift into the horizon of the transcendental notion of value. More specifically, it is a decision about the value of decisions. To move into the horizon of the transcendental notion of value is not to apprehend some categorical value. Again, to decide for the worthwhileness making decisions is not to realize some particular good. Instead, the transcendental notion of value is the ground of all categorical values and the act of decision is the active principle of all particular realizations of the good. Chronologically, we might expect a person to respond first to vital values, then to social values, then to cultural values, and so on. However, as the person develops and is able to respond to ever higher values, the person is not only involved in higher dimensions of values; he or she is also becoming more fully conscious of the unrestricted intentionality of the transcendental notion of value. Moral conversion would occur when the subject realizes that what he or she truly desires is, not this or that particular object, nor this or that subjective satisfaction, but that which is partially realized in each responsible decision and would be fully realized in the totality of all responsible decisions. Moral conversion is a shift into the unrestricted horizon of the transcendental notion of value.

In my interpretation of the notion of conversion in general, the key factor is the act. Intellectual conversion is the act of judgement about the significance of judging. Moral conversion is the act of decision concerning the value of deciding. Religious conversion is the act of loving the unrestricted act of love. In each case, the act fulfills a twofold role. First, it perfects the subject; that is, it is the principle which actuates the subject's capacities. For example, the act of judgment brings thinking to fruition; the act of decision brings deliberation and evaluation to a term; the act of loving fulfills our very being. Secondly, it brings the subject into the horizon of the know-unknown. The subject does not know God, but he or she knows the act whereby God will be known. The subject does not know absolute goodness, but he or she knows the act whereby such goodness will be realized. The subject does not know all being, but he or she knows the act whereby being will be known. In each case, the act is a modality of the act of self-transcendence. Once one is in possession of that criterion—the act whereby the transcendent is known, valued, and loved—there occurs a conversion. Prior to conversion, specific contents conditioned the emergence of the subject's acts; subsequent to conversion, the normative act determines the specific contents.

Conversion is a shift in dominance from content to act. Let us consider two examples. Perhaps the most precise illustration of this point is to be found in the structure of *Insight*. The transition from the first part of the book, "Insight as Activity," to the second part of the book, "Insight as Knowledge," is a shift from content arranged in order to produce certain cognitive acts to cognitive acts methodically guiding the ordering of content. A second and broader illustration is to be found in the methodical understanding of the significance of traditions. Tradition forms the person until he or she arrives at the point where he or she begins to form himself or herself. Insofar as tradition is a communal and historical fund of wisdom, it can be the chief formative influence in a person's life. Insofar as a person is called to conversion, tradition must be transcended. At this point, what becomes normative is, not some cognitional content nor some moral rule, but the act of self-transcendence.

Indeed, traditions can point out their own limitations when they insist that what is most important is loving God and neighbor.

The priority of act over content is not a chronological characteristic. One does not simply spend the first half of one's life unthinkingly absorbing a tradition and the second half criticizing all prereflective thought forms. Without the content of the tradition the normative act has no material basis from which to emerge and without the act of self-transcendence the tradition is not properly realized. The priority of act over content can be understood in terms of intentionality analysis. Children are not expected to fully comprehend the intentions informing the rituals, the stories, and the precepts to which they are introduced. Only as they grow do they come to partially understand the intentions behind their cultural context and even behind their own personal living and doing. Adults are more fully aware of the intentions behind thinking, living, and doing. However, even as they are more aware of intentionality, they are also aware of how profoundly intentionality falls short of its objectives. Adults know that there is a gap between good intentions and good performance; they know of their own limitations, the imperfections of their community, and the wickedness in their history. Nevertheless, between the innocence of childhood and the knowledge of adulthood, conversion can occur.

There is a radical difference between the consciousness that does not realize its own intentionality and the intentionality that is fully conscious of itself. The child is innocent; it does not comprehend the dimensions of its developing aggression and affection. It does not know what its development intends. The adult is not innocent and for two reasons. In conversion, he or she has personally identified with the unrestricted intentionality of the transcendental notions. Thus to withdraw from that full openness to the transcendent is to betray his or her inmost heart. Second, the adult does not operate in a vacuum. Besides the unrestricted intentionality of the transcendental notions, there are concrete factors—physical, psychological, intellectual, sociological, historical—which *de facto* conspire to restrict the act of self-transcendence. For example, one truly desires to help one's neighbor, but that desire is strangled by factors of economic and sociological differences, by fears and suspicion, and so on. In short, the adult who is fully conscious of his or her intentionality must recognize: (1) that he or she truly desires something transcendent; and (2) that immanent within the self, the community, and history are conscious dynamisms which prevent the realization of that desire.

The significance of conversion is that it reverses the priority of consciousness over intentionality. For the child, consciousness is first and it must learn before it can come to understand its intentionality. For the adult, for someone awakened to the unrestrictedness his or her intentionality, intentionality is a first principle and personal, social, and historical consciousness must be transformed according to its norms.

On this analysis, the horizon of the morally converted subject is determined by the act which realizes its own intentionality. It is a critical act in the sense that it proceeds from a reflective self-possession. However, it is not a critical act in the sense that it proceeds from an intelligent grasp and reasonable affirmation of what is meant by value. Indeed, as there is no datum from which we could derive an insight into what is meant by being; so too, there is no content from which we could derive an understanding of what is meant by value. Both notions, in my interpretation of Lonergan's view, admit of only second order definitions. Being is what would be known by the totality of true judgments. Value is what would be realized by the totality of responsible decisions. Accordingly, what Professor Conn writes of in terms of uncritical moral conversion, I conceive of as a consciousness which is unaware of its own moral intentionality.

Professor Conn maintains that critical moral conversion presupposes an implicit intellectual conversion. Intellectual conversion is the discovery of the self-transcendence proper to the human process of coming to know.[45] He calls such an intellectual conversion implicit because it need not involve the explicitly formulated philosophical arguments and notions one finds in *Insight*. However, a critical moral conversion must involve the subject's recognition of himself or herself as the criterion of the truly good. Such a moral recognition, as I understand Professor Conn's point, implies the corresponding cognitional recognition of the subject as the criterion of the real as well. On this basis, critical moral conversion implies a kind of intellectual conversion. Inversely, an uncritical moral conversion is a turn to values, not as mediated by the self-appropriation of the moral subject, but as mediated by someone else. Relating uncritical moral conversion to earlier stages in Kohlberg's six stage theory of development, Professor Conn writes:

> In fact, it is very "natural" for the younger or older adolescent to turn from excessive concern with obedience/punishment and pragmatic self-interest to a genuine desire to be and to do good, interpersonally and socially. Because of the developmental limitations of the adolescent's affective and cognitive resources, however, the desired good, while understood as value rather than satisfaction, is identified uncritically in terms of interpersonal and social givens, as we have seen.[46]

Thus, the uncritical morally converted subject overlooks the necessity of critically grounding values in his or her own acts of evaluation and decision. The critical morally converted subject realizes that as identifying the real with the already-out-there-now is inadequate, so too identifying the good with the already-established-interpersonal-and-social-given is uncritical. Consequently, Professor Conn emphasizes the profound identity between intellectual and moral conversion.

In my interpretation of the development of the notion of conversion, there is a significant difference between the critical exigence and the methodical exigence. The unity and the distinction of intellectual and moral conversion can most fruitfully be understood in terms of the methodical rather than the critical exigence of meaning. The critical exigence pertains to the problem of mediating subjects and objects. It is basically a problem involving the cognitive function of meaning.[47] There are realms of common sense and there are realms of theory. Objects in one realm cannot be understood in terms of objects in other realms. However, both realms include real objects and some way of unifying and differentiating these various realms must be found. Lonergan's answer to this problem came to fruition in *Insight*. He sought to answer three key questions: what am I doing when I am knowing? why is doing that knowing? what do I know when I do it?[48] Of course, the answer is extremely complicated because one needs a full and nuanced account of human knowing in its many realms. The single aspect which is relevant to the present context, however, is the role of reflection. Reflective understanding with its rationally proceeding judgment is the criterion for the real, no matter what realm of meaning one happens to be operating in. It is reflective understanding which grasps the virtually unconditioned. Consequently, the critical problem is profound, but in my view, Lonergan adequately addresses it in his analysis of the act of human reflection.

The methodical exigence of meaning pertains to the self-constitution of persons, communities, and traditions. It is basically a problem involving the constitutive and effective functions of meaning. Before the individual becomes a person—in the sense of one who is reflective and autonomous—he or she must be formed in some tradition. However, if the crucial moment in moral development arises when the subject discovers the potentialities of his or her own act and especially his or her act of decision; nevertheless some traditional and contemporary carriers of meaning are conducive to such an act of self-discovery and autonomy and some not. For example, political systems that depend on fear and coercion must ultimately suppress the need for moral self-determination in their populations. Again, economic systems that rely on the push and pull of pre-reflective mechanisms must ultimately work against the emergence of reflective consciousness in consumers. Accordingly, in the cognitive function of meaning, we can find the material on which to reflect and thereby discover who we are. In the constitutive and effective functions of meaning, we can find the actual tensions which promote or hinder the act of reflection itself. Again, besides the development of the data on which to reflect, there is the development of the conditions of reflection itself as an act. The methodical exigence pertains to the ordering of data so as to most fully actuate the power of human reflection.

Intellectual conversion underscores the critical office of human reflection. Moral conversion underscores the methodical function of the act of self-transcendence. Intellectual conversion overcomes an intellectual problem. How do we know?

Moral conversion overcomes a moral problem. How does one order one's moral life so as to remain faithful to one's pursuit of value? If the critical exigence makes reflection central, moral conversion is concerned with the concrete factors which allow reflection to more fully emerge. Each act of moral self-transcendence, not only perfects the subject by actuating his or her potential, it also transforms the immediate environment. The significance of this second factor is that further acts of self-transcendence, for both the subject and for other subjects, become proximately more possible. For example, in a marital quarrel both partners are hurt. As one overcomes his or her fear and suspicion, his or her desire for vengeance and dominance, and as that person reaches out in an authentic desire for reconciliation, not only is that person constituting himself or herself as more capable of self-donation, but he or she is also creating the intersubjective environment for the other person's self-transcendence. Consequently, the entire context begins to be determined by a reflective dynamism in which persons can emerge as free and giving rather than determined by a pre-reflective dynamism of attack and counter-attack.

On this analysis, moral conversion is a post-critical rather than a critical principle. Inasmuch as moral conversion is a matter of grasping the significance of the moral act, it is a critical principle. However, moral conversion is more. The chief reason that the moral subject must develop is because he or she is only potentially reflective and not actually reflective most of the time. The morally converted subject is aware of his or her own need to develop as well as the communal and historical factors conditioning personal development. Again, moral conversion is critical in the sense that it is an act which is aware of itself; however, moral conversion is post-critical in the sense that it is aware that the act of decision has *de facto* limitations. No one judgment and no one decision can actuate the fullness of human potentiality. Consequently, human development will call forth a succession of judgments and decisions, whose content can in no way be determined beforehand.

In moral conversion the subject grasps that he or she needs to develop. For this reason, the subject may search for a community to support his or her self-transformation. The subject may seek to deepen his or her understanding and appreciation of the tradition which nurtured him or her, in order to strengthen resolve. Thus, the person can realize that it is through one's decisions that one makes oneself into a good or a bad person and still desire to belong to a community and to a tradition whose values one does not fully comprehend. In conclusion, I would say that the critical exigence is met by an understanding of the foundational significance of human reflection; I would say that the methodical exigence is met by actually ordering concrete contents so that they readily promote rather than hinder the emergence of the act of reflection.

In summary, Professor Conn distinguishes between critical and uncritical moral conversion. The differentiating factor is the moral subject's recognition of himself or herself as the criterion of the truly good. I distinguish between a consciousness which is not yet aware of its transcendental moral intentionality and a consciousness which has become aware of its transcendental moral intentionality. Again, Professor Conn points out the identity of critical moral conversion and implicit intellectual conversion. I draw attention to the distinction between grasping the critical significance of the act of human reflection and discovering that the reflective power of the subject is itself in need of development.

Fr. David Tracy

In an article presented to the First International Lonergan Congress, Fr. Tracy raised several penetrating questions about the notion of conversion as a foundational principle.[49] His chief concern was to present his understanding of the contemporary foundational problem. In Fr. Tracy's view, the foundational problem for contemporary theology is twofold. The first aspect concerns the creation of an integrating structure for the diverse types of theological investigation operative in contemporary theology. The second aspect concerns the clarification of the grounds for theology as speech about God. Fr. Tracy wondered whether Lonergan's notion of conversion was sufficiently critical to meet this contemporary foundational problem.

Fr. Tracy was satisfied with Lonergan's conception of the functional specialization of theology. He believed that it did answer the need for an integrating structure for diverse theological investigations. He wrote: "This understanding of theology does permit the methodological collaboration of several disciplines and as such is a major contribution—and, in that precise methodological sense, a foundational one—to the entire theological community."[50] However, there is a further aspect to the foundational problem.

A contemporary foundation for theology must be critical. The notion of functional specialization, in Fr. Tracy's view "does not, however, provide critical grounds for the enterprise itself—more precisely, for the truth-value of the claims to ultimacy of religious and explicitly theological language."[51] Contemporary foundational theology should seek to establish the critical grounds for the entire theological enterprise; it should seek to clarify the conditions of the possibility for any speech about religion, about Jesus Christ, about God. Fr. Tracy wondered whether the notion of conversion was capable of providing such a critical basis.

In the functional specialty dialectic, the theologian encounters the conflicts of the Christian past. He or she meets the traditions, the beliefs, the movements of the past which have contributed to create the present theological and religious situation. The theologian is to decide among them on the basis of conversion. At this point, Fr. Tracy wondered how the theologian was converted in the first place. He writes: "But what of religious conversion? Is it mediated by dialectical reflection upon the results of earlier historical theology—thereby assuming (as a dogmatic affirmation) the truth-value of the data (presumably religious) interpreted and critically investigated by the historian?"[52] Again, Fr. Tracy raises a similar question with regard to the role of conversion in the functional specialty foundations. How is the conversion which foundations objectifies mediated in the first place? In his response to Fr. Tracy, Lonergan formulated the basic thrust of the question as: "Is foundations merely assumed or asserted and in that case dogmatic or, on the other hand, does foundations itself rest on earlier grounds that are critically evaluated?"[53] Finally, I take the basic thrust of Fr. Tracy's question to be: on what basis does the theologian make his or her personal decisions, claims, and statements about God?

In my interpretation, Lonergan's theological method addresses the contemporary foundational problem on three levels. On the material level, the problem is the integration of the advances of contemporary hermeneutics and history. On the formal level, the problem is the construction of the theological method which recognizes the realities of the subject as basic. On the actual level, the problem is the *de facto* limitations of actual concrete subjects—the need for development. I shall briefly comment on each of these foundational elements.

Contemporary hermeneutics and history introduce an array of specialists between the traditional dogmatic theologian and the sources.[54] Scriptural, patristic, and medieval manuscripts are submitted to empirical analyses. Successively more complex levels of organization are conceived in order to reconstruct the initial contexts in which texts were written. However, as competent as such scholarly investigations are, they need to be complemented in two manners. First, they need to be raised to the evaluative level. We need to add to an interpretation that understands a further interpretation that appreciates. We have to add to a history that grasps what was going forward, a history that evaluates achievements, that discerns good and evil.[55] Secondly, besides promoting the object of investigation on to a higher level, the investigators themselves need to be evaluated. The interpreter's self-understanding may or may not be sufficiently developed. The historian's standpoint may or may not be sufficiently cultured, discerning, or wise. Such subjective factors—e.g., the habitual core of insights and presuppositions—include basic philosophic and theological views, whether the scholar acknowledges them or not. Views on religious issues, on morality, and on cognitional theory influence the results of scholarly investigations, even though they properly fall under the competence of more basic inquiries. Thus, if contemporary hermeneutics and history are to be integrated within an overall theological method, we need a way to raise their investigations onto the evaluative level. We need to methodically deal with the issue of value judgments. Consequently, the foundational problem in its material aspect is a matter of integrating contemporary scholarship and such an integration will raise questions about the formal foundations of theological method.

On the formal level, the problem is constructing a theological method which makes the realities of the subject basic. Thus, Lonergan devoted years to "an exploration of methods generally in preparation for a study of method in theology."[56] It was his work in *Insight* which enabled him to investigate, appropriate, and critically explicate the actual performance of the subject. Although he investigated mathematics, empirical science, and common sense, his goal was something more simple and more profound—namely the operations of the subject which provide the condition of the possibility for all ideas, judgments, and decisions. His basic question was: what am I doing when I am knowing? When one can answer that question, one can return to the realms of common sense and theory, of history and philosophy, with a reflective self-possession which provides a critical control of all operations. One can understand, judge, and decide just where investigators in research, interpretation, and history have done their jobs well. One has a basis from which to "appreciate all that has been intelligent, true and good in the past even in the lives and thought of opponents."[57] Accordingly, formal foundations pertain to the *a priori* heuristic structure within which all intelligent, rational, and responsible procedures occur.

Transcendental method provides theology with its formal foundations. As Lonergan remarks: "It supplies the basic anthropological component."[58] It can be invoked to confirm every successful account of human procedure. Lonergan writes: "While transcendental method will introduce no new resource it does add considerable light and precision to the performance of theological tasks."[59] In my interpretation, transcendental method is an expression and objectification of the basic form of human existence and operation. It provides the formal foundations for a contemporary theology.

The foundational problem of theological method on the actual level is the need of theologians to develop. Again, the actual, permanent and radical problem which faces contemporary theology is the reign of original sin. Its specifically theological relevance is that theological operations, occurring in any of the eight functional specialities, are instances of self-transcendence. For example, the actual tension informing scholarly procedure is the effort to intentionally move beyond the initial horizon of the interpreter and into a new horizon which includes the significant features of the intentional context in which a text was conceived and written. But moving beyond one's initial horizon is a matter of raising and answering questions, or continually adverting to what one has not yet understood, or unreservedly surrendering to the pure desire to know; in other words, of cognitional self-transcendence. Cognitional self-transcendence is a difficult reality to isolate for inspection; it is an even more difficult reality to sustain in practice. Consequently, the actual problem facing theological foundations is the promotion of human self-transcendence.

Conversion is the foundational reality which meets and overcomes the actual foundational problem of sustained self-transcendence. The religiously converted subject is moved by an unrestricted state of being-in-love. The morally converted subject is motivated by an unrestricted desire for freedom. The intellectually converted subject is guided by a pure desire to know. Still, even in the case of a converted subject we must distinguish between desire, no matter how unrestricted, and actual performance. In the categories of medieval theoretical theology, besides conversion as an operative grace that turns the will radically towards God as a special end, there is the actual performance of the person which still requires the assistance of cooperative graces. In the categories of a contemporary theological method, besides the unrestricted state of being-in-love which is God's gift of Himself to us; there is the continuing effort of the converted subject to give himself or herself ever more fully over to that love. God's grace fills our hearts in religious conversion, but we must still overcome our fear of death; we must free ourselves from naive and merely extroverted views of reality. Nevertheless, we can affirm that conversion, as a turning towards God, is the foundational reality. It is an ever present norm which can be ever more fully realized.

There is always the danger when speaking of the actual foundations of theology to imagine that one is speaking of an awareness of conversion, an understanding of conversion, an idea of conversion, or a knowledge of conversion. However, it is the reality of conversion that is the actual foundation of theology. Thus, conversion is to be thought of, not as a reality separate from the subject, nor as a reality immanent in the subject. Instead, conversion is to be thought of as an ongoing reality which links the subject dynamically to God. Conversion initiates us, even in this life, into the life which we will more fully share after death. Moreover, conversion continually invites us beyond the present level of development. The objective towards which conversion pulls one is actual union with and transformation into God. Consequently, it is the tension between the immanent reality of the subject and the transcendent reality of God which provides the actual foundational reality for contemporary theological method.

Although the objective of union with God is high and distant, it is also somehow present in our ordinary living. It is even present in the routines of intellectual and scholarly procedure. Most evidently, it is present in the desire to understand, in the desire for the ecstasy of the act of reflective understanding, in the perseverance that sustains scholars in their arduous investigations, and in the historical and communal desire to know. More profoundly, it is present in the desire to contribute to the human good, to promote peace and justice, and to diminish fears and misunderstanding. These are high goals, quite beyond the horizons of the egoist and the ideologue. I believe it is reasonable to discern at the bottom of these desires an unrestricted love that shines deep in the person's heart. It is a love that is both a principle of movement and of rest. It is a love which even while sustaining us, urges us onward

Fr. Tracy seeks to uncover the basis from which we can authentically speak about God, about Jesus Christ, and about religion. I would locate this basis potentially in material foundations—the scripture and tradition; formally in the structure of human subjectivity, and actually in conversion. Initially, we must learn from scripture of the promises which God has made to us. For example, we have been promised the salvation that comes through Jesus Christ, the comfort of the Holy Spirit, and anything we ask for in the name of Jesus Christ from the Father. These are the data on which we must reflect. The meaning of these promises and the understanding of the words of scripture can be mediated via common sense reflections in devotion, via the terms and relations of a traditional theoretical theology, or via the tutored common sense of scholarly investigations.[60] However, a contemporary theology needs to be critical, so we must also mediate our understanding of scripture via the categories of a self-appropriated subjectivity. Most important, for contemporary needs is the actual basis from which theological and religious language originates—that is, self-transcendence. God's love is not meant to be merely a private possession. It overflows; it engages one in community and history. Thus, the actual basis from which theological language must originate is the personal, historical, and communal process of self-transformation into ever fuller union with God. It is in the crucible of personal existence, of community, and of history that we are to find the verification or refutation of our theological understanding.

There is a distinction between religion and theology. While both are promoted by authentic persons and their acts of self-transcendence, theology is primarily cognitive and religion is not. Nevertheless, whether in the realm of cognitive operations or in the realms of moral and religious performance, human wisdom is found in faith.[61] Every act of self-transcendence, including cognitive self-transcendence, demands a kind of faith. The kind of faith we need in theological performance is the ability to be open, to learn from others, to be willing to state our beliefs simply and straightforwardly, and to free ourselves from our fears, our biases, and our blind spots. While this kind of faith does not insure automatic progress, it is, I believe, a sufficient foundation for contemporary theology.

Conclusion

This interpretive investigation has traced the development of Lonergan's notion of conversion. The notion of conversion emerged into prominence in the later period when Lonergan selected it as the foundational reality of theological method. However, as this interpretive investigation has shown, Lonergan's thought on conversion had begun early and had undergone considerable development. In order to understand the notion of conversion in terms of the various contexts in which it was variously conceived, I distinguished among three periods in Lonergan's career. In the early period, Lonergan was chiefly concerned with investigating the realm of Thomist philosophical and theological theory. In the middle period, he moved behind all theory to the realm of cognitional interiority, to the subject as subject. In the later period, Lonergan returned from the realm of interiority to the realms of personal existence, of history, and of community. This was the context for Lonergan's conception of contemporary theological method and for the notion of conversion as a foundational reality. However, conversion does not provide the entire foundation for theological method, and so I distinguished among material, formal and actual aspects of the theological foundations. As a positive conclusion of this interpretive investigation, I would say that the notion of conversion provides the actual foundations of Lonergan's conception of theological method. As a negative conclusion, I would say that I do not perceive a sufficient awareness of this aspect of theological foundations in many of Lonergan's interpreters or critics.

Lonergan has not, of course, uttered the last word on the notion of conversion. Foundational reality is, not a theoretical account of conversion, not a reflective apprehension of conversion. It is the reality of conversion. Again, the most important thing is, not Lonergan's views on conversion, but one's own appropriation of the dynamics of religious, moral, and intellectual self-transcendence. It was the ideal of the early period to apprehend conversion in terms of a theoretical account. But conversion as a foundational notion is not theory. Again, it was the ideal of the middle period to clarify the dimensions of interiority for the subject. In that context, conversion was conceived as a radical clarification. But the notion of conversion as foundational reality is more than a clarification of subjects to themselves. The ideal of the later period, in which the notion of conversion is foundational, is the transformation of the subject. Consequently, Lonergan is offering a formal structure, a framework for collaboration; but the foundation of method is, not an hypothesis or a model which is merely offered for consideration, it is a reality in which we are dynamically enveloped.

Conversion makes the transformation of the subject foundational. As God is the Truth, so conversion awakens one to the dynamic tension which urges one toward an ever fuller realization of the truth. As God is the Good, so conversion awakens one to the dynamic tension which invites one toward an ever deeper desire for the good. As God is Love, so conversion fills one with a peace beyond understanding, a peace the world cannot give. Contemporary method makes foundational what is empirical, what we can be conscious of, and what we can experience. Long ago St. Augustine wrote that God has made us for Himself and that our hearts are restless until they rest in Him. Conversion makes foundational the transcendent orientation of consciousness, our restlessness, vis-a-vis any given situation, fact, or value. As Lonergan writes: "It is something very cognate to the Christian gospel which cries out: Repent! The kingdom of God is at hand."[62] Consequently, conversion makes foundational our discontent with the merely given and our hunger for the all-understanding and all-embracing love of God.

Finally, we need to appropriate the empirical dimensions of the dynamism of self-transcendence. Although that dynamism is an orientation to the Transcendent, it is also a present fact with factual implications. We need to develop the means to heighten consciousness, to become mindful of the movement of self-transcendence. Although it takes us into a further area and a distinct type of investigation, I suggest the tradition of Zen Buddhism as a fruitful area of exploration. As Fr. William Johnston has so gracefully shown, Lonergan's compatibility with Zen is deeper than one might expect.[63] I have long been fascinated with the resonance between two passages; the first from *Insight* and the second from the writings of D. T. Suzuki. Lonergan writes:

> . . .that there are two quite different realisms, that there is an incoherent realism, half animal and half human, that poses as a half-way house between materialism and idealism and, on the other hand, that there is an intelligent and reasonable realism between which and materialism the half-way house is idealism.[64]

D. T. Suzuki writes:

> A mountain is a mountain and water is water before a *sunyata*-experience [enlightenment] takes place; but

> after it a mountain is not a mountain and water is not
> water; but again when the experience deepens, a
> mountain is a mountain and water is water.[65]

There is a perennial materialism, a perennial idealism, and a perennial realism. Still, we need to break out of exclusively European and Western ways of conceiving things. We need to broaden the search for the meaning of human life, for its origin, and for its destiny. Lonergan has traveled the path Western civilization has taken in its ongoing discovery of mind. In my view, he has contributed immeasurably to the clarification of the operations of human intelligence, reflection, and evaluation; and he has exposed the mechanistic determinism of scientific theory as a philosophical error. On the other hand, Zen has devoted centuries to the development of means to awaken people to the truth about themselves. Consequently, we find ourselves in an historical situation analogous to that of St. Thomas' day. He enriched our apprehension of the truths of the Christian faith by integrating those truths with the fruits of Greek philosophic reflection. Perhaps the time is coming when we shall be able to deepen our apprehension of the mysterious and transforming presence of God by opening ourselves to the wisdom of the East.

NOTES

[1] *Insight*, p. 748.

[2] Lonergan writes: "Augustine's penetrating reflections on knowledge and on consciousness, Descartes' *Regulae ad directionem ingenii*, Pascal's *Pensees*, Newman's *Grammar of Assent* all remain within the world of common sense apprehension and speech yet contribute enormously to our understanding of ourselves. Moreover, they reveal the possibility of coming to know the conscious subject and his conscious operations without presupposing a prior metaphysical structure." *M.i.T.*, p. 261.

[3] *Grace and Freedom*, p. 5.

[4] *Verbum*, p. 217.

[5] *Summa Theologiae* I, q. 88, a. 2, ad. 3m.

[6] *Verbum*, p. 87.

[7] *Insight*, p. xviii.

[8] American Catholic Philosophic Association, *Proceedings*, 51

(1977) "Natural Right and Historical Mindedness" by Lonergan, p. 134.

⁹*M.i.T.*, p. 283.

¹⁰While my presentation of religious conversion obviously reveals my dependence on Lonergan's own formulations, I must also acknowledge my indebtedness to the reflections of Dom Sebastian Moore. See his *The Fire and the Rose Are One* (New York: Seabury Press, 1980).

¹¹St. Paul states: "We were helpless when at his appointed time Christ died for sinful men. It is not easy to die even for a good man—though of course for someone really worthy, a man might be prepared to die—but what proves that God loves us is that Christ died for us while we were still sinners" (Romans 5:7, 8).

¹²"Natural Right and Historical Mindedness," pp. 136–37.

¹³This section on moral conversion presupposes Lonergan's account of the structure of the human good as presented in chapter two of *Method in Theology*. The use of the phrase "dynamic state of freedom" is intended to emphasize the close connection between moral conversion and religious conversion as a dynamic state of love. The "dynamic state of freedom" is my own terminology.

¹⁴*M.i.T.*, p. 35.

¹⁵I use the term "object" in this present context in the same sense as the term "body" is used in *Insight*. That is, "a focal point of extroverted biological anticipation and attention. It is an 'already out there now real,' where these terms have their meaning fixed solely by elements within sensitive experience and so without any use of intelligent and reasonable questions and answers." *Insight*, p. 254. More broadly, however, I want to emphasize the dominant role of the subject's intentionality over any merely given datum.

¹⁶*M.i.T.*, p. 156.

¹⁷Ibid., p. 206.

¹⁸Ibid., p. 240.

¹⁹There is of course a material determination to our acts of understanding. We seek to understand some determinate data. Yet, properly speaking, we seek to understand not simply the givenness of the data. We seek to know the intelligibility of the data, a factor which transcends its mere givenness. For the discovery of this further factor, the pure desire to know becomes increasingly influential. The pure desire to know provides both a criterion as well as the meaning. Lonergan had made this point in *Verbum:* "Now this sensitive integration of sensible data also exists in the human animal and even in the human philosopher. Take it as knowledge of reality, and there results the secular contrast between the solid sense of reality and the bloodless categories of the mind. Accept the sense of reality as criterion of reality, and you are materialist, sensitivist, positivist, pragmatist, sentimentalist, and so on, as you please. Accept reason as a criterion but retain the sense of reality as what gives meaning to the term 'real' and

you are an idealist; for, like the sense of reality, the reality defined is non-rational. In so far as I grasp it, the Thomist position is the clear-headed third position: reason is the criterion and, as well, it is reason—not the sense of reality—that gives meaning to the term real.' The real is, what is; and what is' is known in the rational act, judgment.'' *Verbum,* p. 7. In this context, I would substitute the phrase pure desire to know' for the term reason' and retain the substance of Lonergan's early position.

[20] Charles E. Curran, "Christian Conversion in the Writings of Bernard Lonergan," in *Foundations of Theology: Papers from the International Lonergan Congress, 1970,* ed. Philip McShane (University of Notre Dame Press, 1971), pp. 41–59.

[21] Ibid., p. 52.

[22] *Summa Theologiae* 1–2, q. 109, a. 2c.

[23] *M.i.T.,* p. 310.

[24] Lonergan draws a distinction between the religious level and the moral level. He writes: "It is not to be thought, however, that religious conversion means no more than a new and more efficacious ground for the pursuit of intellectual and moral ends. Religious loving is without conditions, qualifications, reservations; it is with all one's heart and all one's soul and all one's mind and all one's strength. This lack of limitation, though it corresponds to the unrestricted character of human questioning, does not pertain to this world. Holiness abounds in truth and moral goodness, but it has a distinct dimension of its own. It is other-worldly fulfillment, joy, peace, bliss." *M.i.T.,* p. 242.

[25] *Grace and Freedom,* p. 16.

[26] For Lonergan's understanding of the notion of abstraction, see *Insight,* pp. 87–89.

[27] *Grace and Freedom,* pp. 4, 5.

[28] Karl Rahner, S.J., "Some Critical Thoughts on Functional Specialties in Theology,'" in *Foundations of Theology,* pp. 194–96.

[29] *Gregorianum* 50 (1969), pp. 485–505.

[30] "Some Critical Thoughts on Functional Specialties in Theology,'" p. 194.

[31] Ibid., pp. 195–96.

[32] "Bernard Lonergan Responds," in *Foundations of Theology,* p. 237.

[33] "An Interview with Fr. Bernard Lonergan, S.J.," in *2nd Col.,* pp. 210–211.

[34] "Theology in its New Context," in *2nd Col.,* p. 233.

[35] "Bernard Lonergan Responds," in *Foundations of Theology,* p. 233.

[36] Ibid.

[37] Ibid., p. 227.

[38] Ibid., p. 234.

[39] *M.i.T.,* p. 283.

[40] Ibid., p. xii.

41 Raymond Laflamme and Michel Gervais, eds., *Les Christ Hier, Aujourd'hui et Demain* (Quebec: Less Presses de l'Universite Laval, 1976), pp. 63–64.

42 Walter Conn, "Moral Development: Is Conversion Necessary?" in *Creativity and Method: Essays in Honor of Bernard Lonergan, S.J.*, ed. Matthew L. Lamb (Milwaukee: Marquette University Press, 1981), pp. 307–24.

43 *M.i.T.*, p. 240.

44 Conn, "Moral Development," in *Creativity and Method*, p. 319.

45 *M.i.T.*, p. 239.

46 "Moral Development," in *Creativity and Method*, p. 322.

47 See Lonergan's discussion of the functions of meaning in *M.i.T.*, pp. 76–81.

48 Ibid., p. 83.

49 David Tracy, "Lonergan's Foundational Theology: An Interpretation and a Critique," in *Foundations of Theology*, pp. 197–222.

50 Ibid., p. 214.

51 Ibid.

52 Ibid., p. 210.

53 "Bernard Lonergan Responds," in *Foundations of Theology*, p. 230.

54 Lonergan, *Philosophy of God and Theology*, p. 32.

55 *M.i.T.*, p. 50.

56 "*Insight* Revisited," in *2nd Col.*, p. 268.

57 *M.i.T.*, p. 252.

58 Ibid., p. 24.

59 Ibid., p. 25.

60 See *M.i.T.* on "Stating the Meaning of a Text," p. 172.

61 In *Grace and Freedom* Lonergan had written: "Just as beatitude is not human but divine and natural to God alone, just as wisdom for us is not understanding but faith, so the highest perfection of man cannot be immanent as are the virtues, but rather must link us dynamically with the sole source of absolute perfection." p. 44. In the context of contemporary theological method, I would locate that highest perfection in acts of self-transcendence which at the same time bring the subject to perfection, as well as transform the worlds of personal existence, community and history.

62 *M.i.T.*, p. 271.

63 William Johnston, S.J., *The Inner Eye of Love: Mysticism and Religion* (San Francisco: Harper and Row, Publisher, 1978).

64 *Insight*, p. xxviii.

65 D. T. Suzuki, *Zen Buddhism: Selected Writings of D. T. Suzuki* ed., William Barrett (New York: Doubleday Anchor Books, 1956), p. 264.

SELECTED BIBLIOGRAPHY

Primary Sources: Fr. Lonergan's Own Works

"Gratia Operans: A Study of the Speculative Development of St. Thomas Aquin." A thesis undertaken under the direction of the Reverend Charles Boyer, S.J., and submitted at the Pontifical Gregorian University, Rome, toward partial satisfaction of the conditions for the Doctorate in Sacred Theology, 1940. I have principally used the unpublished introduction to this work.

Grace and Freedom: Operative Grace in the Thought of St. Thomas Aquinas. Edited by J. Patout Burns, S.J. London: Darton, Longmans and Todd; New York: Herder and Herder, 1971.

Verbum: Word and Idea in Aquinas. Edited by David B. Burrell, C.S.C. Notre Dame: University of Notre Dame Press, 1967.

Collection: Papers by Bernard Lonergan, S.J. Edited by F. E. Crowe, S.J. New York: Herder and Herder, 1967.

Insight: A Study of Human Understanding. London: Longmans, Green and Co.; New York: Philosophical Library, 1958.

Understanding and Being: An Introduction and Companion to Insight." Edited by Elizabeth A. Morelli and Mark D. Morelli. New York and Toronto: The Edwin Mellen Press, 1980.

A Second Collection. Edited by William F. J. Ryan, S.J. and Bernard J. Tyrrell, S.J. Philadelphia: The Westminster Press, 1974.

Method in Theology. New York: Herder and Herder, 1972.

Philosophy of God and Theology. Philadelphia: The Westminster Press, 1973.

"Merging Horizons: System, Common Sense, Scholarship." *Cultural Hermeneutics* 1 (April, 1973), pp. 87–99.

"Mission and the Spirit." *Experience of the Spirit.* Edited by Peter Huizing and William Bassett. New York: Seabury Press, 1976.

"Christology Today: Methodological Reflections." *Le Christ Hier, Aujourd hui et Demain.* Edited by Raymond Laflamme and Michel Gervais. Quebec: Les Presses de l'Universite Laval, 1976.

"Natural Right and Historical Mindedness." *American Catholic Philosophic Association Proceedings* 51 (1977), pp. 132–43.

"Theology and Praxis." *Catholic Theological Society of America*

Proceedings of the Thirty-Second Annual Convention, (1977) pp. 1–16.

"The Human Good." *Humanitas* 15 (February, 1979), pp. 113–26.

Secondary Sources

Books and Articles by Other Authors on Lonergan's Thought

Conn, Walter E. "The Ontogenic Ground of Value." *Theological Studies* 39 (1978), pp. 313–35.

Crowe, Frederick E., S.J. "*Creativity and Method:* Index to a Movement; a Review-Article." *Science et Esprit* XXXIV/1 (1982), pp. 107–13.

————. "An Exploration of Lonergan's New Notion of Value." *Science et Esprit* XXIX/2 (1977), pp. 123–43.

————. *The Lonergan Enterprise.* Cambridge, Massachusetts: Cowley Publications, 1980.

Lamb, Matthew L. *History, Method, and Theology: A Dialectical Comparison of Wilhelm Dilthey's Critique of Historical Reason and Bernard Lonergan's Meta-Methodology.* Missoula: Scholar's Press, 1978.

————., ed. *Creativity and Method: Essays in Honor of Bernard Lonergan,* S.J. Milwaukee: Marquette University Press, 1981.

McCool, Gerald, S.J. "Scientific Theology: Bonaventure and Thomas Revisited." *Thought* 49 (March, 1974), pp. 374–96.

McShane, Philip, ed. *Foundations of Theology: Papers from the International Lonergan Congress, 1970.* Vol. 1. Notre Dame: University of Notre Dame Press, 1971.

————., ed. *Language, Truth and Meaning: Papers from the International Lonergan Congress, 1970.* Vol. 2. Notre Dame: University of Notre Dame Press, 1972.

Tracy, David. *The Achievement of Bernard Lonergan.* New York: Herder and Herder, 1970.

————. "Bernard Lonergan as an Interpreter of Saint Thomas Aquinas." *Listening* 9 (Winter/Spring, 1974), pp. 173–77.

Worgul, George S. "The Ghost of Newman in the Lonergan Corpus." *The Modern Schoolman* 54 (May, 1977), pp. 317–32.

General Background Works Used for the Reconstruction of the Successive Periods of Lonergan's Career

Aquinas, St. Thomas. *Basic Writings of St. Thomas Aquinas.* Edited and annotated with an Introduction by Anton C. Pegis. 2 vols. New York: Random House, 1945.

Copleston, Frederick, S.J. *A History of Philosophy: Vol. IX. Maine de Biran to Sartre. Part II, Bergson to Sartre.* Garden City, New York: Image Books, a Division of Doubleday and Company, 1977.

Cohen, Bernard I. *The Birth of a New Physics.* Garden City, New York: Anchor Books, 1960.

Collingwood, R. G. *The Idea of History.* London, Oxford, New York: Oxford University Press Paperback, 1956.

John, Helen James. *The Thomist Spectrum.* New York: Fordham University Press, 1966.

Johnston, William. *The Inner Eye of Love: Mysticism and Religion.* San Francisco: Harper and Row, Publishers, 1978.

Joseph, H. W. B. *An Introduction to Logic.* Second edition. Revised. Oxford: Clarendon Press, 1916.

McCool, Gerald, S.J. *Catholic Theology in the Nineteenth Century: The Quest for a Unitary Method.* New York: The Seabury Press, 1977.

McShane, Philip. *Randomness, Statistics and Emergence.* Notre Dame: University of Notre Dame Press, 1970.

Moore, Sebastian. *The Fire and the Rose Are One.* New York: The Seabury Press, 1980.

Newman, John Henry, Cardinal. *An Essay in Aid of a Grammar of Assent.* New edition, edited with a Preface and an Introduction by Charles Frederick Harrold. London: Longmans, Green and Company, 1947.

Palmer, Richard E. *Hermeneutics: Interpretation Theory in Schleiermacher, Dilthey, Heidegger and Gadamer.* Evanston: Northwestern University Press, 1969.

Plato. *The Great Dialogues of Plato.* Translated by W. H. D. Rouse. New York: A Mentor Book, 1956.

Stewart, J. A. *Plato's Doctrine of Ideas.* Oxford: Clarendon Press, 1909.

Van Riet, George. *Thomistic Epistemology, Studies Concerning the Problem of Cognition in the Contemporary Thomistic School.* 2 vols. Translated by Donald G. McCarthy and George E. Hertrich. St. Louis and London: B. Herder Book Co., 1965.

Weisheipl, James A., O.P. *Friar Thomas D'Aquino: His Life, Thought and Works.* Garden City, New York: Doubleday and Company, 1974.

INDEX OF SUBJECTS

INDEX OF AUTHORS